LIVE FAST, DIE YOUNG

Summersdale Publishers Ltd
46 West Street
Chichester
West Sussex
PO19 1RP
UK

www.summersdale.com

Printed and bound in Great Britain

ISBN: 978-1-84953-049-1

Substantial discounts on bulk quantities of Summersdale books are available to corporations, professional associations and other organisations. For details contact Summersdale Publishers by telephone: +44 (0) 1243 771107, fax: +44 (0) 1243 786300 or email: nicky@summersdale.com.

PERMISSIONS

From Chris to Courtney:
Twenty thousand roads – and they all led me to you.

From Joe to Nicola, Noah and Addie:
For all the things that have been, and all those yet to come.

CONTENTS

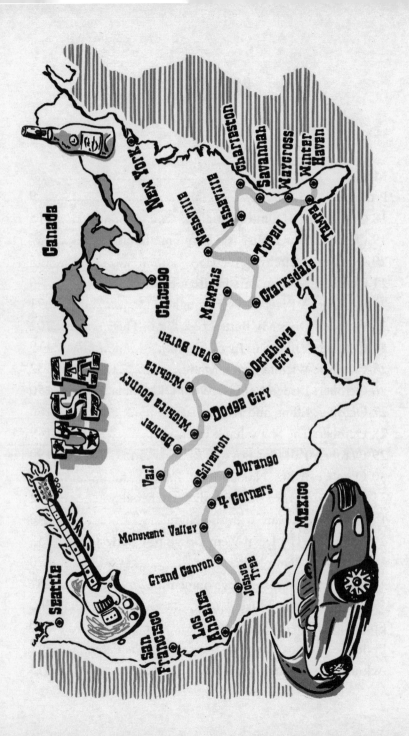

PROLOGUE

Elvis was lying to us. Turns out there's no Lonely Street after all, and definitely no Heartbreak Hotel.

The Eagles, too. Hotel California? Not in the phone book.

And the Highway to Hell? Wasn't on any road map that we could find.

Film buffs can visit the locations of their favourite movies. Bookworms can seek out the real-world setting of their favourite reads. Even soap fans can visit the soundstages. But music lovers... they can't really join in with that game.

Actually, that's not true. You just need to adjust your focus a bit, like one of those Magic Eye posters from the early nineties. Go to America today, and with the right outlook you'll see song lyrics strewn by the roadside and melodies drifting across the landscape on the breeze. You just have to look that little bit harder.

Hello. My name is Chris.

And I'm Joe. Hello.

We're radio and television producers. We play a lot of music. That radio show, where bands cover songs for Jo Whiley in the Live Lounge, that was ours.

Four lines in and already he's trying to turn his life into a movie script. He does that a lot. What he means is we used to work together at Radio 1. That's how we met.

Then I jumped ship and went to work in telly. Which would have been a perfectly good opportunity to let this whole thing drop. But we didn't. Perhaps we should have. (And Joe does the movie script thing too. A lot.)

And that's about as much as you need to know for now. Except to say that most of what follows is true.

See? It's all true. *I'll* start.

Joe and I have loved music since before we can remember. Our friendship is built on it. On being crushed in the mosh pit at a Mars Volta gig; on sharing a bin liner to cover our boots at Glastonbury; on getting the beers in before the Arctic Monkeys come on at the Astoria. It's built on the exhilaration of 'Crazy in Love', the befuddlement of the first time you heard The Darkness, the thrill of clapping ears on *The Marshall Mathers LP*. On the howl of John Frusciante's guitar, the growl of James Hetfield and the wail of Matt Bellamy. It's also built, most crucially, on five years spent arguing about all of this every Wednesday afternoon in the Radio 1 playlist meeting.

On my thirtieth birthday Chris gave me a card with a still from one of my favourite movies, *Butch Cassidy and the Sundance Kid*. It's the scene where the marshal is in town trying to round up a posse and head off Butch and Sundance. The camera pans upwards to the balcony of Fanny Porter's brothel behind him, where Butch and Sundance are drinking beer and watching the goings-on down below. Butch says that when he was a kid he always wanted to grow up to be a hero, to which Sundance replies: 'Well, it's too late now.'

Inside the card, just one handwritten word: 'Hero.' I'll treasure that card until the day I die. Two months later, knowing Chris' obsession with deceased country musician and sometime drug addict Gram Parsons, for his birthday I gave him a home-made card bearing a photograph of his outlaw hero. Inside, one word: 'Heroin.'

Within ten minutes he had lost it.

I don't feel good about it. To be fair, we were in a busy club at the time and my attentions were more focused on not losing the expensive, table-sized work of art that Joe had just presented to me as a birthday gift (more of which later). But this humble exchange of cards turned out to be the beginning of something that got rather out of hand. It was the catalyst for a journey which would see us cross a continent in search of places we weren't even sure existed, of people who were nearly all long dead. A journey that would brush for the DNA of the American music aristocracy and dust for the vomit of a string of deceased rock and rollers. You see, the birthday cards set us talking about Gram, his extraordinary life and the bizarre circumstances of his death on a patch of desert in southern California called Joshua Tree.

Joshua Tree. Two words more exotic and alluring than any travel brochure, more instantly redolent of rock music and all the boundless freedom it implies than any biography I had ever read. Of power chords wrought by rock gods across an infinite, widescreen sky. A sort of imaginary place which exists beyond the law, where the sky's the limit and the streets have no name. Let's face it, who doesn't think of the biggest rock band on the planet™ when they hear those words?

Well me, for one. For longer than I could remember, the words Joshua Tree had been linked in my mind with the story of one man: Gram Parsons. They were words from the pages of a book, the setting of a story which had enthralled me for almost as long as I had loved music. To me they evoked images not of Bono and friends but of the tiny motel room where Parsons decamped with his girlfriend and took a fatal overdose of morphine in 1973. Or Cap Rock, his favoured Joshua Tree perch for UFO spotting and LSD tripping, and the scene of his final, twisted, DIY cremation at the hands of friend and road manager Phil Kaufman. U2 are heroes to most, as Chuck D might just as well have said, but they never meant shit to me.

And, frankly, Gram Parsons never meant shit to me. Chris had been guffing on about him for years but I had never seen the appeal. Country music is for truckers and rednecks if you ask me. But that, I realised, was sort of the point. Yes, Joshua Tree meant very different things to us, but the more we talked about it, the more we realised virtually every song, album or artist we held dear was attached in our heads to some half real, half imaginary place, nearly all of them in America. It seemed obvious to me what the next chapter of the birthday exchange should be.

Two men, a CD player, the open road. On a journey that would span both coasts of the United States we would share great music, good times and rock and roll hi-jinx. Roof down, stereo up, we would create the definitive soundtrack for the ultimate road movie. But more than just listening to our favourite tunes, we wanted to *live* them. We would travel in search of the places and people that would connect us to the music we loved. Stand on the crossroads where Robert Johnson sold his soul to the devil, take a bite of the burger that finally finished off The King, taste the loneliness of the 'Wichita Lineman'.

It could be a birthday present for Gram, who, had he not fouled it up by dying thirty years previously, would have been nearing his sixtieth birthday. So that's why, three years later, Chris and I hired a car and drove from Los Angeles airport, where his body was stolen, via the motel room he died in and the Joshua Tree setting of his makeshift cremation, finally arriving at the Florida town where he was born precisely sixty years earlier. In between, we would tick off some of the most important landmarks in rock music history in the hope of learning a thing or two about America, its music, and each other.

There were several reasons why it took us three years to hit the road. First, Joe had just used up one of the tri-annual 'travel passes' given to him by his partner Nicola. Wonderful wife (and mother) that she is, Nic indulges Joe's near insatiable wanderlust by allowing him a guilt-free pass every three years for a trip of his choosing. Having just completed 'Beijing to Bayswater over land' (Joe is the only man I know who makes travel choices based on alliterating destinations), he would have to wait three years for the next pass.

Which happened to time perfectly with Gram's sixtieth birthday. And besides, we had a lot of preparing to do. We built a website which would give us a platform to blog about our experiences, as well as offering the means of meeting a few interesting people along the way. And the trip, we figured, would make an excellent subject for a documentary. A radio documentary perhaps or, even better, a TV programme. We would shop the idea around to a few of our friends in radio and telly and if no one bit, then – what the hell – we could take a camera and film it ourselves.

No one bit.

So we borrowed a camera and got on with it. We wanted to capture the sights, the sounds, the smells… of two passionate music fans on the road. And we got that. But we got more. A *lot* more.

But hey, enough of my yackin', whaddya say…

Enough.

18 OCTOBER

LA QUINTESSENTIAL

On the flight over I drew up a to-do list. As a birthday present to Gram we planned to end the expedition with a performance, on guitar and ukulele, of one of his most enduring recordings, 'Return of the Grievous Angel'. This would present no significant problem for Chris, who has been performing the song to anyone that would listen for half of his life. I, on the other hand, have never strummed, plucked or struck anything more taxing than an air guitar. Top of my list then, are:

1. Learn to love the music of Gram Parsons.
2. Learn to play the ukulele.
3. Learn to play the music of Gram Parsons on the ukulele.

And for Chris:

1. Grow a formidable moustache.

By 'formidable moustache' he means the horseshoe, or what I'm assured is known in the trade as the 'cockduster'. You will recognise this particular type as the trademark facial adornment of The Village People's 'Leatherman', usually attached to two thirds of Crosby, Stills and Nash, or nestling under the nose of Dennis Hopper in *Easy Rider*. It extends vertically downwards on either side of the mouth, stopping level with the jaw line or, on the more adventurous wearer, protruding very slightly below. *Easy Rider* and CSN were fine by me; Joe's reference points were more James Hetfield (who favours the more flamboyant downward protrusion described above) and Dave Grohl. It's no coincidence that these men wield guitars in the fiercest rock outfits ever to have filled an enormo-dome. In fact it's nigh on impossible to carry one off if you don't. Anyone contemplating wearing a horseshoe, but who shaves less than three times a day, should proceed with extreme caution.

Which is why I was a little uncomfortable with the 'formidable moustache' directive. For one thing the phrase is something of an oxymoron in my case. My beard has never approached respectable, much less formidable, in anything under two months. And Joe has a definite head start in the 'tache stakes. He has been wearing either a full-blown cockduster (don't you just love the use of the verb 'to wear' for facial hair, like it's something you slip into before breakfast), or more often a goatee beard, for as long as I can remember. So for him 'growing' a formidable moustache is simply a case of shaving out a section of stubble approximately one inch by one inch under his bottom lip. (Which is a shame because his beard is an autumn of colour in this area – a fetching vermilion here, a touch of burnt sienna there.) I, on the other hand, must first grow a beard and then shave out as required, which is several weeks in the doing and we only had three. Just as Joe's moustache was entering the realms of the truly formidable, mine would be somewhere shy of barely discernible, and then it would be time to come home.

And so to LAX airport, the setting for the beginning of a journey conceived nearly three years earlier; a dream of the open road in an open-top car, of two fearless explorers driving coast to coast across the land of the free. The flight from Heathrow had lasted about ten hours over a distance of six thousand miles, but we'd come a hell of a lot further than that. This was the culmination of months, *years* of planning, of a trip that would see us catalogue some of the most significant landmarks in music history. A friendship built on a fascination for them was, we hoped, about to find its fullest expression. But LAX was also to be where that same dream, of distant vanishing points sucked in over the windscreen of a two-seater, came within a hair's breadth of being snuffed out.

Renting the car was Harland's job. I had no reason not to believe it was in safe hands: Joe's capacity for forward planning is the stuff of legend. We once made a radio programme featuring rock stars reading books, which required us to roam the backstage area of Reading Festival knocking on tour buses and politely asking their confused, unsuspecting occupants to give a recital from whatever literature they had lying around in their bunks (you'd be surprised). Joe, with his eye on the prize, had made arrangements to be tagged on to the end of the Foo Fighters' press junket for the day. When his turn came to record lead singer Dave Grohl, the moustachioed rock god politely turned him down on the grounds that he had only ever read one book in his entire life – *Catcher in the Rye* by J. D. Salinger. So unless Joe just *happened* to have a copy of it on him right now, it was a no-go. Cue Joe, to the astonishment of both Grohl and his press officer, reaching into his bag and producing a copy of *the only book that Dave Grohl had ever read,* having done his research that morning and popped into Waterstone's on the off-chance. Cue tape, hit record, and two paragraphs later my prized recording of the bass player from Editors reading Brave New World was looking altogether a little pathetic.

So as you can see, I had no reason to suppose he didn't have this all worked out in advance. Arriving at LAX, we hopped onto a shuttle which took us to the car rental dealers about a mile or so away from the terminal. On the way I enquired whether Joe had brought all the necessary paperwork in order to pick up our shiny, convertible Chrysler Sebring.

'Er, they did send me an email, but I don't think I printed it off. Should be fine – they'll have our details on file and I've got the credit card I made the booking with.'

'Welcome to Dollar Car Rental. How can I help you today?' The desk clerk beamed.

'We've made a reservation for a Chrysler Sebring convertible. Name of Harland.'

'Certainly sir – do you have the reservation number?'

'I'm afraid not, but you should have our details on file, and I've got the credit card I made the booking with,' replied Joe.

'I'm sorry sir, but without the reservation number I can't verify the booking.'

'Sorry?'

'Without the reservation number I can't verify the booking.'

She gestured towards her computer, which resembled something out of a seventies science fiction movie. It had a built-in keyboard and VDU, with light green type on a dark screen displaying a single box labelled 'reservation number'. Literally nothing else would allow her to process the transaction. This was a bad start. Jumping back on the shuttle, we turned the dial to 'the future', hoping there might be somewhere with Internet access – and a printer – back at the airport terminal.

There was. We returned to Dollar clutching the reservation documentation like prized lost treasure in an Indiana Jones movie, finally allowing ourselves to get excited about the prospect of beginning our journey. We were *this* close to hitting the road at long last, the wind in our hair and the sun on our faces. Our reservation was processed without a hitch and, with insurance documents and driving licences in hand, we made our way onto the forecourt to get acquainted with our wheels.

'Sorry guys.' The lot attendant tutted as he inspected the paperwork. 'No convertibles.'

'Come again?' spat Joe, as if to say 'I *dare* you to say that again'.

'Nooooo convertibles today. Sorry. But don't you worry, I'll fix you up with an equivalent vehicle in nooooo time at all. I got some great SUVs to choose from.'

'We don't want an SUV, we want a Chrysler Sebring convertible. The one we booked and paid for *six months ago*,' replied Joe. The veins in his neck were beginning to throb.

'They're all booked out,' replied the lot attendant.

'B-but... they can't be. The lady inside said everything was in order.'

Witnessing Joe transform into Basil Fawlty was not, I'm sad to say, a new experience. I had seen it once before when he threatened to set Alan Yentob on a BBC transport executive at Glastonbury Festival. The poor woman made the unfortunate assumption that television's need was greater than that of radio and gave our fleet vehicle to someone from Television Centre, receiving a torrent of invective for her troubles like a thousand slaps to the head of a cowering Manuel. It was a little like watching Bruce Banner turn into the Incredible Hulk. (The phrase 'mild-mannered' was invented for Joe Harland. But so was the phrase 'You wouldn't like me when I'm angry'.) The transformation was swift and terrifying, and by now I was starting to recognise the signs: a bead of sweat at the temples, a change in skin colour, the pulsing of veins in the neck.

'Nooooo convertibles,' replied the attendant, shaking his head emphatically. For our benefit, he went on to explain how the system at Dollar Car Rental works.

It goes a little something like this (and I'm paraphrasing here): the desk clerks accept payment as normal, process the reservation, reassure the customer that everything is in order and, pausing only to try and sell them a variety of expensive extras such as satellite navigation and additional insurance they don't need, invite them to make their way outside to pick up their vehicle. There, the underlings on the forecourt are tasked with finding you an 'equivalent' car to the one you have ordered. It's a very effective arrangement as it apparently dispenses with the need to keep in stock any of the cars that have been (a) advertised or (b) paid for.

'Equivalent to a Sebring is an Aspen or a Land Cruiser,' continued the attendant. 'Great cars. A lotta room in the trunk.'

'I don't care *how* much room they have in the trunk!' exploded Joe, arms flailing, 'It's not the *trunk* I'm interested in! Has it escaped your notice that the Aspen and the Land Cruiser have one very crucial feature in common?'

'No sir. What's that?'

'A fucking *roof*!' For emphasis as he delivered this last point, Joe banged his hand hard against a metal sign just over his left shoulder, swore lavishly and profusely, and began to hop on one foot. This was not going well. Once we'd established that all the 'equivalent' vehicles available to us had a roof – that is, there were no equivalent vehicles – it was time to see the manager. We went inside, approached the customer service desk and demanded to talk to whoever was in charge.

Clayton the manager, bright of shirt and slight of frame, skipped over all smiles and handshakes, trying hard to affect the kind of open body language he had no doubt learned about in a 'dealing with difficult customers' training video. He was going to need all the customer service know-how he could muster, for here were two of the trickiest customers ever to darken his reception area. One of them was angrier than a grizzly bear with a wounded paw, and the other... well, the other had seen an awful lot of high-concept action movies.

'What seems to be the problem gentlemen?' chirped Clayton.

My turn. This called for some Steven Berkoff. Specifically it called for Berkoff as Victor Maitland in *Beverly Hills Cop*. He plays the part with casual, teacherly nonchalance, garnished with the wild-eyed intent of a serial killer about to tuck into his latest victim (always addressing Foley as 'my tough little friend'). Think Hannibal Lecter presenting 'D for disembowel' on *Sesame Street* and you're halfway there. I stepped into character.

'The problem, sir, is that you've had six months advance warning of these two 'gentlemen' walking in here with a credit card and a desire to drive out in a car with no roof. You've failed. What are you going to do about it?'

OK not exactly up to Berkoff's standards, much less Anthony Hopkins', but this kind of thing doesn't come at all naturally to me. I'm just not good at making a scene.

'I'm really not sure there's anything I can do sir,' he squirmed. 'There are no convertible cars available today.'

Berkoff would never have settled for this.

'Now listen to me,' I whispered (I wanted to call him 'my tough little friend', but resisted). 'We're staying in LA for two days. That gives you precisely forty-eight hours to deliver a convertible Chrysler Sebring, as ordered, to the Four Seasons Hotel on Doheny Drive, and then we can forget all about this sorry episode.'

'Let me see what I can do for you sir.'

Crikey, it was working.

Off he went and returned with a pretty blonde in possession of a smile even wider than his and a Master's degree in customer service. She asked us to give her ten minutes while she 'looked into the situation' for us.

Sure enough, eight-and-a-half minutes later she returned (we timed her), and we were dispatched to the lot once more to find a gleaming, silver, convertible Sebring waiting for us with the keys in the ignition. Bingo. I flashed a smug, self-satisfied smile at the lot attendant as I unlocked the boot, placed the luggage inside and slammed it shut. The attendant offered to give us a tour of the controls, but we had no time for that. These jokers had kept us hanging around for long enough already. It was time to hit the road.

I reached for the key. Nothing there.

'Joe, key please. Let's get the hell out of here.'

'I haven't got the key, you have.'

'Mate, I'm not in the mood for jokes. The sooner you give me the key, the sooner we can be sitting by the pool at the Four Seasons sipping a margarita.'

'I honestly don't have the key. You had it last. You put the bags in the boot.'

Shit. I had locked the keys in the boot. In a little under a nanosecond I felt less Victor Maitland and more Frank Spencer. I called the lot attendant over.

'We, er, appear to have locked the keys in the boot.'

'Excuse me?'

'Trunk. I mean trunk. I've locked the keys in the trunk.'

'Absolutely no problem sir. We'll have you a new one cut in no time.' His bubbly efficiency made me feel even smaller than I felt already. Bloody Americans and their impeccable customer service.

In under five minutes we were on our way. Finally, this was it! Santa Monica Boulevard, destination Beverly Hills. The roof was down as planned, but we needed some music to lift the mood. I searched the CD wallet for something to mark the occasion, the auspicious beginning of a momentous journey, a search for the beating heart of rock and roll America. Something that would summon up the spirit of Americana and help us on our way. Something that would send a message beyond the grave in a language the spirits would understand, to say that we were here and we meant business.

Huey Lewis and the News.

Two pasty tourists driving a convertible through Inglewood, one of LA's most notorious neighbourhoods, listening to 'The Power of Love'. Chris was living the dream. I was trapped in his nightmare. We checked into the hotel and resolved to hit the town immediately. Hoping to beat the jet lag by staying up well past LA bedtime (whenever that is), we needed somewhere fitting to raise a glass and give ourselves a rousing send-off. So rock stop number one on the itinerary was the celebrated Chateau Marmont Hotel just off Sunset Boulevard, which competes with the nearby Hyatt for the crown of 'most rock and roll hotel in the world'.

It's a close-run contest. The Hyatt has seen more than its fair share of wild antics over the years and for sheer, clichéd, rock and roll point-scoring it probably has the edge. Television sets thrown out of windows? Check (Keiths Moon and Richards). Motorbikes ridden along corridors? Check (John Bonham). Scenes from famous rockumentary films shot there? Check (*This is Spinal Tap, Almost Famous*). The Hyatt was about as rock and roll as it was possible to get without making three seminal albums of its own and falling down dead of a drug overdose after twenty-seven years.

But for all its irrefutable rock credentials the Hyatt was just a little too obvious for our purposes, posturing and posing as it does on the edge of Sunset Strip like an older, more grandfatherly version of the concrete excrescences that squint out over the Costa Del Sol. It's big, dumb and unimaginative. Aesthetically the Hyatt is the hotel equivalent of the muscle-bound blockhead pumping iron on the front at Venice Beach.

No, the Chateau (as it's known to its friends) was altogether more exclusive, understated, refined. Modelled on the Château d'Amboise in the Loire Valley, it sits above and slightly away from the Strip behind neatly tended hedges and gardens, turning its nose up at the vulgar and frankly rather sordid goings-on down below. Granted, Led Zep had ridden their Harley Davidsons through its lobby and, yes, Jim Morrison had performed the 'window dangling trick' which became the mainstay of his Hollywood hotel sojourns. It even boasted a bona fide rock death in the form of John Belushi's drugs overdose in 1982. The Chateau's proprietors are still a little miffed about all the fuss and bother to this day.

Yes, what went on behind the closed doors of the Chateau Marmont was an altogether more sophisticated variety of rock and roll depravity.

Most exciting of all, for me anyway, was the fact that the Chateau offered the chance of glimpsing the spot where the cover art for Gram's 1973 album *GP* was shot. It's an iconic image: Gram sits alone in a huge, elaborately carved wooden armchair wearing a pale blue shirt, pinstripe trousers and Cuban heels. A Stetson hangs on the back of the chair behind his head. To his left an enormous arrangement of flowers sits on a wide mahogany table in what looks to be a reception area of the hotel. Yellow light spills in from the left of the photograph, casting an amber glow onto the side of his face. With his long, dark hair he has all the trappings and appearance of the LA rock star, but exudes a kind of lord-of-the-manor air that suggests he all but owns the place.

Which isn't as far-fetched as it may sound. He didn't own the place, but he did live there for a time in the early seventies. Not bad for a struggling country-rock aspirant whose efforts to date had failed to trouble anything more than the lower reaches of the hit parade. Gram's family money and privileged background (he was the grandson of the Florida citrus fruit magnate John A. Snively) enabled him to maintain a lifestyle more or less on a par with the contemporaries whose record sales he was so desperate to emulate – the Stones mainly – but had so far failed to match. Many held that this trustafarian spending power was precisely what stopped him from achieving this aim, which is to say he lacked the naked ambition which drove his peers to ever higher heights. Whatever the truth, he was a regular among the circles of the LA rock aristocracy, and that was enough for us. The Chateau was definitely the place to start.

The Chateau was also the scheduled rendezvous for the first hook-up of the tour. We had arranged to meet an Internet superstar by the name of Terra Naomi, a musician and web celebutante who was beginning to attract the attention of the music industry in both London and LA. Her fame so far came from the millions of hits to her YouTube channel, which featured a weekly show chronicling the trials and tribulations of a superstar in the making. She and her producer-manager Paul Fox had offered to show us around LA the following day. Paul was something of an authority on the Laurel Canyon area which, along with the legendary Troubadour live music venue, had been pivotal in turning the West Coast folk scene from a backwater cottage industry into a unit-shifting hit machine responsible for some – in fact most – of the era's biggest names. By bringing her camera crew along, Terra would make us the subject of one of her hit web shows, generating some much-needed traffic, not to mention content, for our own site.

I'll admit it. Arranging to meet Terra at the Chateau felt pretty good. We were two high-powered media execs flying in from London to meet the Internet's newest star. We were staying at the luxurious celebrity bolthole that was the Four Seasons hotel, and despite a touch of jet lag and a sore throat between us (either that or an elaborate ruse on Joe's part to avoid talking to me), we were ready for a taste of the Hollywood high life. A quick call to the hotel concierge was all that was needed to secure a place on the guest list of one of the most exclusive hotel bars in the world. This had been my responsibility, as Joe was doing all he could to save his throat by not speaking. At all. We pulled up outside. I had made that call, hadn't I?

Hadn't I?

Shit.

'Hello, you should have received a reservation from the Four Seasons,' I lied, hoping that by saying the words with enough conviction it would somehow make them true. It was the same combination of hope and misplaced confidence that Joe had injected into 'you should have our details on file' at Dollar Car Rental.

'I didn't receive a reservation from the Four Seasons, no sir, I did not,' said the doorman.

'Well not to worry, there's obviously been some mistake. Pop us down at that table over there and we'll forget all about it.'

'That table is reserved. Yes sir, it is,' he insisted, agreeing with himself. It was like *Rain Man*. Not only were we being denied access, it was happening twice every time the fellow opened his mouth.

'Oh dear. Never mind. Well, anywhere will do, we're expecting a friend along in a minute. Find us a table if you can, old chap.' (If at first you don't succeed, turn the Englishness up to eleven and hope that does the trick instead.)

'There are no tables available tonight. No sir, there are not,' replied the doorman, one hundred per cent in agreement with himself once more.

'Would it help if I told you we come with a message of peace and reconciliation from the Belushi estate?'

'No sir. No it would not.'

This was going nowhere. Rather than be turned away another six or eight times, we elected to cut our losses and leave. Our chance to add a few rock and roll antics of our own to the list of Chateau-related bad behaviour would go no further, this time, than gently taking the piss out of a doorman who had no idea he was having the piss taken out of him. No sir, he did not. Finding a suitable meeting place a little further along Sunset, I sheepishly called Terra to redirect her, explaining that there had been a terrible mix-up at the hotel and by golly there was going to be one hell of a stink when we got back there.[1]

But now that the Chateau was no longer on the agenda, the whole thing felt less like a jubilant send-off and more like, well, two blokes meeting a girl in a bar. And with Joe now virtually mute I felt the sudden pressure of having to carry the whole evening on my own. There was nothing for it but to drink heroic quantities of alcohol. It would make us funnier, more erudite and generally better company than if we'd had none at all. Joe valiantly joined in, quickly establishing that a steady flow of bourbon was just what the doctor ordered to soothe the rasp in his throat. We were starting to loosen up. By the time Terra arrived we were already at least three sheets to the wind, possibly more.

---

1 I have since returned to Chateau Marmont and successfully gained entry as the guest of someone who actually had good reason to be there. The 'atmospheric' lighting in the bar was so low I had trouble finding my face with my wine glass, much less the reception area, and an hour-long excursion to the gents' loos, located eventually by feeling my way along the walls, literally shed no light on the subject whatsoever.

We recognised her immediately from the videos we had seen on the Internet. Inevitably she was smaller than we'd expected. (What's the web equivalent of 'you look smaller than you do on the telly'? In fact aren't people supposed to look bigger than they do on the Internet?) Attractive with striking features, she had long, dark hair and wore a black, short-sleeved blouse with a ruffle at the neck and translucent sleeves which revealed an intricate, swirling tattoo on her upper left arm.

We exchanged kisses to both cheeks – it seemed like the right thing to do when greeting LA cyber-royalty, though to my knowledge there's no established protocol here – and I ordered drinks for us all.

'Do you guys have any money?' she enquired.

Good lord, this one didn't waste any time. I know struggling musicians find themselves short of a dollar from time to time, but hadn't she just pulled up in a Mercedes? And, come to think of it, hadn't she just signed a lucrative publishing deal with Universal?

'The ATM was broken and I don't have a cent on me. I'm so embarrassed.'

Fair enough. Broken ATM or not, I suppose it wouldn't do for a lady, much less a popstar, to be entertained by two gentlemen and have to buy her own drinks.

We sat down and explained how the idea for the trip had been born, talked through our rough itinerary and what we planned to do along the way. Fortified by the booze, Joe and I slipped into what would turn out to be a familiar and well-trodden schtick before we even knew we were doing it. Tonight, as on many others over the coming weeks when faced with a willing American audience, we adopted the patter and dynamic of a TV comedy duo, but with long, overblown anecdotes instead of actual jokes. Out came the favourite about The KLF burning a million pounds of their own money in the name of art, the one about Bill Drummond's travails trying to sell a Richard Long photograph for $20,000 (and how thirty, dollar-sized pieces of it ended up hanging on my living room wall – more of which in a minute), even the one about Joe's mum being a professional chocolate taster who counsels anorexics in her spare time. Our audience was enraptured and we were playing to it, pulling out only our choicest yarns and spinning them out with hilarious asides and amusing bonus content. We were literally the two funniest, most engaging people on earth.

Joe, to give him his due, is a wonderful raconteur. When he's in 'oratorical mode' – usually after no more than one-and-a-half glasses of rosé – you can wind him up, let him go, and settle in for several hours of gripping, ripping entertainment. His capacity for memorising names, dates, quotations, entire speeches, lists or anniversaries, and then weaving them into an exhilarating narrative, is astonishing. Conversationally he can hold his own on any subject you care to throw at him – music, cinema, technology, travel, literature, sport. From Rush to Rachmaninov, Swayze to Scorsese, quantum theory to Timothy Leary, Harland not only knows things that you don't, he'll impart them with all the timing and precision of a seasoned toastmaster. You name it, Joe knows stuff about it. And he's going to tell you.

(What's more – and this delights me and enrages others – he talks like he's on the radio more or less all the time, most often, but not limited to, Radio 4. Give him a call on his mobile some time and have a listen to his voicemail greeting. It has all the hypnotic, undulating timbre of the shipping forecast, rising and falling with the ebb and flow of his carefully constructed message. Or watch his fingers on the table as he's chatting away in a bar and you'll notice him reflexively fading records in and out of his own amusing repartee. He can't help himself.)

Allow me at this point, if you will, a brief excursion into the crazy world of art terrorist and avant-pop artiste Bill Drummond of The KLF. It is necessary here I think because, first of all, the reference above to the $20,000 Richard Long photo probably needs a bit of background. Secondly, it might give you some idea of how unutterably bored Terra must have been by the time we were through with the story. And lastly, it might just give you some sense of the spirit of arty stupidness in which this whole ridiculous enterprise was conceived. It was the same spirit of arty stupidness that led Chris and me to becoming the only two men on the entire planet driving across America to celebrate the sixtieth birthday of a virtually unknown country-rock artist. Drummond, after all, was a man who once drove around London's orbital M25 motorway for twenty-five hours in order to find out where it led.

I'll try and keep it short. *A Smell of Sulphur in the Wind* was a landscape photograph, taken by Long and bought by Drummond, of a small stone circle somewhere in Iceland. Bill decided one morning that the photo, which hung on the wall of his Buckinghamshire home, needed to complete a circle of its own. He planned to sell the photograph for the exact amount he paid for it, bury the cash under the stone circle which featured in the original work, take a photograph of it, and then hang the resulting work – under the new name *The Smell of Money Underground* – in precisely the spot that the original had occupied in his house. You have to admit it has a certain illogical symmetry to it.

How To Be An Artist is a book by Drummond which tells the story of how he tried to find a buyer for the photograph by placing placards in hundreds of unremarkable locations around the country: attached to motorway flyovers and road signs, tied to parking meters or garden gates – you get the idea. Unsurprisingly, he didn't have any takers. The book was also a present from Chris on my thirtieth birthday, the same year as the Butch and Sundance card which started all this.

Undeterred by his failure to flog the photograph by unconventional means, Drummond's next tack was to go one better; he cut it into twenty thousand evenly-sized pieces and tried selling them individually for a dollar each. When the last of the pieces had sold, he would take the cash to Iceland as planned and complete the work of art he had held in his head since he removed it from the wall of his house.

Which is how thirty tiny pieces, or precisely 0.15 per cent, of *A Smell of Sulphur in the Wind* came to be hanging on my living room wall – framed, individually mounted and certified by Drummond himself. Continuing the Drummond-related exchange of gifts, for my thirtieth birthday Joe had bought thirty dollars' worth of the fragmented photograph, one for each of my years, and in doing so completed a little circle of our own. This was the table-sized work of art I was concerned about not losing when I 'mislaid' Joe's home-made birthday card. It is the nicest, most thoughtful present anyone has ever bought me. It's also the only piece of 'real' art that I own. So you can see a sort of pattern emerging: a tradition of marking ridiculous anniversaries in ever more ridiculous ways. You can also sort of see why we sort of *had* to spend nearly a month of our lives driving 4,500 miles in search of rock and roll America as a sixtieth birthday present to a musician most people have never heard of. After all, who else was going to do it?

And there was one more Drummond dictum which had stuck in our minds back in the planning stages. Another of his books – *The Manual: How to Have a Number One Hit the Easy Way* – had asserted that being a Radio 1 producer was one of the fastest ways of losing touch with whatever finer qualities your soul may once have had. We weren't sure whether this was true of us – what would we know, we were Radio 1 producers after all – but surely a quest to find the soul of American music might help us hold onto what few fine qualities we had left.

Several hours and a good deal more Jack Daniels later, Terra finally got a word in edge ways.

'Those guys, the ones that burned a million dollars...'

'Quid,' blurted Joe. 'A million *quid*. That's nearly *two* million dollars.'

'Right, a million quid. Why would they *do* that?'

'Art,' I burped, slamming my glass on the table top for emphasis.

'Art?' replied Terra, incredulously.

'Yep. They made a film called *Watch the K Foundation Burn a Million Quid*.'

'What, and then sold it to a studio?'

'Nope.'

'So how did they make the money back?'

'They didn't. That's the whole point. If they had, it wouldn't have been art,' I explained, as if it were the most obvious thing in the world. And it kind of *was* the most obvious thing in the world, to Joe and me at least.

'But... I don't get it. How is that art?'

'How is anything art?' said Joe, as though by simply asking the question he had settled once and for all a matter which has been taxing the finest minds in the world for centuries.

'It just seems like such a waste,' said Terra. 'Couldn't they have just given it to charity?'

'Of *course* they couldn't have given it to charity,' I jumped in, 'otherwise it wouldn't have been *art*.'

'And *beshides*,' added Joe, his sore throat now a distant, bourbon-tinged memory, 'isn't it fun to do something just for the *shake* of it shometimes?'

'I gue-ess...' said Terra, with a weary look suggesting she was actually thinking '... and I'm going to spend a whole *day* with these losers tomorrow?'

Now don't get me wrong. Neither Joe nor I had any pretensions that what we were doing was art. We were under no illusions that this was anything more than two friends on the road in search of rock and roll America, hoping to learn a little something along the way. What we *were* doing though, was making a grand gesture for the hell of it, because if you can't find a good reason for doing something, then a stupid one will have to do. In our own little way we were burning a million quid, or at the very least circumnavigating the M25 for twenty-five hours. And we didn't care whether people got it or not.

19 OCTOBER

OUR HOUSE IS A VERY FINE HOUSE

The music that moves Chris fills a canyon. Laurel Canyon, to be precise – the location for today's film shoot with Terra. But the magical musical spot for me in this part of Los Angeles is somewhat smaller. It's a house. Well, a mansion really, built in 1918 and owned at one time by Harry Houdini. There's a lot of security around it, and it looks tricky to get into. (But presumably there's a hidden key somewhere nearby so that you can pick the locks without anyone in the audience seeing.)

The Houdini Mansion is now owned by Rick Rubin, a man who has shaped my – and, chances are, your – music collection. On the one hand, Rubin's achievements in music are so extraordinary that he, more than anyone else in the field, is deserving of the prefix 'a man who needs no introduction'. On the other, he is such an enigma, and his work so mysterious, that an introduction is precisely what he needs.

Frederick Jay 'Rick' Rubin, was born on 10 March 1963 in New York and started growing a beard on 11 March. Whilst serving in high school band The Pricks he founded a record label and gave it the rather magnificent name of Def Jam Recordings. In 1984 he met an entrepreneur called Russell Simmons and Def Jam evolved into the most exciting and dynamic record label on the planet. With Rubin handling much of the production work as well as the A&R ('artist and repertoire' in record company speak – the person who says 'Don't record that song it's crap; do record that song it's good' in normal speak), Def Jam signed LL Cool J, Public Enemy, and Beastie Boys. 'Walk This Way'? Yep – that was Rick's idea. Hell, he's even responsible for The Bangles' version of 'Hazy Shade of Winter', one of the most extraordinary cover versions of all time.

Having pretty much brought hip-hop to the mainstream – not a shabby first day in the office – he fell out of love with Def Jam, moved to LA and founded Def American Recordings. Which is where he decided to reinvent heavy metal. Rock music was in good health at this point: Metallica, Anthrax, Maiden, Guns N' Roses were all having considerable success, so the genre wasn't crying out for a new dimension. Clearly no one told Rick. Or for that matter Slayer, a band noted for their recurrent themes of death, deviance, warfare, suicide, religion, necrophilia, Satanism and Nazism. Cliff Richard's a big fan. Impossibly loud, devastatingly thrashing and staggeringly technically accomplished, their masterwork – and their first album with Rubin – is called *Reign in Blood*. It's a classic.

So, having done rap and metal (oh, and having completed an Aerosmith revival by producing the brilliant *Permanent Vacation* album – so that's classic rock ticked off as well), he turned to the fusion of genres being peddled by sock-sporting funk-rock chancers the Red Hot Chili Peppers. Which is where the Houdini Mansion comes in. You see, Rick's vision for them involved recording at his new gaff in LA. The subsequent record, *Blood Sugar Sex Magik*, beat the sales and acclaim of anything the band or Rubin had produced before. No matter what the hip, sneery journos might say – *Blood Sugar* is a masterpiece. From the mono AM radio-style opening of 'The Power of Equality', through the world-dominating 'Under the Bridge', all the way to the Charleston skip of 'They're Red Hot', it's a record of impeccable musicianship, ingenious production and truly awful lyrics.

When I first heard it I found it awkward and terribly long. Yet their tattooed, beachside ne'er-do-well appeal prompted me to do something I had never done before. I tried harder to like it. So when the summer holiday came, I decided I would listen to one album and one album only, so that by the start of the school year I'd have a new favourite band. It worked. I planned to apply precisely this logic to item number one on my to-do list for the trip – learn to love the music of Gram Parsons. A month locked in a car with several albums and a Gram obsessive bleating in my ear was sure to do the trick.

The Houdini Mansion has since been used as a studio for a range of records including such gems as Jay Z's *99 Problems* and The Mars Volta's *De-Loused in the Comatorium*. It's also rumoured to be haunted. Now I'm pretty sceptical about the whole haunting business, but there's a big difference between a house that can scare, say, first lady of the paranormal Yvette Fielding, and a house that scares... Slipknot. That's right – Iowa's purveyors of finest thrash metal recorded at the house and to this day will not go back there, due to what Joey Jordison (the death-mask-encased, crown-of-thorns-wearing drummer) describes as 'an unsettling incident in the basement'. The record they made there, *The Subliminal Verses*, is another of Rick's gems, proving once again that he is a musical alchemist, turning the heaviest of metals into pure gold records.

Everyone owns a bit of Rubin somewhere. If at this point you're thinking that you don't, then I'd suggest a quick look at his discography and you'll find that you probably do. Shakira's 'Hips Don't Lie'? Rubin. Sir Mixalot's bottom-fetish anthem 'Baby Got Back'? Rubin. System of a Down? Rage Against the Machine? Weezer? Rubin. Lil Jon? Metallica? AC/DC? The Cult? Justin Timberlake? All Rick Rubin. Trust me, it goes on. And then there's the reason I love Rick Rubin. Johnny Cash.

Today, Johnny Cash is venerated as one of the greats of American music. His dusty outlaw boom-chikka-boom tales are woven into the fabric of the country's musical history. The mariachi horns of 'Ring of Fire' are as familiar to the American ear as the whistle of a distant freight train. They laughed along with 'A Boy Named Sue', cried along to 'Hurt', and broke into spontaneous applause when he said 'Hello, I'm Johnny Cash.' But it wasn't always this way. After commercial success in the sixties and TV success in the seventies, his star lost some of its shine, reaching its nadir with such country-lite nonsense as 'Chicken in Black' (a song about having his brain put in a chicken – really). Shortly after that particular low point he left Columbia records and exited the mainstream. A little while later, enter Rick Rubin.

In 1993 Rick signed Johnny Cash to his Def American label, and a year later released an album comprising mostly covers, and pretty obscure ones at that. So starts the greatest last act in rock and roll history. Entitled *American Recordings*, the record reminded listeners of one thing – that Johnny Cash was a singer of songs without equal.

In the ten years that followed, Johnny Cash would release another three albums in this vein, each one offering a mix of gospel, country and ingenious covers. Much has been written about his rendition of Nine Inch Nails' 'Hurt', and its quietly devastating video. But for me Johnny Cash did one thing that no one else on the planet could. He made country music sound great. In his hands, with his voice, it no longer sounded like shit-kicking, cousin-shagging fairground music – it was soaring and graceful, evocative and warm. That's why Johnny Cash is the only country artist I love. And that's why I love Rick Rubin.

Not that anyone really knows what Rick Rubin does. I've produced dozens of interviews with people who have worked with him, and none of them – not one – can tell me.

The Gossip: 'Oh, he's a guru.'
Yeah – but what does he do?
Macy Gray: 'He's like a wizard.'
Seriously – what does he do?
James Hetfield: 'You know what, I'd often ask myself that exact same question... What does Rick actually do?'

So after extensive research I can tell you exactly what I think Rick Rubin does. Not much. And that's his genius. Simply by being there, Rick Rubin makes things better.

Production is often considered a black art. There are many schools of thought about how best to produce a record. Some producers almost become a member of the band, some help write the songs, others just set up the equipment and press record. Rick Rubin can do all of these things, but often he is employed simply because, when you need someone to say 'That ain't good enough yet', he's one of few people left on the planet that a band like Metallica will listen to. When you travel to gigs on a private jet with groupies on standby to service you between encores, there aren't many people left who will say no to you. Because of his success, wisdom and skill, Rick Rubin is pretty much the only guy left. And it helps that he has a beard you could lose a bear in.

So I was searching for a mansion, Chris was looking for a bungalow.

> I'll light the fire
> You place the flowers in the vase
> That you bought today.

You might recognise that lyric from Crosby, Stills, Nash and Young's 1970 album *Déjà Vu*. They're the opening lines of 'Our House', a jaunty little portrait of domestic bliss which serves as a homely interlude in an album which is otherwise paranoid, lonely and helpless. It's a very pretty song.

Or you might know them from a nineties advert for the Halifax Building Society – the one with a house made out of people – who used the song to get a little extra help flogging mortgages. Either way, as you hear the song in your head it probably conjures up a picture of conjugal harmony:

> Our house is a very, very, very fine house,
> With two cats in the yard,

Life use to be so hard,
Now everything is easy 'cause of you...

Purty, ain't it? The house in question, a ramshackle wooden bungalow set into the hillside on Lookout Mountain Avenue, belonged to Joni Mitchell during the late sixties. It sat in a quiet district of Los Angeles called Laurel Canyon, a craggy mountain pass which connects, or rather separates, West Hollywood to the south and the San Fernando Valley to the north. Look at a map of the city and you'll notice that just north of West Sunset Boulevard the neat crosshatch of the LA grid system suddenly twists into a knot of elbows as steep, winding lanes tuck themselves into the folds of the Santa Monica Mountains. Cabins, cottages and chalets clamber over one another on dizzying bluffs to sneer at the frenzied affairs of La-La Land beneath them. This quiet and occasionally inaccessible haven was to become one of the most creatively prolific and commercially successful enclaves in rock music.

Mitchell's canyon home had stained glass windows, a grandfather clock given to her by Leonard Cohen, a stuffed elk's head hanging on the wall and all manner of hippie accoutrements besides. She shared this haven of countercultural domesticity with the N of CSNY, Graham Nash, a British singer-songwriter and founder member of the Hollies who had relocated to LA and comprised one quarter of the folk-rock supergroup. Mitchell, one time lover of the C from the same band, David Crosby, had swapped one member for another and moved Nash in with her.

And so it was that Nash came to immortalise this idyllic California setting in song, rhapsodising on his new life and love in the canyon and, without knowing it at the time, selling a few thousand mortgages into the bargain. Laurel Canyon was a tranquil, creative retreat that for a time during the late sixties and early seventies attracted musicians and their coterie almost without number. It was the type of place where you could pop out for some home furnishings in the morning, nip home and pen a song about it in the afternoon, and then release a multi-million selling album off the back of it weeks later. Minutes from the screaming neon cyclone of Sunset Boulevard, LA's playground of debauchery and vice, the canyon was a rambling, shambling collection of houses tucked quietly and inconspicuously into the hills just north of West Hollywood. It was country living, of a type, bang in the middle of Los Angeles, less than a stone's throw away from all the action. If the Troubadour was where this new breed of thrift-shop millionaires went out to play, Laurel Canyon was where they retired afterwards for a nice cup of tea and a sit-down.

It was in Laurel Canyon that David Crosby, Stephen Stills and Graham Nash reputedly first sang together. Exactly where depends on whose account you believe. Some, Nash included, have it that it took place in the front room of 'Our House', Joni's tumbledown cottage on Lookout Mountain Avenue, while others maintain it was at the home of 'Mama' Cass Elliott of The Mamas & the Papas who, along with Mitchell, reigned as de facto 'queen of the canyon', keeping a motherly eye on all the drug-addled goings-on in this curious little neighbourhood.

The fact that nobody can quite remember was all part of the appeal. Probably it was swept away in the blizzard of cocaine that blew through the canyon most days during its heyday, but I prefer to think that this quietly momentous occasion just got lost in the everyday like hundreds of other humdrum happenings in countless cosy areas like it. That was what I loved – the homeliness of it all. The idea that there was a place like Laurel Canyon, packed to the gills with such prodigious music talent, where life just went on like it did for everybody else. A place where Roger McGuinn would pop round to David Crosby's house to borrow a cup of sugar and stop to plot the rise of country rock over a cup of coffee and a chat. Where Jim Morrison could wander over the road to the Canyon Country Store, score a pint of milk and a few tabs of acid, and pay his newspaper delivery bill while he was there. On the way out he might bump into Graham Nash, who would ask him to feed his and Joni's cats while they went on tour. It all seemed so gloriously, thrillingly mundane.

But the reality of life in the canyon was a good deal more industrious than in my romantic imaginings. Its hungry, over-achieving inhabitants didn't just switch off their ambition when they walked through the front gate, and their lives were anything but mundane. Laurel Canyon was a squall of activity, much of it creative, a lot of it business. David Geffen famously announced to four of his artists, whilst sitting in the hot tub at his Laurel Canyon home, that he would keep the Asylum label to which they were all signed very small and intimate, declaring: 'I'll never have more artists than I can fit in this sauna.' Two of them, Glenn Frey and Don Henley, would go on to release America's biggest-selling album of all time – *Their Greatest Hits* by the Eagles. Laurel Canyon may have started out as a cottage industry in every sense of the term, but it was one which had much loftier aspirations than the homespun apparel adorning its hippie inhabitants would suggest. It was where the countercultural ideal met commerce head-on, and the output from both over ten or so prolific years changed the American music landscape forever.

Other famous residents included Frank Zappa, Jackson Browne, Arthur Lee, Carole King, Jimmy Webb, Alice Cooper, Orson Welles, Errol Flynn and Robert Mitchum. More recently, Anthony Kiedis of the Red Hot Chili Peppers, Meg Ryan, Jennifer Aniston, Marilyn Manson and Justin Timberlake have moved in.

And we were about to take a trip through the canyon with one of LA's newest and most ambitious young stars, Terra Naomi, and her producer Paul Fox. There was an aptness to our unintentional selection of tour guide. Terra knew virtually nothing about the Laurel Canyon era we were so keen to explore (beyond what she had been able to deduce from the pissed, rambling account the night before), but showed all the drive and hunger of a young David Crosby trying to make a name for himself on the LA folk scene. She had all the manner and accessories of a celebrity in waiting: an entourage in the shape of a camera crew, a small, fluffy, yapping dog and the kind of self belief that is a prerequisite for anyone wishing get ahead in the music business in LA.

Paul was older and wiser, having apparently worked in music long enough to have seen his fair share of talent through the mill. He was also tuned into the Laurel Canyon vibe, knew exactly the kind of muso-tourists he was dealing with and what kind of sights to show us. It helped that he knew virtually all the houses we were interested in by road name and number.

We followed in convoy into the canyon, the wide roads of West Hollywood sharply giving way to Laurel Canyon Boulevard as we gained height. At the corner of Kirkwood Drive, a short distance from Sunset, the green awning and bright orange facade of the Canyon Country Store peered out over trellis and shrubbery. We parked next door in front of a stone-clad launderette, to the right of which, behind a cascade of rhododendrons, was the wood-fronted villa occupied for a time in the late sixties by Jim Morrison. The store, made famous by Doors tune 'Love Street' as the place 'where the creatures meet', had been the epicentre and focal point of the neighbourhood; the same spot Joni Mitchell et al. had popped out to for their morning papers. The sign above the door was more Grateful Dead tour T-shirt than village corner shop, and to the left was mounted a circular mirror, decorated around its circumference with brightly coloured, psychedelic lettering announcing confidently – and quite beyond argument – that 'You Are Here'.

Inside, yellow strip lighting washed densely-packed shelves with tones of sepia. Traditional convenience store fayre competed for space with more unlikely items: we placed potato chips, some 'Love Massage Oil' and a gourd into a basket before selecting some beers from a capacious cooler at the rear of the store. The purpose of coming had been to set up the trip in a short piece for Terra's YouTube channel, in which Joe and I would be filmed buying supplies for our journey. After all, we had a long trip ahead of us and where better to stock up for it than the place where so many musical trailblazers had done the same? We wandered through the aisles with Terra acting as personal shopping assistant while Joe and I played the role of wide-eyed Brits lost in a bounteous wonderland of unbridled retail opportunity.

Shopping complete, we returned to the car and headed higher into the canyon, Paul pointing out the attractions from behind the wheel. The hairpins grew tighter, the roads narrower and steeper. Houses were crammed into the tucks and turns of lanes overhung with dense green foliage. Each was unique – neat white bungalows alongside tottering wooden villas next to sturdy brick chalets. Often an apparently single-storey house would turn out, upon rounding the next bend, to fall away on the opposite side with a three-floor glass facade onto vertiginous views of Hollywood.

We passed the Houdini mansion, eliciting a small whoop from Joe, on through Lookout Mountain Avenue past the cottage that Joni Mitchell had shared with Graham Nash (just 'very fine') and – this was an unexpected treat – pulled up outside a garage where Boston had rehearsed before hitting the big time. Further up we came upon the house from where 'Mama' Cass Elliott had ruled the canyon roost, cruised past Jimi Hendrix's temporary home and, lastly, stopped outside the reason why Paul knew so much about the area in the first place – the house he himself had occupied during the seventies and early eighties. Joe enquired as to precisely what had attracted so many musicians and actors to this part of LA.

'Well I think part of it was that it was like living in the country right in the middle of the city. It was very free – hey, up this driveway was where Paul Rothschild lived – and because people could walk around doing whatever they wanted, nobody came up here unless they were part of that whole community, which was really just a bunch of hippies. It was just bands playing in their backyards, everybody was high on one thing or another, just walking from one house to the next. People didn't lock their doors. It was just a very communal kind of a feeling. Each one of these houses has its own unique character, and because they were designed not to be year-round residences they were fairly affordable too. I took Dave Gregory from XTC up here and he said this was the "centre of the universe". And in a way it really was.'

Cameraman Matthew asked us to say a few words for the tape about how we were feeling. I clammed up at first – 'You mean you actually want me to actually say something? Off the top of my head?' – before stuttering out something about this being the 'real' start of the trip.

It was true. This magical mystery tour had really kickstarted the journey. Our quest was, after all, about making connections between music and places, and this we most assuredly had done. Joe had snatched a glimpse of the Houdini mansion and I had been able to peer into the front yard of 'Our House'. My only disappointment was the absence from it of two cats.

Terra and I celebrated with an a cappella rendition of the song for the camera. She took the high part and I took the low. Concentrating on the 'la-la-la' interlude towards the end, we made a passable attempt at close harmony, bobbing our heads from side to side and gazing at each other as we sang like Sonny and Cher doing 'I Got You Babe'.

We slalomed our way to the top of the canyon, briefly pausing to take in a spectacular view of downtown LA before dipping down into the Valley on the other side and making our way to the next stop on the tour.

The Alley is a rehearsal space, hideaway and closely-guarded secret located in the San Fernando Valley area of Los Angeles. It is home to more music memories – and memorabilia – than all of the Hard Rock Cafes the world over rolled into one. It's not listed in the phone book and it does not have a website. If you weren't a musician yourself, or closely connected to people that are, you might never even know it existed. The only way of securing a booking is by recommendation or referral by another musician. It is an Aladdin's cave to which only a privileged few are granted access, and our names were about to be added to the guest list.

Terra introduced us to Shiloh, the Alley's proprietor, curator and guardian angel who, along with her husband Bill, had lovingly tended this patch of rock and roll history since they acquired the building in 1973. Shiloh was a softly spoken, bosomy lady in her fifties with long, blonde hair cut into a wispy fringe which looked like it had framed her face unchanged since the sixties. In slow, rounded tones with an accent somewhere between LA and Vancouver, she described how her love affair with the place had begun. She and Bill had set about transforming the place, previously used as a recording studio, into a rehearsal-space-cum-musicians'-retreat from the moment they found it and had been filling its nooks, crannies and cubbyholes with curios, mementos and bric-a-brac ever since.

'Our first clients were Linda Ronstadt, Jackson Browne, Bonnie Raitt and Etta James. Since then we've had Minnie Ripperton, the Eagles, Emmylou Harris, Jack White, Alice Cooper, you name it. Everyone who plays here signs their name on that wall over there.'

Behind the stage a whitewashed brick wall shrieked a scrawl of signatures from floor to ceiling. We wandered over to take a look.

'They're all real people. Some famous, some not. Some alive, some dead,' added Shiloh.

As we marvelled at the roll call of legends who had honed their skills on the very stage we now stood on, Shiloh revealed what she felt gave the place its magic atmosphere.

'I believe that everybody who plays here leaves a little spark of energy, and it's that collective energy you feel when you come in the place, that vibe when you walk in the door.'

Vibe was exactly the right word. Vibe was the only word.

Next, Shiloh led us through a heavy wooden door along a passageway hung with tour posters and other psychedelic artwork. At the end of the corridor a second wooden door, replete with brass porthole and an elk horn for a handle, led to another rehearsal space called The Loft. This room was much larger than the first, with high ceilings and a wide stage occupying almost half the room. To the left a rope ladder led up to the loft which gave the room its name. We went up. A rocking chair in one corner called to me to sit down and, well, rock. Like a ten-year-old in his tree house with nothing but a long summer and a pile of unread comics to look forward to, I was utterly content. I looked up at Joe standing among the rafters.

'Mate, you know that trip we've been planning?'

'I think I know the one you mean.'

'I might just stay here instead. Sit here in this chair and rock. Maybe take up smoking.'

He sighed. 'This place is wonderful isn't it? I just love the fact that everything creaks. There's something of the pirate ship about it. I think we've already found the soul of American music. Why don't we forget the road trip and sit by the pool for three weeks.'

I rocked a final rock and reluctantly prised myself from the chair to return to the rehearsal space below. The wall behind the stage resembled the side of a barn with short, vertical wooden boards between longer horizontal beams that ran the length of the room. Two enormous cross beams extended diagonally from corner to corner forming a huge X behind the stage. A patchwork of patterned material stretched over every second vertical section, like a quilt thrown over the bed in the back bedroom. On closer inspection these turned out to be tour T-shirts for bands that had used the room ahead of going out on the road. They were all there – Alice Cooper, Crosby, Stills and Nash, Lynyrd Skynyrd, the Eagles.

'This is real hallowed turf, isn't it?' I cooed.

'It sure is,' said Shiloh. 'I'm honoured to be a part of it. It's kind of like a living rock and roll museum. A very special place.' She spoke with the reverence of a Westminster Abbey tour guide and seemed to love this place like it was one of her children.

Next we made our way upstairs to the living space. The lounge area was a treasure trove of junk, a mess of rock and roll miscellany strewn over every available space. Every inch of its wood-panelled walls was covered with photographs, mirrors, plaques, plates and other assorted adornments. A cello leaned against the mantelpiece next to a grandfather clock. Guitars of all shapes and sizes were crammed into every available cranny. A television set flickered unwatched in the farthest corner. Every bric, every brac, every knick and every knack was flawlessly arranged to create a harmonious hotchpotch of clutter and clobber.

To the left, two doors stood facing one another across a hallway, painted with what looked like scenes from *Easy Rider*. Each depicted a lone motorcyclist cruising along a highway, one towards us and the other away into the distance. The story behind them, it turned out, made a direct but unexpected connection to the reason for our trip, and it knocked me for six. One of the men in the paintings was Phil 'Road Mangler' Kaufman, the man who had cremated Gram's body. Shiloh will explain the rest:

'This door was on Phil Kaufman's house. When he moved he left the door and we were afraid it was going to be painted over or replaced. So we went and got the door and put it on our bathroom here. It shows Bill, my husband, coming towards you and Phil Kaufman riding away.'

More cooing all round. What a find! The Road Mangler's front door! For rock and roll bounty hunters it didn't get much better than this.

Music, it almost goes without saying, is the product of the people that make it. But it's also the product of the place in which it is made. At The Alley those two things came together in an extraordinarily powerful way. Stumbling upon a direct connection to the very inspiration for our travels in so secret a setting as this caught me completely unawares. I nearly blubbed.

Finally Joe reflected on the magic of the place. 'Every room looks like it's from a movie, except that a set dresser could spend a lifetime trying to get this look and they wouldn't because it's real. There's something quite unsettling about it. That there's somewhere so atmospheric that's just a place to hang out. You feel like it's the entrance way to some sort of ride. Is this queuing time fifteen minutes for the rock and rollercoaster ride?'

The rock and rollercoaster ride, it turned out, was just beginning.

20 OCTOBER

ANARCHY IN THE USA

I like to sleep. I have a young son, so it has become a commodity as prized as gold. Except that I don't ever spend an entire day in a daze because I didn't get enough gold the previous night. Chris is – and I didn't know this until, ooh, let's see, er... today – an insomniac.

Insomnia is no doubt a debilitating and madly frustrating condition, and all you insomniacs out there, you have my sympathies. What I don't understand though is why insomniacs go to such lengths to explain to the somnolent among us just how badly they slept, quite how grating they found their pillow or how much another person's mere breathing prevented them from passing through the fluffy gates to the Land of Nod. Let's say you go to a party, plop yourself down on a sofa and get into conversation with someone who is in a wheelchair. If they were they to start ticking you off for sitting on a sofa next to them as if it were a gratuitous waste of two perfectly good legs when they had none, you would think them a tad unreasonable. Insomniacs, however, never fail to start my day by telling me how awfully they slept, how I don't understand what it's like, and how my snoring sounds like Chewbacca with his tackle caught in a blender.

As I said, today I found out that Chris is an insomniac. Because when I woke up he told me. And all that other stuff too.

I made a brief trip to the bathroom to check my swelling tonsils, and then we headed out in search of breakfast. We had a day to kill in LA before the drive to Joshua Tree late in the afternoon, time enough to do a little more sightseeing, possibly even some celebrity spotting. We made a pretty good start as we exited the lift in the hotel lobby by almost bumping into Lyle Lovett waiting to go up. All those hit songs, I thought, all those arenas sold out, critical acclaim, and yet forever destined to be known as 'the funny looking bloke that shagged Julia Roberts'. (Better than being known as 'the funny looking bloke that didn't shag Julia Roberts' I suppose.)

When you walk out of the Four Seasons Hotel – and for that matter most LA hotels – you become acutely aware that you are both 'somewhere' and 'nowhere'. You are geographically in the heart of the world's entertainment capital, but psychologically the fact you're not heading out for a meeting with Spielberg and Darabont means that you know you don't really belong.

The other reason you realise you're nowhere is that you're walking. Much has been written about LA's love of the car, so it feels a tad clichéd to bang on about it here, but the usual anti-California rant goes like this:

'Seriously, they get in the car to go to the shops round the corner.'

'Really? What terrible, wasteful, polar-bear-killing scumbags they are.'

But there really is no choice but to drive. The shop around the corner is at least thirty minutes' drive away. Not because of jams, but because the streets are huge, and long, and many, and long, and huge. The city evolved alongside the car in a state where space was to be celebrated and exploited. Why put shops next to each other when gas is tuppence a gallon? Spread 'em out, enjoy the drive. See the city as you shop. So don't think of LA as a road planner's wet dream. Think of it as an open air mall where you use a car instead of a shopping trolley. That's how the city has ended up this way.

Inspired by the surroundings, Chris was quoting lots of *Beverly Hills Cop*. Never having been a fan of the film, I was a little confused by this and kept mistaking his one-liners for genuine conversation – bananas in tailpipes, wrecked buffets at the Harrow Club, and how the average American has five pounds of undigested red meat in his bowels by the time he's fifty.

'Must be all those hamburgers,' I said.

'You're supposed to say "Why are you telling me this?"'

'Oh. Sorry.'

'You really don't know it at all do you?'

'Nope. And I never will.'

The story of the making of *Beverly Hills Cop* has been frequently told. Sylvester Stallone, hot on the heels of the success of *First Blood* and *Rocky III* (but before he descended into arm-wrestling pics), decided he was going to make an LA action flick. Creative differences caused him to abandon the project. So off he goes to make *Cobra* with his vision of what *Beverly Hills Cop* should have been, and in comes Eddie Murphy who, so the story goes, improvised most of the great performances in the film.

I have various issues with it, chief amongst them being that it's not very funny and therefore I don't see why so many people I know get all whoop-de-doo about it. And secondly the claim that 'the best bits were improvised'. A great many performances are purportedly improvised, with the claim invariably coming from the actor. Which all seems rather disrespectful to the writer, and greedy on behalf of the star. If Eddie Murphy was that good off the top of his head, how come he couldn't do it ever again? And lastly, as I dismount my soapbox, I ask you to consider a genuinely improvised performance by way of comparison. Marlon Brando did Colonel Kurtz in *Apocalypse Now* right off the top of his tubby dome. Rambling, nonsensical, incoherent – that is what improvisation looks like. So I'd like to take this opportunity to congratulate Daniel Petrie Junior for his work on the *Beverly Hills Cop* screenplay. Because even though I don't like it, *he* deserves the credit.

But back to the breakfast quest. Dizzy with the heat, and determined not to let our growling stomachs go unanswered, we carried on. And on. And then we found ourselves, instead of filling our bellies, outside Doug Weston's Troubadour, where Chris got very excited and distracted us from our hunger with a history lesson.

On the 25 August 1970 a British singer-songwriter just starting to make a name for himself in the UK, but who was so far a complete unknown in the US, played to an almost empty room at a venue on LA's Santa Monica Boulevard. Another unknown by the name of Glenn Frey, who would later find fame, fortune and much else besides in a band called the Eagles, caught a few minutes of the visiting performer's set, having only interrupted his beer in the bar out front to go to the gents. Mesmerised by what he had seen, Frey dragged his drinking partner through to the room at the back of the venue to see the rest of the set. In doing so they witnessed the first performance on American soil of what would turn out to be one of the most enduring – not to mention glittering – careers that the music business has ever seen.

The performer was Elton John, and the venue was Doug Weston's Troubadour. Six consecutive performances at the venue, each more explosive and more talked about than the last, catapulted Elton from visiting unknown to chart-straddling superstar in under a week, and sealed the Troubadour's reputation as the most influential popular music venue in the US, if not the world. That another Troubadour ace face and soon-to-be-colossus-of-country-rock, Glenn Frey, was there to see it happen only added to the sense of magic that surrounded the place.

And our aimless meanderings around Beverly Hills, in a vain attempt at finding some breakfast, had seen us vainly and aimlessly meandering right past its front door. This place is a major entry in the rock and roll history books and as such it had been close to the top of the list of places to seek out when we reached LA. So it came as a shock to find it here, bang in the middle of, well, not very much, as the most diverting places our breakfast quest had thrown up so far were a dry cleaners, a change management firm called Shift Happens and a warehouse store specialising in pet food.

But it wasn't Elton John, or even the Eagles particularly, that we were interested in. For a decade prior to the epoch-changing moment described above, the Troubadour had been steadily growing its reputation as the birthplace of countless new West Coast stars from Jackson Browne to Linda Ronstadt, Don McLean to Joni Mitchell, with Doug Weston as the dictatorial, truculent midwife at the helm. Other regulars at the club included Janis Joplin and Jim Morrison, James Taylor and Carole King. Most importantly though, for us at least, the Troubadour was the closest thing there was to a birthplace of country rock. This was where The Byrds and the Burritos were born. It was also, regrettably, where they in turn gave birth to a bastard child called the Eagles.

It was at the Troubadour that a young David Crosby announced to Jim McGuinn (later to change his name to Roger – presumably because it had a much sexier ring to it[2]) and Gene Clark that they were going to form a group. That group became The Byrds, who would define the marriage of folk and rock by releasing a version of Bob Dylan's as

---

2 The truth is even crazier than that. In 1965 McGuinn joined a 'spiritual association' called Subud, whose leader and founding member Bapak (that's 'leader and founding member' – rings alarm bells straight away, doesn't it?) told him he should change his name, suggesting that something beginning with R would help him to 'vibrate with the universe'. McGuinn came up with a series of names reflecting his fascination with aviation and science fiction, such as Ramjet, Rocket and Roger (as in 'Roger that, Charlie foxtrot'). Bapak selected Roger because it was the only 'real' name on the list.

yet unrecorded 'Mr Tambourine Man', bagging themselves a number one hit on both sides of the Atlantic into the bargain. All of a sudden folk music was commercial, and the new breed of hipsters, shaking off the folksy image in all but the way they looked, were loving it. Crosby typified the ambitious, entrepreneurial spirit that now flowed through the nascent LA music industry, and the Troubadour was the most natural home for it. It was a place where connections could be made, deals done, contracts signed; a place where a determined individual with a handful of songs and a little coke could make friends and influence people. It was where you *got on*.

Later the club would become the epicentre of another growing LA scene, this time the amalgamation of country and rock – first when The Byrds were joined by Gram Parsons and 'went country' and later with Poco, formed from the ashes of Buffalo Springfield. Finally, Gram's post-Byrds project The Flying Burrito Brothers found a more soulful take on the country/rock hybrid, but none of these prototype twang-rockers found any real commercial success, chiefly on account of Gram's voracious appetite for hard drugs, and the fact that his head was jammed so far up Keith Richards' behind for most of the time that his own band became something of a distraction.

But the Troubadour also had another more personal musical connection for me in the form of the song which brought me to this music in the first place. 'Different Drum' was written by the venue's former 'hootmaster' (and later Monkee) Mike Nesmith, who had given the song to his girlfriend and Troubadour debutante Linda Ronstadt, who in turn had a hit with it in 1967. It came to my attention, like so many of my musical mainstays from the time before I was born, via The Lemonheads' Evan Dando, who covered it on *Favourite Spanish Dishes*. I loved it instantly. Along with The Lemonheads' cover of Gram's 'Brass Buttons' on the *Lovey* album, it had been the key which unlocked the door to virtually all the American artists I have since come to love.

Joe insisted I try a piece to camera for our imaginary documentary. Despite a touch of nerves about the prospect of trying our hand at presenting, we felt confident that two wizened media execs such as us had seen too much broadcasting talent in action over the years not to have picked up a trick or two. Really, how hard could it be?

It was then that our preparation for filming – that is, the complete absence of any preparation at all, not even say, working out how to use the camera or thinking about what you're going to say before recording – threw up a few early lessons in documentary film-making.

I fumbled for something to say while Joe squinted into the viewfinder. 'Rolling!'

'Behind me is the legendary Troubadour music venue, where lots of really legendary things happened during the sixties, not to mention the seventies and likewise even the eighties... Sorry, I'll start that again.'

Shit. This wasn't as easy as Kevin McCloud made it look. Take two.

'Behind me is Doug Weston's legendary venue, the Troubadour, the home of live music in Los Angeles for nearly half a century,' – better – 'and *pheeeewy*, this place was exciting in the sixties.'

Joe dropped the lens a couple of inches and peered over the top of the controls. 'Gonna stop you there mate. Wasn't sure about "pheeeewy".'

'Yep, sorry, not sure what happened there. Couldn't think of anything to say.'

'Take your time,' he said, settling into the role of producer-director-cameraman far more comfortably than I was into the role of presenter. He hoisted the camera back onto his shoulder. 'Rolling!'

I paused for a second to collect my thoughts. All it needed was something about Elton John, a bit about folk rock and The Byrds, and a couple of sentences on Gram's connection to the place. No problem.

'Doug Weston's legendary Troubadour music venue, the home of live music in LA for nearly fifty years. It was here that Elton John became dead... er, famous, the Byrds did likewise and ... *pheeeewy*, there was music aplenty.'

Phewy? Music aplenty? What was going on? I hadn't used either phrase before in my entire life, ever. One more try.

'Boy oh boy, am I excited to be here... Shit!' Apparently I was now filing a Blue Peter special report on the birthplace of country rock.

'Sorry mate.' I squirmed. 'This may take some time. The light on top of the camera is erasing everything just as I open my mouth. Mind if we pop back to the hotel for a bit to do some research?'

Which is how we came to learn a valuable lesson about talking to camera. Work out what you're going to say, write it down even, so the laser beam can't make you say things you've only ever heard in Roy Rogers movies, *then* say it. We got better, honest.

Once we'd finished admiring the Troubadour (a less time-consuming pursuit than you'd imagine – when the history lesson is over you realise it's just a closed-up bar and you're still hungry), we decided we needed a tour guide. It was time to visit Punk Rock Mike.

'Punk Rock Mike' is not one of those tiresome, ironic nicknames in the vein of *Robin Hood*'s Little John or Bill 'The Hotness' Gates. Punk Rock Mike is thus known because punk rock – specifically the contemporary form of punk rock coming out of Los Angeles, California – is his life. It's the reason for his abundant and impressive tattoos. It's the reason he married his punk-band-fronting wife Stacey, and it's the reason he is the host of Radio 1's Punk Show. Mike lived in London for many years and recently moved back to the States, which is why Punk Rock Mike with his punk rock wife and his punk rock tattoos lived with... his dad.

Mike's home was in Culver City, which is in fact not really a city but one of the many suburbs which have coalesced into what we now know as Los Angeles. Like Tooting but with film studios instead of kebab shops.

After introducing us to his genial dad, a retired Welshman who had been one of Hollywood's finest location managers, Mike offered to show us around his manor while we captured the tour on film. Punk Rock Mike may be steeped in the ethos of London circa 1976, but he's very much a twenty-first-century tour guide. We jumped in the wheels and drove all of two yards.

'Pull over. We've reached our first landmark.'

'Really?'

'Yup. Gentlemen, that piece of sidewalk right there is where Erick Estrada sat me on his bike during a break in filming for *CHiPs*. You can carry on driving.'

Three right turns later we approached the entrance to a huge golf course – or something that looked very like one – that looms over Mike's house. The sign above it read 'Holy Cross Cemetery'.

Mike was very proud of his turf, even – in fact especially – turf that contained dead people. And understandably so. The roll call of famous and infamous personalities interred in the hill overlooking his pool was impressive. It was an enormous place. So big in fact that after twenty minutes of driving around we couldn't actually track down a single famous dead person. For us there was no Bing Crosby to pay our respects to. No Rita Hayworth, no Sharon Tate. We couldn't even find John Candy's grave, which is surprising as unlike most of his films his final resting place apparently has a sizeable plot. We cut our losses and gave up.

From the graves we went, if not to the cradle, then to one of the places Mike first made his mark on the world. Bill Botts Field is the baseball pitch where he found little league fame as a heavy hitter before his rotator cuff failed and forced him into early retirement at the ripe old age of eleven.

There can't be many sports fields with the sort of views enjoyed by Bill Botts. The whole of LA lay before us like a dirty Legoland. The Pacific glinted to the left, muscular hills rose to the right. You could even see the Hollywood sign. Behind the batting cage a handful of nodding donkeys loped and clanked at depleting wells of oil. 'Mike, have I seen those pumps somewhere before?' I asked.

'You seen *LA Confidential*, *Beverly Hills Cop II*, *Swordfish*?'

'Yeah.'

'Then you've seen them somewhere before.'

He pointed out the key landmarks: the Police Headquarters, the business district and nearby rooftops where state troopers had settled with sniper rifles during the Rodney King riots. I'm pretty sure you don't get that depth of information from a commercial guide.

'OK – let's go watch the junkies at Venice.'

You don't get that from a commercial guide either.

We freewheeled down from Bill Botts Field and hit the pedal towards Venice Beach. Mike pointed out the enormous white frontage of 9336 Washington Boulevard, instantly recognisable as the house from *Gone with the Wind*, even to those who, like me, have never been arsed to sit through the film.

Nearby is the Culver Hotel. Countless Hollywood stars stayed here in the classic era and the rooms have names like 'The John Wayne Suite' in their honour. But even the Duke's visit is overshadowed by the Culver's most infamous guests. In 1938, while filming *The Wizard of Oz*, MGM studios announced, with no hint of irony, that they were 'short of midgets'. And you can't take a trip to Munchkinland without munchkins. So 'little people' from across the country were bussed in to take their place on the yellow brick road. And they all stayed at the Culver.

It was, at that time, probably the largest gathering of little people the world had ever seen, and with the added excitement of movie-making it seems that many got a little carried away. In fact the stories of what went on in the hotel during their four-week stay have long since passed into legend. My favourite was regularly told by David Niven, who recalled walking past the Culver one evening when the police were called. He asked one of the attending officers as to the nature of the incident, to be told that several munchkins had become drunk and disorderly and were currently resisting arrest. With hands too small for cuffs and no restraints of a suitable size, the hotel laundry had been called on to help. Niven watched as nine policemen emerged from the foyer, each holding a wriggling, writhing and rather heavy... pillowcase.

We sluggishly stop-started our way across the gridlocked LA sprawl to Venice Beach, the Camden of the coast. We parked the car and I feigned sunny nonchalance, leaving the roof down as we wandered off and casually bibbing the car lock over my shoulder.

'Dude, you gonna leave your car like that?'

'Yeah, Mike. This is Venice Beach. It'd be square to put the roof up, no?'

'No.'

'Really?'

'*Really* not square. Square is coming back to find a Chrysler-sized hole in the parking lot and a car-sized hole in your insurance claim.'

Evidently Venice Beach was the Camden of California in every sense. Roof up, doors firmly locked, we continued the tour.

First we reached Muscle Beach, which of course is not actually a beach but an open-air gym. An open-air gym designed not so much for working out as for a very particular brand of muscle-bound, homoerotic exhibitionism. Rollerbladers and skateboarders, henna tattooists and hair braiders, basketballers and basket cases all played out their roles in this pantomime. But despite the temptation of a temporary tour tattoo, we walked down to the sea to dip our toes in the Pacific and mark the true beginning of our coast-to-coast undertaking.

'Don't take your shoes off until you have to. There are needles and drugs and shit everywhere round here.'

'Mike – you're not imbuing the moment with appropriate road-trip romance.'

'Just being realistic.'

'You come here often Mike?'

'Nope. Only with tourists.'

'Thanks.'

'Though I used to go to school just a ways down the coast there. They used to film *Baywatch* on the beach by our school. Early mornings were the only time they could have the beach, so my bus would pull up just in front of where Pamela and Yasmin were wrapped in towels freezing their asses off.'

The Pacific Ocean rolled in, sinking our feet into the sand. We tried hard to savour the moment, gazing meaningfully at the horizon while simultaneously scanning the surf for hypodermics.

That evening, Mike treated us to dinner courtesy of Culver's finest Mexican food outlet, Tito's Tacos. We ate by the pool in his garden, watched by a flotilla of hummingbirds. Their anxious buzzing was a reminder that we needed to move on. LA had been good to us, but now was the time to clock up some miles. We bade our host goodbye and pointed the car towards the Mojave Desert.

On 14 July 1973, Byrds guitarist Clarence White was killed by a drunk driver while loading gear into his car for a gig. Following the funeral, his friend and band mate Gram Parsons got drunk, as he was wont to do. He had been deeply affected by the burial of his close friend and told his tour manager Phil 'Road Mangler' Kaufman that when he died, instead of a conventional funeral he wanted to be cremated at his favourite place in the world, Joshua Tree in the Mojave Desert. Kaufman promised that if he was still around when it happened, he would do right by his man.

Two months later, Gram took a trip out to Joshua Tree to hang out with friends, sing songs and take drugs, as he was wont to do. He checked into room eight of the Joshua Tree Inn with his girlfriend and two days later 'checked out', having overdosed on booze and either heroin or morphine depending on whose account you believe. His body was taken to Los Angeles International Airport to be prepared for shipping to Louisiana for burial. If the story had ended there, then Parsons' infamy probably would have ended with it. It didn't, because at this point in the tale things got weird.

Kaufman, who by his own admission was twisted with a heady mix of grief and alcohol, resolved that he would honour his friend's wishes. He borrowed a hearse, drove it onto the tarmac at LAX and persuaded the ground crew that they should give the body to him. Convinced by his wheels if not by his unusual appearance, they handed it over and Kaufman headed east. He drove as fast as his little legs would allow and screeched to a halt at Cap Rock, a massive outcrop in the middle of the desert all of fifty yards from the road. Unable to lift out the coffin, he drove off the road and tipped it onto the scrub. Then he doused Gram in petrol and set fire to him.

As with all legends, there is of course so much more to Gram's story than that. There's a man called Coon Dog, a millionaire orange farmer, Charles Manson, a suicide, an alcoholic mother, and – because it wouldn't be a proper rock and roll story without him – ladies and gentlemen, please welcome Keith Richards.

The first time I ever heard the name Joshua Tree was, I think, when Roger Scott talked about the new U2 album on Radio 1. Great album, crap name. As a result I have always associated the place with the Larry Mullen Band more than anyone else. When you are actually in the Joshua Tree National Park however, the only obvious musical connection you can see is at Cap Rock. This is where the 'Grampires' come to pay their respects, down a shot and share in a bit of rock and roll history. Keep on driving through the desert and you reach a rocky escarpment from which you can look across a twenty-mile-wide valley that marks the exact point at which California is trying to break away from the mainland. One day the faultline will give way, the ocean will rush in, and we'll be left, as Bill Hicks put it, with the natural beauty of 'Arizona Bay'.

As we headed out of LA along Interstate 10 it occurred to me that, other than the tale of his drunken DIY cremation, I knew very little about the man whose birthday we were supposed to be celebrating. When I say 'very little' I actually mean 'pretty much nothing other than his name'. So with the strains of his second solo album *Grievous Angel* quietly plink-plonking on the stereo, I flipped through a Parsons biography in the hope of learning a thing or two. The salient points, from where I was sitting, looked like this:

1946: Ingram Cecil Connor III is born.

1957: Sees Elvis in concert and resolves to become a rock and roller just like him.

1958: His father, 'Coon Dog' Connor, commits suicide two days before Christmas. That's right, 'Coon Dog'.

1959: Gram's mother Avis marries Bob Parsons.

1963: Joins first professional outfit, the Shilos.

1965: Attends Harvard University to study theology. Drops out after one semester.

1966: He and friends from the Boston folk scene form the International Submarine Band. His daughter, Polly, is born.

1968: Relocates to Los Angeles and releases the album *Safe at Home*. Leaves the band before release and joins The Byrds, at that point one of the biggest bands in America. Gram instigates a new vision for the band, taking them in a country direction for the album *Sweetheart of the Rodeo*. Refuses to tour South Africa with The Byrds, ostensibly because of apartheid. Many speculate it is actually because he would prefer to hang out with his new friend Keith Richards of the Rolling Stones. He is fired from the band. Starts visiting Joshua Tree.

1969: Forms new band The Flying Burrito Brothers with Chris Etheridge and pedal steel player 'Sneaky' Pete Kleinow. Releases *The Gilded Palace of Sin*. It is a fine album but not a commercial success.

1970: Releases second Burritos album on a very tight budget, comprising of swiftly penned numbers, rushed recordings and a couple of *Gilded* out-takes. It's called *Burrito Deluxe*. It tanks.

1972: Now fat from too much drink and Southern food, Gram is signed to Reprise Records.

1973: Releases first solo album, *GP*. Accidentally burns down his Topanga Canyon home. Starts dating Margaret Fisher. Dies from an overdose in room eight of the Joshua Tree Inn on 19 September, despite Margaret's attempts at resuscitation by putting ice cubes up his bum.

1974: His second solo album, *Grievous Angel*, is posthumously released.

As we drove toward the fabled Joshua Tree National Park I started to think about where we were going. And I realised that everything I know of the place is based on a 'Classic Album' documentary I once made about the U2 album of the same name. Sadly these memories told me nothing of topography, geography or climate. In fact, all it told me was why the album is so called:

'What are those things over there?' Bono asked the driver as they scouted for locations to shoot the album cover.

'Those? Oh, those are Joshua trees.'

'I know that look in his eye,' thought Edge as Bono continued to look out the window at the gnarled cacti waving their fists in the air. 'So that's what the album's going to be called, isn't it?'

And that is how Joshua trees entered the popular music conscience. Not because of any mystical, hippy, Stones-tinged majesty. Not because of runes or ouija boards or wizardry. No magic involved at all, unless like some you think Bono is the Messiah.

At least that's how Edge tells the story. They had recorded an album that everyone was telling them was the best thing they'd ever made, and it was untitled – until they went to do the photo shoot for it, and in the landscape around them Bono found his inspiration. Chances are if you've heard of Joshua Tree before, it's because of that album.

We arrived in the dark with a scuff of tyres on dusty forecourt. Joe rolled camera as I approached the office to pick up the keys. A brief introductory conversation with innkeeper Yvo Kwee and we were in possession of the key to room eight of the Joshua Tree Inn, the place where it had all gone horribly wrong on 19 September 1973.

The room itself was smaller than the one I had held in my head for the past fifteen years. Even as I sat scanning it, the mental image of the 'original' room eight was hard to shake off. If I closed my eyes I still saw that imagined room and not the one we now occupied. It felt prefabricated, built quickly and cheaply without ostentation save for a nod to the

Spanish in style. The walls were painted salmon pink, which looked uncomfortable on exposed brick, which in turn jarred with the chintz of the tasselled curtains and wrought-iron lampshades either side of the double bed. In all it had the feel of a tiny scout hut decked out by a fussy housewife.

At the foot of the bed were two doorways, one with no door which opened onto a space about the size of a walk-in wardrobe, but which contained nothing but an empty fridge. To the left of that was the bathroom, spartan but with neatly arranged towels and showy net curtains above the toilet. It crossed my mind that this bathroom must have been where Gram took the dose of morphine that finally finished him off. (Then again maybe not: if you choose to rent a motel room in the middle of the desert for the express purpose of taking drugs, perhaps you wouldn't feel the need to retire to the bathroom to do it. Unless junkie etiquette dictates that the actual doing be done behind closed doors or whilst sat on the toilet. He did have company after all.)

Above the bed hung a black and white photo of Gram in a grand wooden chair – a section of the same picture on the sleeve of *GP* – flanked by two posters for Byrds gigs, one with Fleetwood Mac, the other with Joe Cocker, both at the Fillmore West. A guest book sat on the dresser, filled with touching tributes from other weirdos who had gone before us. Flipping through I felt a little pathetic; just another sad 'Grampire' among thousands that pass through, eager to leave a message for 'Brother Gram' and thank him for the music. But stumbling across a message from the Charlatans' Tim Burgess we began to feel as though we were among much more auspicious company.

It didn't feel at all weird being there. Not ghoulish or macabre or morose, not 'like staying in a mausoleum' as Joe put it. To know that Gram lay dying on this floor just feet from where ours were now didn't feel in the least morbid or sinister. But it must have been strange for Joe, whose connection to him goes no further than tolerating my unusual obsession and tireless evangelism.

A word or two about Joe then: if it were possible to like him more than I do already then he'd given me every reason in the last few days. Here are some of them:

One: I have closer friends who actually *like* Gram's music, but they weren't with me now, nor did they suggest the trip, as Joe did, on the grounds that, well, you're my mate, you love this guy Gram Parsons, so why don't we throw him a proper party and see a thing or two on the way? Two: he'd separated himself from his wife and child for three-and-a-bit weeks in order to be here, missed them like a hole in the ozone layer and hadn't moaned once beyond a brief 'homesick moment' as we left LA. Three: he indulges an obsession in me which borders on the compulsive, even though he still doesn't understand it. Four: anyone prepared to embark on a month-long journey across America just because they don't understand something deserves a medal. I don't understand Sudoku but I'm not about to go to Japan to find out what the fuss is all about.

But he snores like a congested hippo.

21 OCTOBER

MISSING PARSONS REPORT

Body clock still running fast, I woke up at 5.30 a.m. for the third day in a row despite a concerted effort the previous evening to give myself a fighting chance of sleep – by staying up late and getting drunk on the Coronas we'd bought at the Canyon Country Store. I should have known better. Here of all places I was never going to get more than a few snatched hours. After all, this was no ordinary motel room. It was room eight of the legendary Joshua Tree Inn, the very same room where Gram had his last fix, put one last notch on the bedpost (possibly not in that order), and then drew his last breath. Sleeping wasn't why Gram came out here, and it wasn't what brought me here either.

Aside from all of that, Joe and I were sharing a bed. We had agreed in advance that, despite there being only one queen-size double in room eight, it would be better for the project (and for our wallets) if we 'shared the experience' in every possible sense. We had done this once before when I found myself without a hotel room or tent to doss down in at Reading Festival. We were sure we could manage it again. So after much manly posturing and strategic placement of pillows, Joe nodded off as usual and left me to contemplate the spirit of Gram Parsons wafting through the rafters.

Next day, instead of wasting the dawn lying awake in bed next to the perpetually slumbering Joe – technically a lie-in and therefore definitely a little weird with someone you're not shagging – I chose to get up and photograph the motel in the gentle light of the desert at daybreak. It was a treat to have the place to myself for an hour or two and take my time overwriting the version which had occupied my head for the past fifteen years. The creeping morning light made for a beautiful photo of a silhouetted Joshua tree by the pool, another showing a warm glow through the window diffused by the fading orange curtains, and a very cheesy shot of Joe waking up underneath a picture of Gram looking dazed, confused and faintly stupid with his new cockduster moustache.

Breakfast was cereal and muffins in the reception area of the inn, a cosy dining space hung with maps of the National Park, local artwork and leaflet displays. Pictures of Gram competed for space alongside photographs of Bono and friends, but despite the colossal profile of the latter compared to his lesser-known wallmate, this place, for the hundreds of fans who pass through each year, will always be linked to Gram and Gram alone. Margo the matronly innkeeper gave us directions to Cap Rock, Gram's favourite spot in the desert for getting high with friends (Keith Richards among them) and the place where his manager Phil 'Road Mangler' Kaufman had whisked and then flambéed the body, having stolen it from the airport hours before.

The approach to the Joshua Tree National Park is littered with drooping, ramshackle cabins that desert dwellers apparently call home. Cacti, the like of which I had seen only in Road Runner cartoons, line the roadside like Venice Beach muscle-men flexing their biceps for an all-over tan. Anxious not to miss anything, I jumped in the back of the now topless Sebring and shot some film of the junkyard of rusty rock formations and Joshua trees that scatter the Mojave landscape. This was our first taste of the in-through-the-nose-and-*relaaax* kind of driving we had envisaged before we arrived, a welcome decongestant spin after the asphyxiating rush hour choke of LA the day before. We shot endless reels of passing roadside, figuring they would make great general views (or 'GVs' in telly parlance, *daaahling*) should we ever need voice-over material for a proper programme.

Cap Rock was easy to spot. A barn-sized yellow outcrop sitting lonely in a wide expanse of desert with nothing for company but Joshua trees and a huddle of smaller rocks at its feet, it takes its name from the flat, rounded boulder which glints on top of it like a cap perched on the scalp of a balding, sweaty trucker. We pulled off the road and embarked on what we supposed would be an arduous search for the sacred spot of Gram's cremation, where the rock is scribbled with fans' dedications to commemorate his passing. I had noted down the complicated directions given to us over breakfast: 'Start out from the car park and proceed in a north-north-westerly direction (NO trail), turning left at the fourth tree past the heart-shaped rock after the weeping cactus.' It all sounded fantastically secret and esoteric, a hidden desert grotto to which all but the most intrepid were denied access.

In the event it was disappointingly easy to find. Margo could have saved herself the trouble ('It's on the opposite site of the rock to the car park' would have sufficed), but we were learning that there are many minor and harmless embellishments to the GP legend that serve to make the trail that little bit more satisfying in the pursuit.

We arrived to find two people already there. One was a lean and lithe rock climber type with a bewildering capacity for meaningless chatter and inappropriate candour, preparing to embark on a 'Gram Parsons Memorial Hand Traverse', as tradition has it for the more outward-bound among GP pilgrims. This involves hanging with your fingertips from the uppermost edge of one of the smaller rocks, swinging your legs sideways over a clutch of thorny bushes which crouch menacingly beneath your rear, then sliding your hands along until you can negotiate another foothold. This you repeat until you've made your way along the entire length of the rock, before dropping several feet onto the sand below. All in the name, apparently, of showing Gram just how much he means to you.

I had planned on completing a memorial traverse of my own, but quickly realised I was woefully unprepared. For one thing I was wearing all the wrong clothes. Our rock climber friend was decked out in all manner of technical gear, including fingerless climbing gloves and rubber-soled pumps that seemed to stick to the rock like Spiderman. Despite this, and his possessing the physique of an Olympic gymnast, he still looked like he was having difficulty, made worse by the fact that he was attempting to hold a conversation with an onlooker as he went. In between grunts he relayed to the second Parsons pilgrim, a bald but bearded, matchstick-chewing biker, the details of his disastrous personal finances and the demise of his last relationship.

'It all started to go wrong for us – ooh, ouch – when I lost my job. Cindy was the kind of girl that liked the finer things in life, you know?'

'Uh-huh.'

'And when I couldn't provide the material things for her any more – whoa! nearly lost it there – things started to go downhill in our sex life too.'

'Sucks.'

'We were arguing a lot anyway, which was worse when Cindy got her period – man, she had *really* heavy periods – and I think the job thing was the last straw, you know?' His left buttock was suspended inches above a nest of thorns.

'Sorry, man.'

'That was when I started to hit the booze real hard – ooh! ah! – and Cindy took off with a guy from work…'

'Bummer.'

And so it continued, the climber ever more generous with the depressing details of his personal life, the biker always monosyllabic in reply, until finally the climber completed his traverse, dropped onto his feet and with a 'Nice talkin' to ya!' was gone.

I lingered and read the dedications scrawled onto the rock. Many quoted lyrics from GP songs, often incorrectly, but if the grammar was a little out the sentiment was still there, even in the tribute from one touchingly misguided fan of 'Graham Parsons'. But, as I was later to write in the guest book at the Joshua Tree Inn, we came in search of the spirit of Gram Parsons and found it written all over Cap Rock. We made a quick, unsuccessful attempt to clamber to the top before returning to the car park, where we found the rock climber unburdening himself of some recent health scares to a family of day-trippers. He's fine now though, so don't worry.

Lunch at Denny's before a haircut at Twentynine Palms' famous Barber Judi, the only hairdresser I have ever visited who faces the customer *away* from the mirror as they are being shorn, presumably so that (a) your travelling companion can wince theatrically and suck through his teeth as she goes about her toil and trouble, as Joe did now, and (b) you have 'a nice surprise' to look forward to at the end of the whole terrifying experience. Proudly boasting marine-style grade fours, we returned to the Joshua Tree Inn. It was at this point that the day took a turn for the unexpected, if not for the truly inconceivable.

We had made an arrangement with Yvo at breakfast that morning to interview him and Margo on camera in room eight, possibly to be posted on the website if all went well. When we were ready to roll I popped out to the pool to fetch our interviewees, who were chatting to a group of friends. Yvo introduced them one by one. First a glamorous all-American girly type named Mary, who looked like every sunkissed Californian model hanging off Stephen Stills in Canyon-era rock photography, and second a grinning South American hippie named Arturo. Lastly I found myself shaking the hand of a diminutive figure of fiery red hair and piercing blue eyes by the name of Polly.

Polly.

Polly?

It was a name I'd read many times in books and magazine articles about Gram. Had I remembered it right? Polly *Parsons*. Yes, Polly was *Gram's daughter*. And she was stood right in front of me. For years I had devoured every word written about the man, learned every chord of every song, bought every album, reissue and biography several times over, and here I was staring his DNA in the face by the pool of the Joshua Tree Inn where he had died thirty-five years before. Gulp.

I struggled for something to say, very nearly telling her it was an 'honour' to meet her, but fumbling for 'pleasure' just in time.

She jumped in and spared my agony. 'Great to meet you. I heard about your trip. I think it's great what you're doing for Dad.'

Did you hear that? Polly had heard of *us* and thought it was great, what we were doing. *She*'d heard of *us!* And she approved!

Now forgive me while I pounce on a passing remark uttered only to spare the blushes of a man finding himself stuck in a conversational cul-de-sac, but Polly Parsons' endorsement was not something I'd ever imagined this trip would attract. Here was a direct line to Gram himself putting the Parsons seal of approval on the whole ridiculous enterprise. All of a sudden we had a higher purpose for what we were doing. And God knows we needed one. Yee-ha! Yee-fucking-ha!

The interview with Margo and Yvo was fine. He was monosyllabic and distracted, she engaging and articulate. Joe filmed, I fawned. It passed in a haze. Having just met Polly Parsons, our exclusive interview with Margo and Yvo suddenly didn't quite feel like such a scoop.

Later we were introduced to another friend of Polly's named Shilah, and learned what had brought them out to the Mojave Desert on precisely the night that we happened to be there. Shilah works in the music industry and an attorney friend of hers in LA – who also happened to be the attorney for one Terra Naomi – had told her about two crazy English guys who were celebrating Gram's birthday by driving across America in search of rock and roll hi-jinx, and suggested we hook up. Shilah was promoting a gig nearby, so they'd decided to head out to Joshua Tree and see if there wasn't some fun to be had. Brash, buxom and bonkers, Shilah was the life-and-soul type you warm to instantly. This we did, and an invitation to join them that evening at Pappy and Harriet's Pioneertown Palace was issued. We accepted without hesitation.

But first we had to take a second drive out to the desert. The sun was about to go down and we had resolved to be sitting underneath Cap Rock when it did, raising a beer to Gram. Cap Rock was the closest thing Gram had to a grave, closer than the Louisiana cemetery where his charred remains were buried following the botched desert cremation. As the place he had spent many a night stargazing with friends, it was only right that Joe and I should do the same. We sat down, leaned against a boulder graffitied with a cross – the same one embroidered into the nudie suit he wears on the cover of *Gilded Palace of Sin* – and cracked open a couple of Heinies.

'Cheers Gram,' said Joe with a clink of his bottle against mine.

'Yeah, cheers Gram,' I said. 'Hope you like your birthday present.'

'Thanks for sending us your daughter by the way.' He turned to me. 'So what did Polly say to you?'

'She said she knew who we were and asked if we'd had much response to the website, to which I lied that we had. And then one of her friends came over and she told her about us. She said, "This is Chris, he's on a road trip to celebrate Dad's birthday." *Dad's* birthday. I've never heard him called that before.'

Another clink of bottles and a 'cheers' from us both. From our twilit Cap Rock vantage point, following an encounter with the ghost of Gram himself, it seemed our quest had got off to a pretty good start.

'I'd love to know what Gram would think of all this,' I pondered. 'He'd probably think it was a really, really stupid idea.'

'Probably.'

The sun had gone down and a cold desert chill swept in behind it. We finished the last of our beers, returned to the car and hit the road to Pioneertown, where we planned to party like it was 1969.

Purpose-built in the forties, Pioneertown started life as an Old West motion picture set. Designed to look like an 1870s frontier town, countless westerns including *The Cisco Kid*, *Jeopardy* and *The Gay Amigo* had been filmed there. The idea had been to create a living movie set, a community in which actors could both live and work. If you've ever wanted to know what it feels like to burst through swinging saloon doors on a darkened and deserted film set, Pioneertown is the place to find out.

Pappy and Harriet's Pioneertown Palace is a barbecue canteen and live music venue at the end of Mane Street. It was exactly how I imagined a juke joint would be (though in truth I had no idea what a juke joint was) with real life sawdust on exposed wooden floorboards, *ginuwine* cowboys in authentic plaid shirts and country music so loud we had to shout to make ourselves heard. Spotting Polly and friends at a table near the stage, we shuffled in. We hung back at first, still unsure whether they had us down as fellow music industry types or just another couple of Grampires passing through. Shilah saw us and waved us over.

'Hey guys! So glad you could make it. Tonight is kind of my night – I'm promoting the show. Really it's more like hosting a few friends. Take a seat.'

We sat down between Mary the impossibly-beautiful-Californian-model-type and Arturo the Chilean hippie. Polly was on the edge of the group, quietly observing but letting Shilah do all the talking.

'I hope you can stick around. Marc Olson is playing later on.'

This was all the invitation Chris needed. Marc Olson is the lead singer of the Jayhawks. The Jayhawks are one of his favourite bands.

We ordered a round of whiskies and settled in. Shilah told us a little about the group of friends.

'Polly and I grew up together. My mom knew Gram and took me to see the Burritos when I was a kid. She says Polly and I used to run riot at the Troubadour together when we were three years old! I introduced Polly to her husband Charlie, *and* I was maid of honour at their wedding.' With the addition of Mary to the group – head of marketing at Amoeba Records, who were releasing some newly discovered Parsons recordings – a girly threesome was born.

But it was Shilah who took centre stage. Mama Shi, as she is known to her friends, was evidently something of a local celebrity. She ran Sin City Social Club, a marketing company she described as a 'renegade collective of musicians, artists and industry executives brought together by a shared appreciation of Americana'. Apparently the members' list extended to virtually everybody in the place, as was made evident by the steady stream of friends who, spotting Shilah's trademark Stetson hat, would make a beeline for our table to say hello. Every one of them was smothered with a bear hug, handed a drink and invited to join our table. This was a lady who knew how to make a party swing.

Later Shilah and Mary took us for a midnight tour of Pioneertown by torchlight. We strolled past the Bath House Hotel, the law office and the jailhouse.

'So what about you guys,' probed Shilah as we crossed Mane Street towards the saloon. 'What's your story?'

I scuffed a trainer through the dust. 'Well it's not as interesting as yours. I'm a fan of Gram's music and wanted to see where it all went on. And apparently Joe and I can't have a perfectly ordinary exchange of birthday cards without it turning into a four-and-a-half-thousand-mile road trip.' I explained how the Butch Cassidy birthday card had started it all.

'Well you're in the right place for some Butch and Sundance action, that's for sure. But what about you Joe, I still don't get what's in it for you.'

'That's a question I've been asking myself for three years.'

'And?'

'God knows. I don't even like country music.'

'You don't like country music?!' squealed Shilah, discharging a full-throated Marlboro guffaw. 'That's the funniest thing I ever heard!'

'I pretty much hate country music in fact. Except for Johnny Cash, obviously.'

'Well you've got that right at least,' said Mary, 'they don't come much better than Johnny. Even Gram would tell you that. Hey, let's go rob that bank over there!'

She galloped to the entrance of Pioneertown Bank, Joe trotting after her. With palms clasped and held tight to their chests, index fingers tucked under their chins like Smith & Wessons, they pressed their backs to the wall on either side of the entrance and surveyed the street for officers of the law. The coast clear, first Mary then Joe disappeared inside.

'It's pretty amazing what Joe's done for you,' said Shilah as we shuffled a little further along Mane Street. 'Coming here, I mean.'

'It is, isn't it? Especially when you consider this was all his idea.'

'That's a true friend you've got there.'

'Yes ma'am,' I attempted in my best Southern drawl. 'It sure is.'

A silence hung heavy in the darkness. It was Shilah who broke it.

'Are you planning on going through Nashville?'

'Not a chance I'm afraid. I'd have loved to, but Joe's been before and hated it. Probably something to do with all that country music. We're heading south to New Orleans instead.'

'That's a shame. A friend of mine in Nashville – Jack Fripp – might be able to hook you up a visit to Johnny Cash's place in Hendersonville.'

'Really? That would be incredible!'

'It's a long shot, but worth a try. Johnny's son John Carter is running the studio down there now. It's in a cabin in the grounds of the estate. But I guess if Joe hates Nashville he won't be in a hurry to go back.'

'I guess not.' I shrugged.

Joe and Mary crashed through the doors of the bank, whoopin' and hollerin' in celebration of their imaginary haul. We chased after them.

'Let me speak to Jack,' panted Shilah as we reached Pappy's. 'He owes me a favour.'

More whiskey ensued, followed by the worst Mexican food we'd ever eaten at a drive-thru on the way back to the motel (Joe: 'We're eating dog food aren't we?'), followed by more booze and an impromptu jam session with Marc Olsen in room nine. It was quite a night. Later, as I lay awake in bed enjoying a particularly rousing rendition of Joe's now nightly olfactory symphony, I reflected on the day's events.

I imagined being able to talk to the eighteen-year-old version of myself, a fresh-faced university undergraduate arriving at Gram's music via The Lemonheads, The Charlatans and Primal Scream, and discovering an artist that would change the way he thought about music forever. Gram's songs taught me to let go of any notion of cool when appreciating music. His stock in trade, after all, had none that he didn't give to it himself. Back then country music, with only very rare exception, was the preserve of rednecks and racists. He turned it into rock and roll.

I tried to imagine what that eighteen-year-old me would think of all this. I pictured his reaction to the news that in his early thirties, the love affair with Gram's music undiminished by fifteen years of familiarity, he would meet Gram's daughter by the pool at the Joshua Tree Inn, she would be sweet and welcoming and open and – get this – she would *approve* of what you're doing. I'm not sure he would believe it.

But something was nagging at me. Shilah's words, about what Joe was getting out of this, what a friend he was for even being here let alone suggesting the whole thing, were running around in my head. What *was* he getting out of this?

I reached over and switched on the bedside lamp, then prodded his arm.

'Joe, wake up.'

Nothing. Another prod, a little harder than the first.

Still nothing.

Grabbing him by the shoulder, I shook him as hard as I could. 'Joe – wake up!'

'Wh-wha —?' he grunted. 'Sorry, was I snoring?'

'Yes. But that's not why I've woken you up.'

He rubbed his eyes. 'Ri-ight. Then why exactly *have* you woken me up? I was having a lovely dream about helicopters.'

'The itinerary's changed.'

'What?'

'The itinerary's changed.' A pause for effect. 'We're going to Nashville.'

22 OCTOBER

A RIVER RUNS THROUGH IT

'We're not going to Nashville.'

'What?' croaked Chris, his first word of the day.

'I know what you're like. For the past few hours you'll have been working on a cunningly worded 'invite' coercing me to go to Nashville. So I'm not bothering with cunning wording. We're. Not. Going. To. Nashville.'

'Why not? How bad is it, really?'

'You want to know why I hate Nashville?'

'Yes.'

I should have started by saying that Chris must appreciate the context of my contempt. That I've been lucky enough to travel a bit, from Camden to Calcutta, Gretna to Guatemala, and Nashville is the most dismal place I've ever been. I should have explained to him in sesquipedalian detail that Nashville is the dreariest place in all born-again-Christendom. That to visit the US and go to Nashville is like being invited to the

Playboy mansion and spending the evening with Brett Michaels from Poison. There are thrills, spills and jaw-dropping views everywhere you look, but you're stuck with the most boorish company in the room. Its glory days are long gone, it's falling apart despite extensive retouching to its decrepit exterior. And it's wearing a cowboy hat.

What I actually said was: 'Because it's really horrible.'

Way to go Seinfeld.

'Well, how can I disagree with that reasoned and rational appraisal?' Chris tutted, heading out of the door to grab some breakfast.

Defeated, I thumbed through the room eight guest book – an embossed and leather-bound notepad for Gram fans to pen a line or two about what he means to them. I felt like a fraud because of my slightly false motives for being there. Everyone else in the book had been truly moved by the work of Parsons, whereas I still think of country music, with a handful of exceptions, as the soundtrack to fertilising your sibling. And the whining of the pedal-steel guitar – one of Chris' favourite sounds in the world – makes my ear canals contract. With this in mind I didn't want to write something disrespectful or phoney. So I decided not to put pen to paper and trailed after Chris to the breakfast room.

Breakfast dispatched, we packed the car and reluctantly bade farewell to the ladies who had made the previous night such an exceptional experience. Shilah was as effusive with a hangover as when she was acquiring it, Mary still smiled with the consistency of a synchronised swimmer, and Polly was quiet and sweet. A quick photo, then it was into the car to get some proper mileage away. Today was day five of the trip.

Nearly a quarter of it done and so far we had covered precisely 150 miles. 4,000 still to go. There was a balance that needed redressing.

Chris took us along 62 through Twentynine Palms, the scene of our brutal shearing the previous day at the hands of Barber Judi, and then out through some equally brutal scenery. Reddish-brown crumbling hills rolled in like great stone waves breaking and receding just short of the roadside – geological tides for mile after mile. After a couple of hours we stopped at a petrol station to switch drivers. It had Portaloos for toilets; four plastic booths full of trucker shit baking at ninety degrees. Not even vultures were circling.

Onwards from the befouled Portaloos to the interstate through Arizona. We put the roof up to prevent our scalps turning to crackling, and made the slow journey towards Grand Canyon. While we do that, a few words about my travelling companion.

Chris is the smartest guy I know.

That's not to say he's my most 'intelligent' friend, statistically speaking. That title probably goes to Big Jim, a man whose party trick is to ask you to name any date in the last two thousand years, or any in the next ten thousand, and then tell you what day of the week it is.

Chris is smart, but he isn't the most forward-thinking person I know either. That one goes to a friend of mine by the name of Jesus Jim, who was using the Internet before it was even called the Internet, when there were about as many websites as most people have names in their mobile phone. (It was so embryonic, in fact, that in late 1992 Jim managed to bring the entire Internet down for a day by telling his friends – who all told their friends – that they could download a game called *Castle Wolfenstein* from his computer. The next day he was escorted from his university lodgings by the local constabulary, who had been told from on high that this young lad had done something very wrong indeed, but weren't entirely sure what it was.)

So, to get all *Top Gear* about it, Chris may not be the fastest or the loudest, and he may not have a flappy-paddle gearbox, but he is the smartest, wittiest, wryest, most withering, best read, most musically-gifted person I've ever had the privilege to call a friend, and there's frankly no one else I would have wanted to do this trip with. He was the first person to tell me on hearing their debut album that The Darkness were amazing, and the first to tell me on hearing their second that he was wrong about the whole 'The Darkness are amazing' thing. And he was the first to tell me that James Blunt was total shite, as well as the first person to tell me seconds later that he was definitely right about the whole 'James Blunt is total shite' thing.

Christopher Price also has one other extraordinary quality. He can *focus*. Chris can focus like – well, in the absence of an appropriate human simile – he can focus like a microscope. In his mind there is no point doing anything unless you're going to give it everything you've got and try to be the best in the world. If he buys a guitar he'll play it until his fingers bleed. When he runs his stride is precise, his breathing regular and his pace swift. And when he does DIY it has to be nail-for-nail perfect or those shelves he's just spent three days erecting are coming straight down. Which to my mind makes him a pretty exceptional chap and, one imagines, an absolute nightmare to date.

Oh, and he's really, really hairy. He might not be able to grow a beard in anything less than one revolution of the earth around the sun, but he makes up for it in almost every other department. Sit with him for a while in a soundproof radio studio and you'll notice a slight squeaking noise. That's his hair growing.

Most of all, Christopher Price is a good man. And I like him very much.

In his determination for the ghost of Gram to be around us at all times, he had christened the car the 'Grievous Angel'. This was in reference to the lyric:

Billboards and truck-stops passed by the Grievous Angel
Twenty thousand roads I went down, down, down
And they all led me straight back home to you.

The car, however, was a touch more grievous than angel. It had two peculiarities worth highlighting. The first was the CD player. It skipped a bit. This didn't particularly bother me, not least because it seemed to skip songs that featured pedal steel. This meant that either (a) the CD player had my taste in music; (b) I was kicking it from under the footwell whenever a song came on that I didn't like; or (c) the machine struggled to play slightly scratched CDs. Which were invariably the ones that he liked most. Which of course were the ones that featured pedal steel.

Whatever the truth (and I think he suspected my footwork to be at play somewhere) Chris was fabulously and ragingly agitated by this. When it skipped, he would fast-forward the track, hoping this would fix the problem. When it didn't, he would go to the next song. And when that continued to jump, skip and click, he would let it play for up to a minute to try and outstare the CD player. All of which I found highly amusing. Which, of course, annoyed him even more.

The other grievance with the Grievous Angel was the electric shocks. Whether it was bad wiring or just static build-up in the nylon carpets we knew not, but each time you got out of the car and closed the door, you were guaranteed a little electric livener. Sometimes it was no more than a delicate nip, other times it sent enough voltage up your forearm to make your fillings glow and cause you to swear out loud in public, thus ensuring that in one brief moment any passer-by knew two things about you – one, you were English, and two, you were talking to your vehicle.

In the car, however, we were oblivious to the static built up on the seemingly endless tarmac. Mile upon mile, the road towards the centre of the continent pounded on with rumbling predictability. The monotony was relieved by the occasional and welcome diversion – always greeted with a wave and a toot of the horn as we passed – of sighting a 'truck mullet'. Truck mullets – and if that isn't their proper name then it really ought to be – are pretty much as the name suggests: a vehicle-wide, two-foot-long hairpiece that clips under the rear bumper of a pick-up or RV and brushes along the ground like the mane of a proud mullet-wearer over the collar of his overalls.

With the possible exception of furry dice, British drivers are much less enthusiastic about automotive adornments than our American counterparts (our rear bumpers, for instance, are viewed more as an aid to parallel parking than a place for stickers advertising how funny, Christian or Republican we are), so at first we were flummoxed by the truck mullet. We wanted to believe it was about pimping your ride so that driver and wheels hummed in perfect fashion unison, but that was almost too perfect to be true. Was it the latest innovation on the rubber travel sickness strips that once hung ineffectively from the back of Escorts and Allegros in the late seventies? Surely not that either.

After much debate, and the sighting of a mullet used for its proper purpose, we finally worked out that they are in fact used to stop the back wheels of the 'lead vehicle' showering gravel over the vehicle it is towing. (Forgive the rather vague terminology there, but this is a country in which trucks tow trucks and caravans apparently pull cars. Serious motorhome fanatics often tow a car for greater freedom of exploration once they've dropped anchor in a trailer park. The first time we came across this arrangement on the interstate I winced and told Joe that the guy in the sports car was dangerously close to the RV in front.)

The glory of the Grand Canyon comes from its facility for catching you unawares. High up in 'Marlboro Country', the Colorado River has spent six million years (some say considerably more) carving, grinding and sculpting a blasthole in the earth; clapping eyes on it for the first time is one of the rare occasions when the American fondness for the word 'awesome' is entirely justified. The surprise is due in no small part to the slow incline that most visitors – the ones who don't arrive by helicopter – drive up to get there, a climb which takes you unsuspectingly to around twice the height of Ben Nevis. A very slow rise, over a very long time, which we now embarked on.

There was a problem, and I had no choice but to tell Chris.

'Mate, I think we've got a fuel leak.'

'What?' came the panicked response.

'We've gone through a quarter of a tank in the last twenty miles.'

'Really? Are you sure?'

'The backs of my calves have started sweating, so yeah, I'm pretty sure.'

'How much have we got left?'

The needle on the fuel gauge was pointing menacingly and inescapably at a capital letter: E.

'Well, not to be melodramatic about it, fumes.'

'What do we do?'

With a fuel leak you have two options. Keep moving and hope, or stop and try to fix the leak. The former is potentially foolhardy and runs the risk of losing power just when you don't want to in, say, the outside lane of a contraflow, where we were now. The latter is probably just as risky and definitely just as foolhardy in the outside lane of a contraflow.

Chris sized up the situation. 'Let's keep going. Maybe we can make it to a garage.'

Ten miles later the reassuring red T of Texaco hove into view. Soaked in a sweat of panic and relief, we pulled off the road and freewheeled up to pump number seven. Chris got out to fill up. He reached for the nozzle, then stopped as he caught sight of the display, his jaw sagging with disbelief.

'Pricey is it, Pricey?' I jested.

'Come and have a look.'

I got out. Where you would normally expect to see the price per gallon, a very different message blinked at us in tones of L, C, and D:

GOD BLESS AND SUPPORT OUR TROOPS IN IRAQ.

After fifteen years listening to politicians tell the world that the war in the Middle East had everything to do with human rights and nothing whatsoever to do with oil, the unmistakable truth had popped up in the unlikeliest of places. Pump number seven at a Texaco petrol station in Ash Fork, Arizona had 'fessed up. We thanked it for its honesty. Then we crossed our fingers and looked under the car. Nothing. Not a drip. Confused as to what to do next, we filled up and chose to keep moving and keep hoping, rejoining I40 as the low sun cast long shadows over cornfields stretching as far as the eye could see.

After ten miles the fuel gauge had noticeably declined.

'It's doing it again,' I tried – and failed – to say without fear or frustration.

'How far do you think we can get on this tank?' replied Chris calmly.

'To the canyon and maybe a bit further,' I guesstimated.

'Let's just get there then,' soothed Obi-Wan.

Whether to ease the rising fear of being stranded in the dark, or perhaps because he just wanted to hear some familiar tunes, at this point Chris did something rather brave.

'Have a listen to this,' he said, and slid his own album into the CD player. By that I don't mean one that he owned, but one he wrote and recorded himself with his friend Simon. They call themselves Missing Parsons.

Being as our relationship is founded on music and – crucially – the honest appraisal of it, this was a very ballsy move indeed. All the more so when you factor in my ever-increasing disquiet over the fuel situation. It was never going to get a fair hearing.

A pedal steel chimed in. I looked at Chris and raised a brow. His eyes narrowed. Strumming, more steeling, and more narrowing. Then a rich, slightly twangy vocal filled the car. I laughed, at which Chris looked rightly annoyed. I wasn't laughing at him though. I was laughing because it was good. Really good. It was also, to my immense relief, country music of a sort, which meant that when the inevitable moment came for him to ask 'What do you think?', I would be able to say, hand on heart, 'Well I really can't give it a fair appraisal. You know I don't like country music.'

We raced the setting sun towards Grand Canyon, listening to Missing Parsons. The vast crop fields all around turned from yellow to gold to grey and then to Stabilo-Boss pink as the sun sped towards the horizon. The music was working. Our minds were lost in Missing Parsons' quirky tales of love lost and found. As the road wore on, Chris flipped through the car manual for 'how to fix a fuel leak', while doleful final album track 'Half-Remembered Memory' – a break-up song about a girl we both knew – distracted me from my weapons-grade sore throat. As the song drew quietly to a close, we entered Grand Canyon National Park.

And Chris did a wonderful thing. He didn't ask me what I thought. Instead, he just carried on leafing through the manual. 'It says here that fuel consumption varies according to altitude.'

'OK...'

'You know what that means?'

'What?'

'For the last two hours we've been driving at something like five thousand feet. We don't have a fuel leak at all.'

'What have we got then?'

'A car. At altitude.'

23 OCTOBER

DOES MY BUTTE LOOK BIG IN THIS?

'What have I got then?'

The analgesic throat spray, menthol lozenges and salt water were no longer doing their job. I had been left with no option but to enter the realms of the US health care system and pay for a consultation at the Grand Canyon Medical Centre.

'Herpes.'

'In my throat?'

'Yes sir,' chirruped a white-gowned lady doctor.

How was this possible? No, I didn't want to know. Actually, yes I did. If only so I could explain to my wife how I went on holiday with a mate, shared a motel bed with him, and came back with a sexually transmitted infection down my gullet.

'Herpes isn't always an STI.'

'Thank God. I mean, thank Chris – Christ! – er, thank goodness.'

'It can be transmitted through air or contact with hard surfaces. Which is probably what happened to you.'

'Is there any treatment available?'

'Sure. Here's a prescription. Take it for a week, you should be fine.'

Outside in a convertible sports car sat a lightly sunburnt Englishman in a snug Fred Perry shirt. 'What is it, honey?' he camped from the driver's seat.

'I've got herpes.'

Chris' face strained with competing desires to panic and take the piss. Flumping into the passenger seat I answered the question posed by his wide eyes and slack jaw.

'Apparently it's a viral throat infection related to the herpes virus. No biggy.'

'Is it contagious?'

'Very,' I coughed. 'Let's go.'

Joe had seen the Grand Canyon before, a few years previously on holiday with his partner Nicola. I hadn't. This presented something of a problem.

When two male friends do something fun or exciting together – climb a mountain, see a band or go to a comedy club perhaps – and one of them has done that thing before, there is a protocol which must be adhered to rigidly. Man A (who has done the thing) must first spend several hours explaining to man B (who hasn't) that he cannot possibly imagine how life-changing the experience will be in order to impress upon man B how impoverished his life has been up to now for not having done the thing already. Man A must also pre-empt every response man B could possibly have to doing the thing ('You're going to shit/cream/wet yourself') so as to divest the experience of any newness or novelty in the actual doing. Lastly, once the thing is done, man A must make plain to man B just how much funnier it was the first time, how comparatively clear the sound or tough the climb. Throughout, man B must try at all costs *not* to have a good time, so as to deprive man A of the satisfaction of seeing him enjoy something that man A enjoyed last year, last month or last Tuesday.

All of which meant I would have to be completely unimpressed by the Grand Canyon.

We parked and walked towards the viewing area, Joe hoisting the camera onto his shoulder and following close behind as I approached the rim in order to capture my awe on tape. 'However big it is in your head mate, it's *waaaay* bigger in real life.'

'It's a hole in the ground.'

'You wait.'

As we neared the edge I reminded myself to remain calm, collected and nonchalant, and under no circumstances to utter the words 'goodness', 'crikey' or 'fuck me'.

I stepped onto the viewing platform. 'Fuck me.'

Shit.

I had seen deep holes before. Looking into a hole – a well perhaps, or a deep crevasse – and not being able to see the bottom was not a new experience for me. Looking into a hole that is *four miles wide* and not being able to see the bottom definitely was. We stepped onto a lower platform and joined a large crowd of people, mainly Americans, 'wow-ing' and 'ooh-ing' into the emptiness, their voices muted by the nothingness all around. A hazy autumn sun bleached the colour from the pinstripe of reds, browns and yellows visible on the opposite side of the gorge, each layer representing millions of years of erosion and earning themselves such incomprehensibly ancient-sounding names as Palaeozoic, Precambrian and Triassic. The Grand Canyon was, ahem, awesome.

There are two things that you cannot prepare for on a visit to the Grand Canyon. The first, of course, is its perspective-shattering dimensions. The Grand Canyon operates on a scale which demands you abandon your everyday frames of reference with regard to size and distance and shift up several notches. How far is it to the other side of the canyon? How deep is it? There is only one answer to every question about the Grand Canyon: 'Very.'

The second thing we noticed upon arriving in the car park at the south rim, was the profusion and seriousness of signs screaming 'Do NOT attempt to walk to the bottom and back in one day', a precaution also necessitated by the dizzying incomprehensibility of the canyon's vastness. Lacking the wherewithal to work out how far it is to the other side (it varies along its length from four to eighteen miles), any guess as to depth will be just that – a guess. To the untrained eye it could be 500 metres, could be 10,000, which is the difference between a brisk scenic stroll and a fatal gallop into the lungs of hell. Hence signs which combine text and imagery in a terrifying mix that is one part Orwell to two parts slasher flick. And with some justification, as people die in the canyon with alarming regularity. If visiting the Grand Canyon is on your list of 'things to do before I die', try very hard to ensure you aren't one of the four or five people every year for whom a canyon visit jumps to the top of a very short list of 'things to do immediately before I die', either from falling, dehydration, heat stroke, hypothermia or drowning.

'Shall we try and get down to the river and back?' I swaggered.

'Can't you read?'

'Yeah, but we've run marathons. We'll be OK.'

Chris pointed a finger at one of the signs along the rim. 'You reckon?'

'COULD YOU RUN A MARATHON?' it shouted. 'THIS GIRL COULD, AND NOW SHE'S DEAD.'

Why?

'BECAUSE SHE TRIED TO GET TO THE BOTTOM AND BACK IN A DAY.'

This is going to sound very churlish, but I can't help begrudging America the Grand Canyon a tiny bit. 'Bigger and better' is virtually the national motto, and by a geological quirk they have ended up with the biggerest and betterest natural phenomenon of them all. And there's a part of me that wishes it was much harder to get to. As it is, you can order a drink at your Vegas hotel bar, leave your air-conditioned lobby and get into an air-conditioned limousine to the steps of an air-conditioned private plane, see the canyon and be back in your seat by the time your margarita arrives. Surely the wonders of the natural world should demand a little more effort than that?

We attempted a brief stroll down the pathway which zigzags into the first few hundred yards of the canyon.

After twenty minutes Chris started to grimace and groan. 'Mate, my leg's starting to hurt.'

When Chris' leg hurts you have to be careful. It's a proper, bona fide injury. While training for a marathon in 2003 he overdid it and detached the muscle lining from the bone in his left leg.

'Oh. OK. How much further can you go?'

'Probably make it back to the top.'

I feel bad for admitting it, but this pissed me off a bit. The downside of Chris' ability to focus is that, rather like a spider under a magnifying glass on a sunny day, he has a tendency to burn out. Deep down I couldn't help feeling his injury was down to his not being able simply to *run* a marathon, but having to do it faster than Haile Gabrsellassie or not at all. So when he said 'My leg's starting to hurt', what I heard was: 'I deny you this once-in-a-lifetime moment because of mistakes I made several years ago which we're both paying for now.'

Yep, I do feel bad for admitting that.

Despite best efforts to carry ourselves like intrepid fit folk, we shuffled back to the car like a couple of fat kids, electing instead to take a bus tour of the south rim. The tour guide announced it was a round trip of seventy-five minutes. Chris was indignant. The canyon may have taken 5.4 million years to create, but seventy-five minutes! I mean, we're busy people.

One hour and sixteen minutes later we were back behind the wheel, controls set to sea level. The road east from Grand Canyon, Highway 64, leaned lazily downhill. Even a swarm of Harley Davidsons with sidecars – and wow, trailers too – failed to add any of yesterday's tension to the easy calm of descent.

Chris looked puzzled. 'Doesn't a sidecar and trailer sort of defeat the point of having a motorbike?'

'To normal people, yes. To Harley riders, probably not.'

'But surely – and stop me if I'm missing the point here – those bikes, when you factor in the sidecars and trailers, are wider than a car, longer than a car, and have one more wheel than a car?'

'Harley riders are a strange breed. You hear that clanking sound their engines make?' A five-wheeled fandango glugged past on our left. 'A few years back Harley Davidson spent loads of money fixing the sound so it was clean, rhythmical and didn't make those odd plopping noises. But all the Harley riders complained, so they spent even more money making it sound like a steam engine again. Logic isn't a word in the Harley vocabulary.'

As ludicrous as five-wheeled motorbikes are, they looked right at home in scenery this big. The easy riders pulled in for gas, and so did we. Unable to compete with the classically American iconography of the bikers, we decided to try out something equally American and iconographic: beef jerky.

How lucky Americans are to have beef jerky, and how apparently limitless the opportunities for enjoying it. Inside, a breathtaking array of 'Jack Links' jerky varieties hung on branded racking occupying one entire end of an aisle. Variations on standard beef – peppered, teriyaki, sweet and hot, hickory smoked – were presented alongside jerky made from quite different types of meat altogether – ham jerky, buffalo jerky and, my favourite, turkey jerky (high fives round the marketing department that afternoon no doubt).

We selected a large bag of original beef and a smaller one of sweet and hot, and made our way back to the car chomping enthusiastically on this classically American delicacy. (Not that it's exclusively American. Jerky is essentially just dry cured meat, and as such is found in South Africa as biltong, Ethiopia as *qwant'a*, across pretty much the rest of the world, in fact, wherever people eat meat. The only country you won't find it would appear to be Great Britain. But then we've got Scotch eggs and pork scratchings, so who's laughing now?)

While we cruised and chewed on mouthfuls of leathery, salty hide, Chris put another album of singer-songwriter western crooning – another attempt at preaching to the averted – into the CD player and gave me the back story. Stay with it (I had to).

Let me introduce you to a remarkable lady by the name of Bette Nesmith Graham. In 1951, Bette was a single mum with a young son to support, working as a secretary to the chairman of the Texas Bank and Trust. Her brand-new IBM electric typewriter was wonderful. Fast, quiet and ergonomically designed, it delivered even spacing and left-hand margins straighter than any she had seen. It had multiple copy control and a fancy 'Impression Indicator' which prevented her from hitting the keys too hard. But there was a problem: the new carbon-film ribbons made correcting mistakes virtually impossible, at least in the way she was used to – with an eraser. Which was an issue, as Bette was a terrible typist.

So Bette, bless her Christian Scientist socks, had a bash at mixing some tempera paint at home in her kitchen blender – the same stuff she had seen used by signwriters who painted the holiday windows at the bank each Christmas. If they made a mistake, she noticed, they simply painted over it. With a few improvements courtesy of her son's high school chemistry teacher, Bette's homemade concoction was ready. She took a bottle to work and – right under the nose of her disapproving boss – used it to paint out her mistakes. Before very long she was struggling to keep up with colleagues' requests for more and, recruiting little Michael to help her fulfil the orders, 'Mistake Out' was born. Later she changed the name to 'Liquid Paper', which became a lucrative sideline with which to supplement her income at the bank.

But in 1959 she was fired by the bank after absent-mindedly typing her own company's name at the top of a letter. She threw herself into the business full time. By 1967 she had patented and trademarked her product, and the operation had moved into an 11,000-square-foot automated production plant. She eventually sold the company to the Gillette Corporation in 1979 (having been turned down by IBM) for close to $50 million.

I just love this story. I love Bette's humble but Herculean insight that mistakes could be painted over rather than erased, which, self-evident as it seems to us now, demonstrates a level of lateral thinking that even Edward de Bono would be proud of. I love the fact that it was a mistake left uncorrected which got her sacked and presented the opportunity of correcting mistakes full-time. And I love that IBM turned down the chance of making even more money from their flawed typewriters. But what I love most of all – more than any of this – is how Bette decided to spend all that money.

But we'll come to that in a moment. First I'd like to tell you what happened to her little boy. Remember Linda Ronstadt's boyfriend, the 'hootmaster' at the Troubadour in LA? That was him. In 1965, Michael Nesmith responded to an ad in the *Hollywood Reporter* looking for 'four insane boys' to join a Beatles-inspired pop group and television series called

The Monkees. Beating off competition from, among other noteworthy auditionees, one Stephen Stills (reputedly rejected because of his thinning hair and bad teeth), Mike added another household name to the Nesmith product portfolio as one quarter of the world's first manufactured pop act.

But it was 'Different Drum', the song he had given to Ronstadt and which I'd fallen in love with via The Lemonheads, which was running around in my head. I made another decision.

'We need to go to New Mexico.'

We were on US160, headed north towards Monument Valley on the border of Utah and Arizona.

'What?' huffed Harland, head buried in a road atlas. 'Why on earth do we need to do that? New Mexico isn't on the itinerary.'

'Mike Nesmith lives there. In the Nambé Valley. We could go to his house.'

He interrupted his map reading and looked across at me in the driving seat.

'Mike Nesmith? As in the twat in the hat from the Monkees?'

'That's the one.'

'And what, pray tell, makes Mike Nesmith worthy of...' – a glance at the map, a thumbing of pages and a sucking of teeth – '... a two-hundred-mile detour?'

'He's important.'

'Important how, exactly? I don't think made-for-TV popstars qualify, do you? Mike Nesmith is about as important as Joey from New Kids.'

This was supposed to rile me. It did.

'You're being deliberately obtuse,' I sulked. He was.

'Oh, come *on*. We're supposed to be looking for the beating heart of rock and roll America. Mike Nesmith's contribution is hardly coursing through the veins of the American music corpus...'

'But there's more to him than meets the eye,' I said, but he wasn't listening. He was on a roll with his beating heart metaphor.

'... In fact "Daydream Believer" is more like a relentless, twitching nerve in your elbow. Nags away until it drives you potty. So before we consider even setting foot in New Mexico, give me one good reason – *one* – why Mike Nesmith deserves our attention.'

'I'll give you several.'

'Please do.'

'He's one of the great polymaths of the modern age.'

'He was a Monkee.'

'Singer, songwriter, film producer, novelist, entrepreneur, philanthropist...'

'Philanthropist? Really?'

'Yep. And stepfather of country rock.'

'I thought that was Gram?'

'Gram was the godfather of country rock. Do try and keep up.'

'Of course. Silly me.'

'*And* Nez was the grandfather of MTV. So I sort of owe my living to him. I really ought to say thanks.'

'Sorry?'

'Mike Nesmith invented MTV.'

'Now you're just making things up.'

'It's true.'

'Hmmm. And you think he deserves thanks for that?'

He had a point I suppose, but Mike Nesmith is a much more noteworthy fellow than most people give him credit for. That he was a popstar with a penchant for woolly hats and sideburns is where most people's acquaintance with him starts and ends. In fact, not only does Nesmith's post-Monkees output embrace ideas in virtually every field of creative endeavour, I can tell you without fear of hyperbole that one very specific enterprise is devoted to nothing less than the furtherance and elevation of ideas themselves (more of which in a minute). His Monkee beginnings are by far the least interesting chapter in his life story. And there was one particular entry on this list of achievements for which I personally owed him a debt of gratitude. In a very roundabout way I owed my living to the man, and surely that deserved at least a polite thank you if ever the opportunity should arise.

So for Joe's benefit – and, I hope, yours – a handful of reasons to love Nez.

He invented MTV. Kind of. In 1977 he made a promo clip for solo hit 'Rio', a conceptual rock video which received very little play in the US and was never a hit there. But it was played heavily on New Zealand channel TV2, which aired a late night music show named *Radio with Pictures*. Inspired by its success, Nesmith piloted a show called *Popclips* for cable channel Nickelodeon, which he later sold to Warner Communications as the concept for a twenty-four-hour-a-day music channel. That channel became MTV.

Precisely who 'invented' MTV is a matter of some debate. In the glory days of global domination and multimillion-dollar music videos, pretty much anyone who had uttered the words 'music' and 'television' on the same day would attempt to claim credit. These days it's a little like owning up to a silent-but-deadly in a lift. But I latched onto the Nez connection straight away when I left the BBC for the Viacom Corporation. Invention by one of my favourite songwriters was one helpful way of easing my conscience over jumping into bed with the enemy. (A terrible one I'll admit, roughly on a par with 'Darling, it didn't mean anything.')

But back to Bette, and how she decided to spend all that money. In 1978, just before she died, she established the Gihon Foundation, a mysterious organisation dedicated to the pursuit of entrepreneurial philanthropy which, among many other wonderful things, runs the ambitious and loftily entitled Council on Ideas. This forum, hosted by Nez himself at his Nambé Valley home every two years, gathers together a handful of the world's most respected thinkers – Nobel and Pulitzer Prize winners, professors and university fellows, journalists and company CEOs – to identify and recommend solutions to the most pressing issue of the day. Nez, in the role of intellectual midwife, pays each of the invited visionaries five thousand dollars from the foundation coffers, sits them around a table in a converted barn on his estate, and then disappears to let the ideas gestate. The goal is one 'extraordinary moment' of insight – a solution to the most pressing issue of the time.

Whether that extraordinary moment is even possible remains the subject of some debate (two members of the 1990 gathering clashed so angrily that the entire group walked out), but you can't blame him for trying.

And there's something very heart-warming about Mike's determination that the cash from Ma Nesmith's own little moment of insight – correcting typos – should be put to use with the aim of correcting nothing less than the world's problems.

And that, along with production credits on several great movies (*Repo Man*, *Tapeheads* among them) and a strange but beautiful sci-fi novel called *The Long Sandy Hair of Neftoon Zamora* to his name, is why I think Mike Nesmith is a pretty wonderful fellow.

But more important than any of this is the fact that, post-Monkees, Nez released several albums of the most sublime country rock ever committed to tape. Three of them are of a quality most artists never manage once in an entire career, let alone three times in one year, as was the case with *Magnetic South*, *Loose Salute* and *Nevada Fighter*. And if Gram was the godfather of country rock, Nez was definitely the stepfather. If anyone can lay claim to having begotten the bastard child that was the Eagles, it's Nez. Have a listen to Ian Matthews' Nesmith-produced 'Seven Bridges Road' on the 1973 *Valley Hi* album, then flip to the Eagles' so-called definitive recording of the same song seven years later. They're note-for-note identical.

'OK, he's interesting,' said Joe, 'but he's not beating-heart interesting, and definitely not two-hundred-mile detour interesting.'

'But maybe we could be on his ideas council!'

'We're not knocking on Michael Nesmith's door and asking if his ideas council is coming out to play. No. No way. Anyway it's enough that we're making a detour of nearly a thousand miles via a city I hate on the off chance we might be able to pop in and say hi to the ghost of Johnny Cash.'

'Don't you want to go to the Cash estate?'

'Of course I do. I just think it's a long shot.'

'But it would be *amazing* if it comes off.'

He smiled. 'It would be, to use the Bronx vernacular, "the shit" if it comes off. Let's hope Shilah comes through.'

Late in the afternoon we became dimly aware of the buttes and mesas of Monument Valley rising slowly in the distance, realising some time and several miles later that they were considerably larger and much further away than we had first thought.

I almost hesitate to describe them; aside from being robbed of both the breath and words to do so upon first glimpsing the formidable red bulk of the 'Mittens', two enormous, straight-sided sandstone plateaus bookending the desert view ahead of us, I'll wager you already know what Monument Valley looks like anyway.

No? Picture John Wayne on horseback contemplating the unknowable vastness of the Wild West; that monolithic stack of sandstone silhouetted behind him is the Totem Pole. Or think of any seventies TV space explorer teleporting onto the surface of a strange, uncharted planet. The red dirt at his feet is the Monument Valley floor. Or a Road Runner cartoon: the anvil with which Wile E. Coyote hopes to crush his lightning quarry is hanging from Ear of the Wind Arch. Yes, you've definitely seen the bizarre rock formations and lunar landscapes of Monument Valley before.

We had made a reservation at Gouldings Lodge just off US163, a motel which must surely lay claim to one of the most panoramic, most iconic and, if you'll excuse me while I put down my rhyming dictionary, most tectonic locations on offer for the guest in search of a room with a view. And what a consciousness-expanding, ego-thwarting view he is confronted with: a wide, flat, landscape punctuated by vast, crumbling towers of red rock which pierce the endless blue sky and betray the millennia of desolation like headstones.

Joe was right about the Grand Canyon. It was wider, deeper and more deathly quiet than I could have imagined. But, impossible as it may be to compute the numbers attached to it – 277 miles long, 18 miles wide, 6 million years old – the average brain has no trouble with the general concept of a river carving a hole, albeit a comparatively small river and a very large hole, further and further down through the earth over time. It's what rivers do.

Harder to conceive of – and this I think is what gives Monument Valley its eerie, 'what-planet-have-we-just-arrived-on' ambience – are features of geology which apparently do the opposite. Colossal, straight-sided red mountains appear to rise vertically from the vast, flat plains to heights of over 1,000 feet through shallow, sloping shale collars which seem to stretch the surface tension of the earth like tent poles poked through a flysheet. The ground just isn't supposed to do that – doesn't, normally.

And the numbers are even more stupefying: 160 million years of erosion and uplift over 2,000 square miles have sculpted a landscape more unsettling than anchovy cheesecake washed down with a marmite and tonic. What better backdrop for conveying the mysterious and unearthly frontiers of outer space and the wild Wild West.

Gouldings Lodge is named for the man who brought all of this to the notice of Hollywood, and by extension to the world. Harry Goulding was the first white man to own land in Monument Valley. In 1925, Harry and his wife Leone, to whom he referred affectionately by her fabulously come-hither pet name 'Mike', packed a truck with all of their belongings and some merchandise to trade with the Navajo Indians, and trundled off into the wilderness to start a new life together. Decades later their prospering trading post had comfortable cabins and running water. By the time we arrived it had been turned into a modern motel with air conditioning, a gymnasium and cable TV.

We checked in with just enough time to be on our balcony as the sun set behind us. The iridescent red sandstone of Sentinel Mesa – a rectangular, titanic island mountain rising vertically from the flat plains on top of a sloping, stratified bedrock – turned brushed-steel grey from the ground up as the shadow of Olijato Mesa behind us crept slowly skywards like a fish tank filling with water. I could hardly get to sleep fast enough to watch the whole spectacle in reverse the following morning.

24 OCTOBER

VAIL TO NO AVAIL

I was having a perfectly lovely dream about hovercrafts when the skirt on my vessel made an alarming 'zzzzzzpp' sound. At which point I realised it was Price opening the curtains of our slightly shabby motel room to reveal the not-remotely-shabby view of Monument Valley. He hopped onto the balcony to take some shots, then raced back in. 'Quick, where are the car keys? The view will be better on the other side of that headland.'

Put a camera in Chris' hands and he will constantly dart into awkward spaces to get arty shots, run off in search of better light or simply stand still, incapacitated by the artistic options in front of him. I was relieved to get him out of the Grand Canyon alive, as there was every likelihood his search for the perfect shot would involve leaning just that little too far over the edge and tumbling, cheap-sitcom-style, thousands of feet into the Colorado River. Except with added death.

Ten minutes later he marched disgruntled back into the room and threw the keys on the bed: 'Fucking missed it.' In the time it had taken him to drive to the perfect spot to watch the perfect sunrise, the sun had risen and the magical moment was lost. Me? I watched it from my bed. It looked very nice.

Hollywood showed the world how to make westerns. Monument Valley showed the world how they should look, and the stationery in our motel room bore the name of the man responsible. Harry Goulding grew up in the Rocky Mountain gold rush town of Durango. Having scrapped, scrabbled and hustled a living from the hills for twenty-five years, and later moved out to the plains of Monument Valley, in 1938 he did what millions of others were doing and headed for Hollywood. But Harry wasn't looking to settle under the bright lights of the big city. He wanted Hollywood to come to him. Having heard that Tinseltown was looking for great locations in which to set their westerns – and believing that the valley in which he lived was just what they were looking for – he had a series of photos taken and set out for Hollywood.

Harry parked up outside United Artists and went inside to try and charm the receptionist while Mike waited in the car with her knitting. Exasperated by his refusal to leave or make an appointment, the receptionist summoned a location manager to provide a more authoritative flea for his ear. Goulding was about to be thrown unceremoniously from the building when the location manager spotted the photographs. He showed them to director John Ford, who was in pre-production for *Stagecoach*, and in that moment Monument Valley started its journey towards becoming cinematic shorthand for the Old West.

Stagecoach was Ford's first valley effort, starring a B-movie-swagger-for-hire by the name of John Wayne. He followed it with *My Darling Clementine* which, for my money, makes best use by far of Monument Valley's towering crags. In the romantic showdown between Wyatt Earp and Clementine Carter, each of the actors is positioned before a silhouetted stack of sandstone. Clementine is framed by an appropriately feminine slither, while Wyatt gets an altogether more massive eminence. As the romantic tension builds and the sense of longing becomes more palpable and intense, the camera dollies downwards so that Wyatt's 'rock' appears to grow. John Ford: king of the western, prince of geological knob gags.

But *Butch Cassidy and the Sundance Kid* was the one that we were interested in. When I first saw it as a child I liked it so much I watched it another three times straight afterwards just to check it was as good as I thought. 'When I grow up,' I resolved, 'I'll go there, ride where they rode, talk their talk and walk their walk.'

Four days later an edition of BBC1's *Holiday* programme featured a package entitled something like 'Dreams of the American Old West' featuring scenes from *Butch Cassidy* and other westerns. The host rode horses up escarpments, gazed contemplatively upon widescreen sunsets and ate beans from a billycan by an open fire. At the end of the piece, a graphic totted up how much a holiday like this would set you back. And, cards on the table here, I cried. I cried because it was so beautiful. I cried because it was so much money. I cried because I knew I'd never convince my parents to take me there. I cried because I was ten years old and confused.

But here we were, looking out onto those very vistas, and my eyes misted at the thought of it. Millions before us had sat and contemplated the view we now saw through the windscreen of the car. Like us, many of them will have had their own romantic reasons for being there. *2001: A Space Odyssey* perhaps. *Thelma & Louise*. *Forrest Gump*. Or the cover of the biggest-selling 'best of' of all time, the Eagles' *Greatest Hits*. I'll wager I'm the only person who can say he was inspired by seventies TV host Cliff Michelmore.

We continued east along US163 past Mexican Hat, which I eagerly added to the list of 'geological features resembling headgear' that I had been keeping since Cap Rock, now pleasingly doubled in length. We made a brief detour via Four Corners to experience the thrill – fleeting, expensive but unmissable – of being able to stand in Colorado, New Mexico, Arizona and Utah all at the same time. Joe opted for the civilised 'heels and toes' approach, while I resolved to get my three dollars' worth with an ungainly but enthusiastic face-down star jump, pushing off from feet planted in Arizona and New Mexico onto hands in Utah and Colorado. This technique afforded the additional (if admittedly adolescent) gratification of disproving Joe's earlier assertion that we would not set foot in New Mexico. I derived extra value for my dinner money by giving him a dead arm and a Chinese burn.

Just over the Colorado state border we rejoined US160 heading for Durango, the southern end of a stretch of railway as scenic and spectacular as any in the world – the Durango & Silverton Narrow Gauge Railroad. The 'D&SNG' steams and woofs for forty-five miles across viaducts through the San Juan Mountains, whose silver and gold ore it was built to carry to neighbouring towns in the late nineteenth century. It has been running continuously ever since. Threading a similar path through the Rockies is US Highway 550, which we planned to follow to the opposite terminus at Silverton. US550 is known as the 'Million Dollar Highway', possibly because it cost a million dollars to build in the twenties, or maybe because the grit and hardcore used to make it was mined from such gold-rich environs that the tarmac on which we now drove had a higher gold content than an Elizabeth Duke clearance sale.

As the road began to climb, the grass on the roadside became wilder and paler, then grew jewels of ice around its tips, and soon disappeared completely beneath a slim ermine of snow. The trees became sparser, the air cooler, the fuel tank emptier and petrol stations fewer and further between. In his perpetual and admirable quest for music to match the scenery, Chris rifled through the CD wallet. He pulled a CD out, thoughtfully held it up to the light as might a wizard a new potion, and then loaded it. A distinctive Canadian falsetto cut through the speakers.

'Neil Young, right?'

'Yup,' said Chris. 'Fan?'

'Not so much.'

'Give it a chance.'

Track one, 'Out on the Weekend', passed me by. I was too busy concentrating on the twists and turns of the climb, and the fuel gauge as it yet again sped ineluctably towards empty.

Track two, 'Harvest', didn't particularly register either, lost under the approaching snowdrift forcing two lanes of traffic into one, as well as the sudden and repeated braking required to avoid ending up under the wrong end of a concrete mixer nearly two miles up.

By now we were looking down on mountain peaks which had towered over us only a short while before. The air was not just desperately cold but also, on account of the nearest open water being something in the region of a thousand miles away, almost impossibly dry. As we approached the ten-thousand-foot-high brow of Coal Bank Pass, the CD moved onto track three. A delicate piano chord chimed like an icicle, and over it a mournful, almost unbearably poignant voice began singing about life's unsettling twists and turns.

Neil Young's 'A Man Needs a Maid' was as cold, bleak and desolate as the world outside the windows. It's a remarkable song – the perfect keening poem for grizzly, cabin-dwelling mountain men to cry their lonely eyes out to. Three-quarters of the way through, as the back wheels of the car skittered on the ice along to the piercing crescendo of the London Symphony Orchestra, every part of my body flashed, flickered and flared. As we reached the highest point of the pass, my heart shattered into a thousand tiny shards. Then, lifting my foot off the accelerator, we freewheeled down through steep hairpins towards Durango.

The overall appeal of Neil Young still eluded me, and the universal acclaim accorded to 'Harvest' is still a little confusing I must confess, but 'A Man Needs a Maid' had won me over a thousand times. If you ever find yourself navigating your way through the freezing temperatures and imposing scenery of

Coal Bank Pass in western Colorado, I heartily recommend you bring Neil Young along with you for the ride.

On the face of it 'A Man Needs a Maid' does sound a tiny bit misogynous. On first hearing perhaps you can understand why some women were offended by the idea of a young man, now famous in his own right and rich from platinum-selling albums with Buffalo Springfield and CSNY, singing about hiring in some help to cook his meals, ease his loneliness and then go away. Maybe you can sympathise with anyone upset by the apparent implication that, in substituting a lover for a maid, the role of lover is reduced to cleaner and cook.

But if you really listen – not just to the words, but to the doleful opening piano chords, the cinematic orchestral arrangements, the heart-rending chimes and lilting oboe of the middle eight, the piercing flute and racing violins that signal the final chorus – you realise it's about something else entirely. On second listen you hear the fear and confusion of a man for whom wealth and fame had brought the inescapable truth of no longer knowing who to trust. You hear the desperate longing of someone in search of love, but too frightened to go in search of it.

Joe didn't need a second listen. He got it in one.

And then we were in Silverton, terminus of the narrow gauge railroad, which had special significance for many reasons. Chief among them was that it was where several key scenes from *Butch Cassidy* were filmed, including the Hole in the Wall Gang's repeated ambushes of the Union Pacific Flyer. And as

Butch Cassidy was the birthday card which started all this, he was pretty central to the plot of our road movie too.

The real Butch, from all anecdotal evidence given, was the most charismatic gunslinger of the era, to the point where even the law were taken in by him. At the beginning of 1896 Robert LeRoy Parker (as Butch was then known) was in jail in Laramie, Wyoming, serving time for racketeering and that most quintessential of cowboy crimes, horse rustling. The story goes that the governor of Wyoming, William Alford Richards, went to visit him and said that he would release Butch on one simple – and you have to say quite reasonable – condition: that he stop breaking the law. Butch gave this a moment's thought before offering the governor a deal of his own. He couldn't promise to stop breaking the law, but if he were released he wouldn't do it in Wyoming any more. And with that Butch walked out of jail, across the state border and back to his life of crime.

Maps are an unnecessary luxury for visitors to Silverton. There is only one proper road, and it winds down from such a dizzying height that the entire town is laid out like a perfect model village. From the dense pine woods to the east, the Durango & Silverton steam train billowed in, puffing cotton wool from its smokestack. I half expected an enormous hand to reach down and change the signals. We cruised down from the mountains, turned off the main road and bumped across rutted frozen earth, stopping so close to the parked steam engine huffing impatiently alongside us that it made our cheeks glow when we stepped out of the car.

In its prime, Silverton was a one hundred per cent, bona fide, spit and sawdust, take-your-pardner-by-the-hand old-time Wild West town. The mining boom of the 1860s had brought hundreds of workers from across the world to the San Juan Mountains, and Silverton sputtered into life almost by accident. The layout was agreed in 1874 (and with just one main road it was, I imagine, a very short meeting).

How wild was Silverton in those days? Well, by 1883 it had acquired two banks, five laundries, and twenty-nine saloons. In that same year there were 117 indictments against lewd women. Today the cemetery testifies to the harshness of life in the time of the gold rush: the crumbling headstones tell of 161 locals who died from pneumonia, 117 in snow slides and over 200 who passed away in mining accidents. The number of men whose bodies were never recovered will never be known.

Today, Silverton's mines are closed, but there are still a dozen saloons where you can order a steak and sarsaparilla and feel like a cowboy. We opted for Natalia's 1912 Restaurant, situated in one of the town's oldest bordellos, ordered steaks and sarsaparilla, and felt like tourists. Sated by meat and fizzy pop tasting of Germolene, and fearing snow slides or bouts of pneumonia, we hit the road once again.

We fell short of reaching Denver by sundown and settled instead for Vail, which competes with Aspen, a couple of hours west, for the title of 'American ski resort most likely to cripple you financially if not actually'. (Aspen holds the record currently; killing a member of the Kennedy family scores triple points.) Excited at the prospect of enjoying a night on the tiles in one of the world's most prestigious mountain resorts, we checked into the least prestigious lodgings we could find in order to conserve pennies for a 'massive night out' in the village.

In season, Roost Lodge is the ideal place for Vail's youngest and least affluent visitors to sleep off a hangover. Off-peak, it apparently served as a dosshouse for the hundreds of construction workers bussed in to make the place shipshape for the start of the season. And us. We checked in, then immediately jumped in a taxi up to the village in order to avail ourselves of all that's available in Vail.

Pre-season Vail at night is what Harrods must be like after the doors have been locked and the cleaners move in. It's pristine, unspeakably pretty, but unutterably dull. After a brief look around we found the only place with more customers than staff, an Italian restaurant and bar called Vendettas, and tucked into a pizza just smaller than our table.

But pizza wasn't why had come to Vail. We were two red-blooded males starved of excitement from days in the desert, and we wanted action. I quizzed the waitress as to the possibilities for stimulation in Vail off-peak. She disappeared and returned a moment later brandishing a card detailing something called a 'Pub Crawl' taking place every Tuesday night in the village. All we needed to do was drink one beer in each of five bars dotted along the main street, and we would be entered into a prize draw by the host venue after midnight. Prizes included tickets to see the Denver Broncos, and a snowboard.

We did the math. There were approximately fourteen people in the resort at the time, most of whom were either behind a bar or at the wheel of a taxi, so the odds were stacked in our favour. How could we lose? Drink some beer, stay up until midnight and win a prize. This should present no significant problem for two hard-drinkin', street-fightin' fellas like us. Bring it on.

In fact, we turned out to be a couple of softies for whom the prospect of drinking more than three alcoholic beverages in anything approaching quick succession was scarier than a baby with fingers for eyes. We managed one more beer in a bar round the corner, which turned out not to be a participating venue anyway, and retired to bed, pooped. We tried our best to convince ourselves that, well, it had been a long drive hadn't it, and this prissy place probably couldn't handle us anyway. But there was no escaping the fact that we were two grown males faced with near-certain odds of winning a prize relating to extreme sports or football, and neither of them were sufficient incentive to put away a measly five beers. We picked up our handbags and left.

Dumping our handbags on our separate beds in our separate rooms, we separately flicked on our separate televisions. The men on mine were playing rounders, only not.

It's all too often said how bemusing and baffling cricket is. But the implication has always seemed to be that all other sports are simple by comparison. Football, bar the offside rule, is almost as simple as it's possible to be, with the possible exception of boxing (or 'hitting' as I've always felt it should be called), but baseball seems every inch as complex as cricket.

And I now had the perfect forum to learn the complexities, the peculiarities, and the delights of a sport that my father first tried twenty-six years ago to get me into. That forum was the World Series. This year the St Louis Cardinals faced the Detroit Tigers. We didn't know that the series was on until meeting up with Punk Rock Mike in LA, where we had watched part of the deciding game which took St Louis to the final. The Mets lost, but if you get the chance to glance at YouTube, look up 'chavez catch mets' and witness the most extraordinary catch you will probably ever see in sport. The ball was not just heading out of the ground, it *was* out of the ground. Chavez, though, ran to the fence and jumped so high, arched his arm back so far, and tilted his glove so much that he caught the ball despite it being almost two feet over the fence. When he landed he had the same look of disbelief that was on every face in the crowd. If life were the movies they would have gone on to win the game, and then the series. It isn't, and they didn't.

Which brought us to where we were today. After three games of the World Series, St Louis led two games to one. This, we were told in a barrage of bellowed sportspeak, was a big deal for them. Seventy-two per cent of game three winners in the last nine years had won the series, and sixty-four per cent of away teams with pitchers over 6' 2" had won two consecutive games in Detroit in the last four seasons. And of course ever since Roberto Alomar hit the winning home run for the Toronto Blue Jays back in '92, no avian-themed team with Hispanic lead batsmen had lost in the World Series. I made some of those statistics up, but in the context of the absurdly over-analytical world of baseball stats, they're entirely plausible.

Baseball coverage has long since crossed over from meaningful interpretation of events to a hybrid of statistics and superstition. And how baseball fans love statistics. It seems they simply can't bear to admit that this might be just a sport, susceptible to human error and – dare we say it – luck. Apparently it is a holy sporting algorithm that one day men with abacuses will be able to predict with total accuracy. At which point presumably the teams won't even have to play – the managers can just announce the teams and the bean-counters will determine in a matter of minutes who the winners would be, thereby saving the messy business of actually having to play the game.

It was too early to know who the star of the series would be. We couldn't yet know which batsman, pitcher, catcher or baseman would be the hero of this year's contest, but I already had a favourite. I'm sorry to say that he was my top choice not for his skills on the field (though he appeared to be something of a talismanic bat for St Louis), but for his name. Whilst the name Albert Pujols didn't make me laugh per se, I was cheered when he took the field by thoughts of small children across America falling to the floor and choking on their chips when the commentator said (and the phonetics are important here): 'We're in the eighth innings and it's getting pretty sticky at the bottom for St Louis – which means one thing – it's time for poo-holes.' If I listened carefully I could hear moms all over America tutting as they wiped spittle-flecked popcorn from their fifty-six inch plasma screens.

25 OCTOBER

WICHITA LINES, MAN

Next morning over breakfast at a nearby Holiday Inn (Roost Lodge offered about as much in the way of breakfast as it did in the way of comfort), I checked my email. There was a message from our Joshua Tree hostess, Polly Parsons' best friend Shilah.

```
From:     Shilah Morrow
Date:     24 October
To:       Chris Price
Subject:  Re: Thanks


Hello Chris!

You're so very welcome... I love being the
maître d' of Joshua Tree - it makes my trips
out there more interesting. So, Wichita huh?
Let me know if you spot a lineman. That's
```

one of my favorite songs. The melody makes my heart hurt. 'And I need you more than want you, and I want you for all time...' What an incredible line!

Now... Are you sitting down?

I spoke with Jack Fripp who runs the studio, and apparently John is out of town working on a biography about his mother until Sunday. *But* he said I could pass on his info and he'd be more than happy to show you around even if John Carter wasn't there! So if your voyage didn't include a trip to Nashville then you should look at changing your routing asap!

OK, must go wash the ol' bones now! Keep me posted on your travels and let me know how the Cash Cabin Studio thing works out! And remember to call me on the cell when you're having an exceptionally good time!

Love & Rockets,
\m/
Shilah

Yee-es! Shilah, you beauty!

Instantly I felt the scores had evened up a little. Finally Joe would get something more out of this trip than several pairs of reasonably priced Levis and a tanned forehead. Not that I wasn't excited about visiting the Cash estate myself (because boy was I excited), but Johnny Cash is one of Joe's favourite singers and Rick Rubin is one of his favourite producers and the Cash Cabin Studio is where... Well, you can see why I was excited. And relieved too, that this barmy idea might actually end up being as much fun for him as so far it had been for me. I could stop worrying that he was quietly rueing the day he ever suggested it.

Yes, the trip had been his idea, but still I couldn't shake the feeling that I was on my own little journey of discovery while Joe tagged along for the ride. Deep down I knew that none of this was true – we had been planning it together for three years – but still I wanted him to have a 'Joshua Tree moment' like the one I'd had meeting Polly. If we were really lucky he might even get to rub shoulders with country music aristocracy itself in the shape of John Carter Cash. And if I was really honest, meeting John Carter Cash – the only child in the Cash dynasty from Johnny's marriage to June Carter – would be at least as big as meeting Polly Parsons, if not just a teeny-weeny bit bigger. The progeny of the Cash and Carter families is the closest thing America has to blue blood.

But I was getting carried away with myself. Shilah had saved my bacon and my conscience, as well as saving Joe from death by a thousand pedal steel riffs, and that was enough for now.

'Mate, get a load of this!' I squeaked, spinning the laptop around to face him.

His eyes darted over the screen. A smile started to grow, dipped at first, then full beam.

'Shilah... you... fucking... beauty!'

I think we actually high fived.

'Doesn't sound like John Carter's going to be there,' he said, scanning the email a second time, 'but just think, we'll get to see where *The Man Comes Around* was recorded!'

'Do you hate Nashville now?'

'I fucking *love* Nashville now. Let's go.'

But first we had a date with Wichita, Kansas. And finding a lineman, as Shilah had guessed, was our business there. The loneliness of Glen Campbell's 'Wichita Lineman' had been regularly breaking my heart for a decade, and we planned to get a taste of it. Joe called for the bill.

It was my turn to pay for breakfast. The bill arrived with a 'tipping suggestions' breakdown at the bottom: 'A 10 per cent tip would be $2.38. A 15 per cent tip would be $3.57. A 20 per cent tip would be $4.76.' I put $2.52 on the plate and refused to hand it over until the waitress could tell me what percentage that was. No, you're right, I didn't.

The road out of Vail to Denver was pretty for exactly half of its length. The first half, winding slowly up into snow-dusted mountain tops, was just lovely. The second half, heading down into Denver under a smoggy sky the colour of skid-marks, was not. The guide book boasted that Denver stands proudly at the foot of the splendid and stoic Rocky Mountains. It doesn't. Denver skulks, embarrassed by its averageness and by the cancer-coloured cloud of car fumes it sits under like a yellowing Tupperware sky.

We hurried through, making a brief pit stop at Radio Shack to buy some cabling for the laptop, then pressed on, wondering quite what nothingness lay ahead of us. Several people, upon hearing of our planned route through western Colorado, Kansas and Oklahoma, had warned 'Man, there's nothing there... Except fat people.' Let me take this opportunity to set the record straight. There's nothing out there – not *even* fat people. Several times we drove for over half an hour without seeing another vehicle. That might not seem odd in some parts of the world, but in America it makes you wonder if you're the only two people left alive on the continent after a devastating nuclear catastrophe.

We had hit the Bible Belt, and judging from the radio stations the car stereo was scanning, it was buckled up *reeeeal* tight. East of the Rockies the dial seemed suddenly to offer up a smorgasbord of Christian radio listening catering to all tastes along the musical and denominational spectrum. There was gospel music, pop, rap, country obviously, and a genre which one station referred to rather vaguely – if a little tautologically – as 'inspirational'. (If you're making Christian music that's not inspirational, then perhaps you ought to be looking for a new career.)

Christian radio, of course, is all about keeping the Lord first. And keeping the Lord first was the number one priority for Colorado's KTLF – can you see what they've done there? – whose *Light Praise* afternoon show we now tuned in to. (Light praise during the week I imagine, and save the heavy stuff – the really serious praise – for Sunday.) KTLF was a music network which served up a hale and hearty diet of God-fearing modern rock with titles such as 'Just to Know You Lord', 'Above All', 'Salvation is Here' and – my favourite – 'Our God is an Awesome God (Much Better Than Buddha or Any of Those Other Ones)'. It was, in every possible sense of the word, awesome.

Alongside KTLF on the dial was Air One – the 'Christian alternative' (that's Protestantism surely?) – followed by K-LOVE, whose sole *raison d'être* was apparently to provide you, dear listener, with an endless list of ways to part with your hard-earned cash. Why? To keep the station on the air. That way, they will have the funds to carry on telling you how to raise more funds. It's ingenious.

There were many ways to make a pledge. Every link detailed one of the myriad opportunities for filling the K-LOVE coffers, suggested starting pledge forty dollars. Call 800-525-LOVE and have your credit card ready. Make your pledge online. Shit, crack open the kids' piggy banks and haul your arse down here with the small change, we're not fussy. But *do* make a pledge. Who knows, you might even get a mention on air, and surely that's worth forty dollars of anyone's money. And if God has blessed you, be generous.

In case it wasn't enough just to know that our hard-earned moolah would keep K-LOVE in the lovin' game for a few more minutes, the excited presenter kindly furnished us with a number of other reasons why donating was a good idea. It was a positive influence in our lives and the lives of our children. Hundreds of suicides were prevented every week because lonely people wouldn't feel so lonely any more (which is as foul and cynical as it is unprovable). And don't forget what you get for your forty dollars. Not just great music, but the satisfaction of knowing that you're 'helping people out there who are really in need'. This last point made me feel slightly less nauseous – at least they were using the money to support the needy and desperate. I was beginning to think it all ended up in K-LOVE's pockets.

But no, it turned out the needy didn't see a penny. K-LOVE apparently helped these people simply by being on the air, because *desperate people can listen too*. And what better way to cheer them up than with an endless stream of anodyne, soulless MOR.

The difficulty with Christian music is that, if praising the Lord is your thing, then surely all of it, regardless of artistic merit, is good by definition. Or praiseworthy at least, and definitely good in the sense of 'not evil'. So even if, say, rock music isn't your thing, 'Wings of Change' by hard rockin', strong-believin' David Lee Williams must have *some* appeal for Christian music lovers, because that rockin' has a higher purpose. Those axes are being wielded in the name of the Lord, and that has to be good, right?

And there's the rub. As a genre, and therefore as a radio format, Christian music is utterly meaningless. It is no more a genre than 'songs about California' might be considered one, or love songs. I'm a sucker for an honest tear-jerker – 'The Power of Love' by Frankie Goes to Hollywood I could comfortably listen to all day – but not all of them are great, are they? 'One More Night' by Phil Collins, to pick just one example of many, is shit. So is 'The Lady in Red' by Chris de Burgh. And so, unfortunately, is 'Above All' by Women of Faith, even though it deals with a very different kind of love, a higher love if you will – the love of the Lord.

Don't get me wrong, I don't hate all Christian music. Or even all music made by Christians. There's plenty of great stuff – try virtually anything by Johnny Cash for starters – which has soul *and* a higher purpose. But they choose not to play it on K-LOVE. Christ knows why. Perhaps we should ask him.

We pressed on through the infamous and disquieting Tornado Alley, whose named turned out – today at least – to be inaccurate on two counts.

When I was a kid there was a lane behind the cornershop near my house known to locals under the age of fifteen as Piss Alley. For a narrow thoroughfare between two buildings which stank of piss, 'Piss Alley' strikes me as a very apt name. But an expanse of central North America including Texas, Oklahoma, Kansas, Nebraska, Iowa, Missouri, South Dakota and Colorado – a land mass roughly ten times the size of Great Britain – to my mind stretches even the most generous definition of the word 'alley'. And happily, today there turned out to be nothing but cloudless skies and the curvature of the horizon to concern ourselves with.

The destination was Wichita, the route simple. We had entered rectangular Kansas in her north-eastern corner, cruising calmly and smoothly east along I70. Calmly and smoothly that is, until the perfectionist co-pilot growled a hesitant 'errmm' whilst moving a finger from one point on the map to another quite different point on the map.

'What is it?' I asked.

'Well, the thing is...'

'Yes?'

'We're heading to the *city* of Wichita.'

'Yes,' I said as forcefully as possible, fearing where this was going.

'Well the lyrics of the song go, "I am a lineman for the *county*".'

'Nothing contradictory in that. He's from the city of Wichita and now he's a lineman – whatever that is – for the county. Hence "Wichita Lineman".'

'And you'd be right, only there's also a Wichita *county*.'

'Which is how far from Wichita *city* exactly?'

'About 200 miles due south of where we are now.'

Jesus. 'What should we do?'

A slip road approached on our right. Chris slammed the map on the dashboard. 'Exit here!'

With a squeal of brakes and the squeak of rubber on tarmac, we pulled off I70 and darted south through Sharon Springs towards Leoti, the county seat of Kansas. Time, miles and beef jerky disappeared. As the late afternoon sun scrolled from yellow to ember-red, we reached the edge of Wichita County.

Chris finished a mouthful of jerky. 'Shit.'

'What now?'

'There's another Wichita County.'

'What? Where?'

'Texas.'

'Well that's all right then.'

'Sorry?'

'If it were within two hundred miles of here you'd want us go there too. As it isn't, we won't be going anywhere.'

Jimmy Webb, who wrote 'Wichita Lineman', never lived in either of the Wichita Counties, nor indeed in the city of the same name, so we'll never know which of them, if any, was the real inspiration for the song. For all we know he wrote it in High Wycombe and just liked the sound of the name. But by now it didn't really matter. For approaching on our right under a row of sagging telephone lines was a rusty, faded metal sign which said 'Welcome to Wichita'.

I can remember the first time I heard 'Wichita Lineman' as clearly as if it were yesterday. It was in the front room of a very dear university friend by the name of Mauro, whose London flat for a period in the mid-nineties became a playground of discovery for four pals bonded by a passion for two things: music and gin.

Dan, Steve, Mauro and I would retreat to that front room every weekend after club or gig to share music with one another. Taking turns to choose the next tune from Mauro's expansive CD collection covering one entire wall from Abba to ZZ Top and all points in between, a series of random, gin-soaked playlists would emerge from the near infinity of possibilities like an old-world iPod on shuffle. Every now and then we would allow guest selectors from outside the group, and occasionally even girls, to join us for the evening and spice things up a bit.

Some time in the early hours of the morning, after eighties hair metal but before ambient, surfaced a period of quiet, country-tinged reflection where Gram Parsons, the Burritos, Nesmith et al – for we were all fans of one sort of another – would get a run out. And it was here that one night Steve suggested it was high time Glen Campbell got an airing.

'Glen Campbell?' I snorted, 'as in "Rhinestone Cowboy"?'

'Yep, that Glen Campbell'.

'Isn't he sort of... rubbish?'

Glen Campbell was an artist who occupied – typified – the 'crooner' end of the country spectrum. He was establishment – a singer whom, by denying everything that he and his contemporaries stood for, I used as a means of asserting my love for all things outlaw.

'Have you heard "Wichita Lineman"?' asked Steve.

I admitted that I hadn't.

'You've never heard "Wichita Lineman"?!' squeaked Dan, sensing the thrill of two lifelong pals about to meet for the first time.

'Well you're in for a treat,' said Steve. 'Check this out.'

He slid *Twenty Golden Greats* into the CD player, selected track six and hit play. A brief silence, then a five-note hopscotch of bass guitar – doo-do do-be-doo – and a string section which turned my blood to wine before even the first line had been sung.

I am a lineman for the county
And I drive the main road,
Searchin' in the sun for another overload.

I had no idea what a lineman was. Probably some kind of railwayman out repairing damaged track, or – more likely – a phone maintenance guy up a telegraph pole fixing lines. Either way he was out in the middle of nowhere with nothing but his thoughts for company.

I hear you singin' in the wire
I can hear you through the whine
And the Wichita Lineman
Is still on the line.

Must be the phone guy. Strings again, pizzicato this time, like the glint of scorching sun on telephone wires like tiny, repeated stabs to a lonesome, lonely heart.

And I need you more than want you
And I want you for all time
And the Wichita Lineman
Is still on the line.

'Wichita Lineman' is one of the greatest songs ever written. Anyone who tries to tell you otherwise doesn't like music. My guess is that when Jimmy Webb was inspired to write it, he was driving through Wichita County late in the afternoon in early autumn, the sun just reaching the end of its slow arc west and close to dipping below the telegraph lines that run the length of Highway 96. He sees a man working alone in the sun under a vast expanse of sky and imagines him pining for a distant love.

Even knowing the power of Webb's songwriting, Wichita County line – the Kansas version – still knocked me for six when we arrived. No matter that there was some other line by the same name several hundred miles away. This one matched exactly the image I'd had in my head since first hearing the song in Maz's front room. But this was no approximation, it was a carbon copy. A sense of déjà vu stronger than any I had ever experienced.

We pulled the car off the road onto a dusty track behind the rusting metal sign. Behind it a row of telegraph poles stretched off to a vanishing point just beneath a sun which bleached the colour out of everything in view. A string section blew in on the breeze and caused the telephone lines to hum. The rays of the sun pounded out a rhythm on the road. This was a more visceral experience of music than we ever imagined possible. We were there.

We never found a lineman. We'd had an idea we would look one up in the phone book and talk to him. Find out what it was like out there working the lines all on your lonesome. But that was when we thought we were going to Wichita City. The chances of finding anyone – any*thing* – out here were somewhere shy of zero. And in a way I'm glad we didn't – it might have spoiled the tranquillity of what turned out to be as perfect a moment as any we experienced on the trip; a quiet intermezzo in the symphony, if you will. I thought about the boys back in London – Dan, Steve, Maz – and considered texting them. But in the end I thought I'd keep this one for me and Joe.

A few days earlier, as we were walking along the rim of the Grand Canyon, Joe had asked me to describe my favourite place in the world. I told him about Lake Tekapo on the South Island of New Zealand, where I had witnessed a sunset and moonrise more perfect than I had thought possible. Next time I'm asked that question I'll have a tough time answering it. To arrive somewhere for the first time and know that you've been there a hundred times before must make it a pretty good contender.

Beauty, we are told, is in the eye of the beholder. But let me tell you – that ageing sign, that setting sun and those telephone lines vanishing into the distance were one of the most beautiful sights we had encountered by a country mile. Roof down, we put 'Wichita Lineman' on the stereo. And for a moment we were Jimmy Webb. We were linemen. And we were happy.

Reluctantly we re-boarded and headed for Dodge City, the most notorious point in the cowboy world, home to the aptly named Boot Hill Cemetery and a ginuwine high-noon history of buffalo-slaughtering and Injun-burying.

The glow of the Kansas sunset gave way to a clear-skied chill. We hummed 'Wichita Lineman' while the car tyres hummed on Wichita lines, man. On the open plains of America, darkness descends like a blackout. There are no road lights, and the only illumination other than your own headlamps are gas stations that bob in the blackness and cars that wobble towards you like a close encounter of the road kind. It's an experience akin to driving through an early nineties screensaver.

I wasn't tired, but the headlights hovering across the pancake landscape became hypnotic. Twenty minutes of total darkness swallowed up with just yards of road in front and a few feet of red glow in the rear-view mirror. Then a distant white flicker like a dying torch would appear over the horizon and for a full ten minutes seem to hang in space. Suddenly the glimmer would grow, the car would whip past – its rear lights briefly dancing in the wing mirrors – and it was gone. I've been in photographic darkrooms brighter than the Kansas night sky.

'How come we can't see any stars?' I wondered out loud.

Splat.

'Clouds probably,' said Chris. Splatsplatsplat. 'Rainclouds.'

Splatsplatsplatsplatsplat. I turned on the windscreen wipers.

The crisp aura of the mid-western emptiness swiftly disappeared under a smeared re-imagining of the Kansas night. The gas stations became smudges of neon and the hovering headlights took on the menace of a joust. Instead of the slo-mo anticipation of passing fireflies, my muscles tightened as the lights got brighter and the rain threatened to send them aquaplaning into our path. Somewhere up ahead, Dodge City awaited.

Dodge was very, very famous in the forties, fifties and sixties. The radio serial *Gunsmoke* (later turned into a TV series) was set there, turning Dodge into a kind of colloquial shorthand for 'Wild West town'. Even today people in quite other parts of the world, probably without knowing why, are heard to say 'Let's get the hell out of Dodge' when they mean 'We should leave now, it's getting a little rowdy and I'd rather not get caught up in a kerfuffle.'

Westerns are usually simple affairs: small on plot, big on hats. The iconography is simple too; there are the hats, the guns and the spurs of course, but the other essential item is coffins. Just as a love story must have a kiss and a wedding, so a western must have a death and a burial. In *Gunsmoke* – and in nineteenth-century Dodge City – that meant a trip to the place where gunslingers were buried with their boots on: Boot Hill.

Boot Hill is also where one of the greatest sequences in cinema – a key early scene in *The Magnificent Seven* – was shot. Yul Brynner plays Chris, a man determined to outsmart a trigger-happy racist mob who are trying to prevent an Indian being buried on the hill. He needs someone to sit upfront with him on the wagon – to literally ride shotgun. Enter Vin, played by Steve McQueen. The scene is acclaimed not for the setting, or the cinematography or the script. It is wheeled out on clip shows and in film-school lectures because of the *silence*. By barely speaking – four sentences at most – McQueen stole the scene, made his name and became a star. Ever since I was a kid I have wanted to be Steve McQueen and take a trip to Boot Hill.

It came as something of a disappointing inevitability then to find that Dodge City was about as dangerous as a pillow fight and as edgy as in-flight cutlery. The only discernible connection to the town's gunslinging past was that, like the residents of its most famous landmark, it was completely dead.

We cruised into town along Wyatt Earp Boulevard. A green sign said: 'Welcome to Dodge City.'

Chris looked pensively out of the passenger-side window. 'You know, some place names make total sense straight away, don't they?'

'Such as?'

'I don't know, Oxford for instance. Presumably it was where you took your cattle across a river.'

'Makes sense.'

'Then there are the weird American ones like Wichita, which probably have some Native American dialect meaning like "place where the buffalo sit under the trees".'

'Where are you going with this?'

'Well, I'm just wondering, under what extraordinary circumstances would you want to call a town "Dodge"?'

'Maybe "Avoid" was already taken.'

Yellow and blue neon announced a vacancy at the Firebird Motel on our left. We pulled onto the forecourt, wandered into reception and checked in.

I picked up the keys. 'Can you recommend somewhere to eat?'

'There's a Mexican further along Wyatt Earp,' said a weary, elderly landlady. 'But you better hurry, most places close around nine.'

We went to our room to drop off the bags. The guide book had recommended the Firebird Motel as being 'clean and run by friendly people', but neglected to mention it's the kind of place you book by the hour where truckers relieve the loneliness of the open road by strangling each other in French maids' outfits. Stacey, wife of Punk Rock Mike in LA, who had stayed in her fair share of motels during her time as a touring musician, had given us a piece of advice for the trip: never stay in any hotel, motel or other lodgings whose reception smells (the rationale being that if they can't keep that clean then the rooms are very likely even worse). Sage counsel.

What she didn't tell us – but which we could, and probably should, have worked out for ourselves – is that the same should apply to any motel whose rooms featured metal hooks hanging from the ceiling above beds already occupied by crawling, non-paying residents. We were in no mood to hang around.

First we tried the Mexican. 'Sorry sir, we're closing.' Perhaps we could grab a beer next door. Just locking up. Could they recommend somewhere to go bowling? It was a drive away on Kliesen, but yes, we could go bowling.

We drove through the deserted streets, past the darkened restaurants, across the carless junctions of downtown Dodge to the bowling alley which was, yes, completely rammed. Seems the entire population of Dodge had gone bowling. We asked for a lane and were told that there should be one available some time after nine.

Now, here's the odd thing. The lady at the Firebird had told us that most restaurants shut down around nine. What she hadn't said, but which became abundantly clear as everyone filed out of Spare Tyme Bowl on cue as if the fire alarm had sounded, was that everyone in Dodge goes home at nine. We didn't know why, and couldn't work it out. This meant that Chris and I, self-conscious bowlers not blessed with a winning grip, were the only people on the lanes, watched intently by a small crowd of a barman, two security men and the owner.

We bowled briefly and badly and then departed to find the car alone in a car park which an hour earlier we had circled several times in order to find a space. Perhaps *American Idol* was on at 9 p.m. and a Dodge City hopeful had made it to the final. Or maybe there was a still a curfew on from the hell-raisin' days. Whatever the reason, if you ever find yourself in Dodge City after 9 p.m., you shall find yourself very much alone.

26 OCTOBER

DODGE KANSAS, AVOID OKLAHOMA

For the first time I woke up before Chris and resolved to give Dodge a second chance by daylight. Chris declined my offer of a little early morning tourism, preferring to get up and post a blog to the website. While he tapped and huffed (it was not going well for him), I took the car out to a legendary spot.

Dodge City's reputation is built on buffalo hunting. Its notoriety is built on Boot Hill. Humming Iron Maiden's 'Die With Your Boots On (Live Version)' I parked up, strolled past the wrought-iron fence in front of Boot Hill Museum and went straight to the Dodge City Laundry to get some washing done whilst I touristed. I immediately noticed – and perhaps this shouldn't have surprised me, but it did – that the staff and clientele were exclusively middle-aged and male. I was taken aback, I suppose, as these were the Dodge citizens I had imagined would be hard at work in the fields and farms on a Thursday morning in Kansas. Instead they were meekly showing idiot tourists how to put four quarters into a tumble dryer.

The penny dropped along with the quarters. The bowling. The laundry. The sweet but down-at-heel motel. Dodge City may have witnessed its fair share of death over the years, but these days it was the town itself doing the dying. Two hundred years earlier Dodge City had not existed and it seemed to be heading back that way pretty fast. With my pants left to get a whole dollar cleaner, I went back to Boot Hill Museum. Nine dollars to get in and I had the whole place to myself.

It didn't look like it had in *The Magnificent Seven*. The long carriage ride up to the graves was little more than a brisk skip up some concrete steps. Instead of being on the dust-blown edge of town it was smack dab next to some recently-built brick houses on the main road. Damp grasslands instead of beige badlands. The cemetery was all of five metres square with a sprinkling of fake headstones marking graves whose original occupants were disinterred at the turn of the century and taken to a range of less touristy but more appropriate plots.

I closed my eyes and thought of Vin. It was no good; this was as much the Boot Hill of the movie as I was Steve McQueen. I slunk back to the museum. A smiling, round-faced girl sat behind a counter, wearing a name badge which said 'Ellie'.

'Are you enjoying your visit, sir?'

'Very much, thank you. Although it's not quite like I'd imagined it.'

'Really?'

'Well, I know it was the movies, but I thought it would be a bit more like the Boot Hill from *The Magnificent Seven*.'

'I guess maybe that was one of the other Boot Hills.'

'Sorry?'

'It could have been the one in Tombstone maybe?'

Balls. There was another Boot Hill. But all was not lost. If it wasn't too far away we could still go there and I could fulfil my dream.

'So... There's another Boot Hill then?'

'Oh yes,' she enthused. 'There are Boot Hills in Dead Wood, Cripple Creek, Leadville, Montana, Iowa, Idaho, New Mexico, four or five in California. It's a real common name for a cemetery.'

'Oh. I see.'

Not only had I screwed up, I knew it was exactly the sort of stupid mistake that Chris had saved us from when we nearly ended up in the wrong Wichita. Which made it as annoying as hitting your head on a 'mind your head' sign.

On the mock-up of the original Main Street was a barber, a sweet emporium, photographic shop and restaurant, all of which were closed. I walked a few blocks along the wooden sidewalk listening to the distinctive clack of my own boots on wood, normally accompanied by the jangle of spur. The famous lawmen of their age had once walked this stretch. Lawmen who shot first and asked questions later – or more often not at all. Hell, Wyatt Earp strode through here striking fear into the hearts of the guilty, and most of the innocent too. He might have enjoyed a sarsparilla, a gunfight and some casual misogyny on this very spot. Possibly all at the same time – he was a hell of a multitasker.

My undergarments would be ready, so I passed through the gift shop and ignored the passing desire to spend lots of money just to give Ellie something to do, as I didn't need a Boot Hill licence plate or sheriff's badge. Dodge had taken me by surprise. Having embarked on a trip to celebrate the lives and deaths of legends, it seemed we had extended the brief from individuals to whole towns.

Dodge City hadn't been on the itinerary at first, but was added after the hasty diversion via Wichita County. It had looked on the map like the only town in south-eastern Kansas which was big enough to offer decent accommodation. Plus of course there was the anticipated satisfaction the following morning, with a screech of tyres and the smell of burning rubber, of hollering 'Let's get the hell out of Dodge' and then getting the hell out of Dodge. As Joe delivered the line to camera, the pleasure was fleeting, nowhere near enough to compensate for the dismal experience of a restless night in the dodgiest motel in the dodgiest town west of the Mississippi.

A quick stop for breakfast at McDonalds, pausing only to reflect that in these parts at least a Big Mac was perfectly acceptable breakfast fayre, judging from the forest of shuffling ankles stuffed into sneakers under sagging trays. (Personally I would feel better about myself pouring whisky on my cornflakes of a morning, but I suppose we all draw the line in different places.) Joe overheard a snatch of conversation between two breakfasting ladies, one explaining to the other that she just *couldn't* do bacon on her burger that early in the morning, which is about as restrained as sticking to pints for breakfast.

Today was a driving day. We aimed to reach Little Rock by sundown, three states away in Arkansas, electing to drive on

153

interstates where we could engage cruise control, sit back, and watch the miles clock up. The weather appeared to be determined by whoever was behind the wheel. Joe took the first few hours from Dodge to Wichita through a cloud of fine rain, followed by a canopy of sunshine for my three-hour southward stint through Oklahoma City. As evening approached we broke just outside Fort Smith, Arkansas to put the roof up. Joe pleaded that we stop in nearby Van Buren, for the purposes of a gag that only fans of finest Dutch trance will appreciate: the opportunity of saying 'I'm in Van Buren.' (Bear in mind this is a man who once dragged a friend – thankfully not me – for thirty-six hours across Honduras into coastal Guatemala so that upon arriving in the region's main town he could say 'Livingston, I presume.' He wasn't about to pass up the opportunity of a similarly futile gesture in honour of the world's number one DJ.) Cue thunder, lightning and rain so torrential it took a combined effort from both Joe driving and me in the passenger seat to stay between the road markings.

As we squinted our way along I40, the car headlights were rendered virtually useless. On full beam they reflected in the sheet rain like a torch shone into a mirror, blinding us with white light. Dipped, they lit a section of road approximately four feet in front of our noses. I turned the music down and shouted instructions – 'bear left, bear left!' – over the drumming on the roof and the flapping of wipers frantically bailing oceans from the windscreen. Mile after mile it continued, barely another vehicle in sight.

Somewhere around Clarksville another set of headlights appeared behind and tailed us for several miles.

Joe adjusted the rear-view mirror. 'I was starting to think we were the only ones stupid enough to be out in this.'

'He's probably sitting on our tail so he can see where the road is.'

'I don't blame him. I can't see a fucking thing. Where the fuck are we?'

I turned around in my seat to retrieve the road map from the back seat. As I did, a pirouette of blue light danced above the car behind us, accompanied by the whoop of a police siren.

'Fuck.'

'Fuck.'

'You'd better pull over.'

Quite what went through the mind of the patrolman as he stepped up to the car I can only guess at. Joe whirred the window down.

'You was gittin' kinda close to the ve-hicle in front sir,' he began, bending to look into the car. He double took upon seeing two men sporting horseshoe moustaches and a look of quiet terror on their faces, the strains of *Sweetheart of the Rodeo* softly a-honkin and a-tonkin' on the stereo. It must have come as quite a shock. (Or perhaps this was normal in Oklahoma: 'Hi honey, I'm home. Oh, the usual – fightin' at the Broken Spoke, couple o' fags out on forty sniffin' tailpipes.')

'Vehicle, officer?' said Joe. 'We can't even see the road.'

A quizzical look as he tried to compute what he'd heard. Perhaps it was the accent. Certainly the cockdusters taxed him some.

He leaned in a little closer. 'Say, yew boys're brertherrrs, ain't yew?'

The rain dripped from his Mountie hat, whose broad rim was protected by a neatly fitted, ruched and elasticated rain cover. As he scanned the car and its contents it felt like cross-examination by a prissy headmistress who had just stepped out of the shower.

'Brothers, officer?' quivered Joe. 'No, not brothers.'

He tipped his head to one side as if to get a better look. 'Yew boys ain't brertherrrs?'

'N-no officer, we're just good friends!' I stammered, trying and failing to make the situation look less weird than it already did.

'Well, yew shurre do fayvurre each utherr.'

Now we were confused. Favour each other? Was he speculating as to our sexual orientation? Terribly forward don't you think, officer? Whatever he meant, we were so terrified by now that we would happily have revealed every tiny detail of our personal lives just to make him like us.

Joe bit his lip. 'Favour each other?'

'Shurre. Yew lerk jerst laaake each utherr.' Favouring someone in Oklahoma evidently means resembling them, which came as something of a relief all round. 'Say,' he went on, 'whirr yew boys frerm?' The words 'where are you' elided gloriously into a single, elongated diphthong – whirreeoo – the same collision of vowels that for years had me thinking George Bush was asking us to join him in the fight against tourism.

'London, England, officer!' we chorused.

'Lerndon, Eeenglund, huh? Aaah shurre laaake yurre akseeunts.'

'Thank you, officer! Yours is jolly nice, too!' squeaked Joe.

'Kinda stormy to be out in a convertible ve-hicle, doncha thank? Whirreeoo headed?'

'We're trying to get to Little Rock. But we might just find a motel at the next exit and get out of the rain.'

'Good thankin'. Yew boys draave sayfely now.'

Documents verified, we edged back onto the highway and carried on our way.

Forced by the rain to overnight sooner than our scheduled Little Rock stopover, we sought and found comfort at a Comfort Inn in Morrilton, feasting on a TV dinner of Subway, Michelob, Letterman, Leno and O'Brien. Fat on chat and a foot-long Spicy Italian Melt, I blogged while Joe watched baseball on TV.

I started typing. Then deleting. Then typing again. And deleting again. Reflecting on the last few days' events, I realised that, brushes with the law excepted, I didn't have an awful lot to say. There was huffing.

Joe was transfixed by the baseball. 'Doesn't sound like it's flowing for you tonight.'

'It's not. What have we actually *done* in the last few days?'

'Loads. We've done... loads.'

He was right. We'd had some exceptional, extraordinary and exhilarating experiences; I had lived out the lyrics of 'Wichita Lineman' on the Wichita County line; Joe had virtually walked between the lines of his favourite western movie script in Silverton. But none of this came close to the experience of Joshua Tree; meeting Polly and Shilah, Cap Rock, room eight, Pappy and Harriets. Yes, the trip was about tying music to places. But so far it was the people, not the places, who had made it. We needed more people.

I'd had an idea during the planning stages that we might use the website not just as a way of meeting people but of keeping costs down too – by staying in their houses. How cool would it be, we thought, to cross a continent relying entirely on the kindness of strangers? Coast to coast, couch to couch. Cool idea perhaps, horrible reality. But it was an idea which, long since abandoned, had helped us make a number of cyberfriends, many of whom were now following our progress and providing welcome commentary to our blogs. I reached out to them:

```
Date: 26 Oct, 11.21 p.m.

Folks,

Thanks for your comments! We wanted to let
you know the itinerary for the next few days.
We're loving that people are tracking our
progress and suggesting we hook up. But as
the blogs are usually about 24 or 48 hours
behind by the time we post them, we're missing
each other.

So - today is Thursday 26 October.

Friday 27 - Little Rock to Memphis
Saturday 28 - Memphis/Clarksdale
Sunday 29 - Memphis/Clarksdale to Nashville
Monday 30 - Nashville
Tuesday 31 - Nashville
Wednesday 1 - Waycross via Atlanta? Charleston?
Thursday 2 - Arrive Waycross
Friday 3 - Waycross
```

Gets a bit sketchy after that, but the plan is
to be in Winter Haven, Florida on 5 November.
Do get in touch if your plans coincide with
ours at all. We've met some great people and
want to meet more.

Chris & Joe

I closed the laptop and flopped against the headboard. With batting averages and pitching stats swirling in my head I started to drop off. Tomorrow was a big day. We would make our way to Memphis on the trail of two men. One was the most famous dead person in the world. The other released one album, went paddling in a Memphis river and was never seen alive again.

27 OCTOBER

EFFING AND JEFFING

No prizes for guessing the most famous dead resident of Memphis. And whilst we would obviously do some Elvis business in town, Memphis was on the itinerary for a quite different reason. It was where another of our musical heroes died – or if not exactly where he died then certainly where he last drew breath on solid ground. This one, unlike all the others so far, had been equally central to both our lives and was, importantly, dead. At a slightly older age than the fashionable rock star innings of twenty-seven, he took a swim in Wolf River at the age of thirty-one and was spotted three days later by a tourist on a riverboat.

But before we get into that, I'd like to get something off my chest. For most of my adult life I've had to deal with an embarrassing problem. It's a condition which is difficult to bring up even among close friends, let alone in the pages of a book, so this isn't at all easy. It never used to be a serious problem – God knows after twenty years I've learned to cope with the staring and the tutting from passers-by – but today the symptoms got much, much worse. I know I'll feel much better if I just get it out in the open.

I'm a slow driver. Always have been. Being overtaken is as much a part of the driving experience for me as changing gear. Milk floats, street cleaning vans, children on bikes, wheelchair users – they've all whizzed past me at some point with my 'every day's a Sunday' approach to getting from A to B. I've grown accustomed to it. But I have never, so far as I can recall, been overtaken by a house. Or, for that matter, a shed.

American roads are bigger than British drivers are used to, and so, it follows, are the vehicles that travel on these continent-spanning highways. Having become used to the trucks, the monster trucks, the articulated lorries, the reticulated lorries, the ship-sized RVs towing Range Rovers and the trucks towing trucks carrying four other trucks, it was going to take something pretty remarkable to jolt us from our cruise-controlled calm. A two-bedroomed house passing in the inside lane did the trick. A huge wooden bungalow, split down the middle with its two halves placed side-by-side on a massive yellow flatbed truck, rumbled past announced by flashing yellow lights. In its wake blew a shower of chipboard which tumbled onto the road and then bounced over the windscreen of the Grievous Angel. The house was followed a minute later by a shed, complete with rakes and lawnmower jangling away inside. It seems the phrase 'moving house' isn't as simple a concept as I once thought. (Boom, and if you will, boom.)

Last in this curious line of passing traffic was part of the lorry itself. With a barely detectable shudder from the house on top, one of its wheels flew off and raced down the outside lane. It had been going for well over a minute by the time we finally overtook it, and was still doing around fifty when we turned off the interstate. As you read this it should just about be reaching the Appalachians. Be sure to give it a wave if you see it pass.

There, did it. And I do feel better.

While we're in the mood for confessions, I'd like to put something out there too. (You don't mind, do you?) Mine involves a petty crime I committed in my early twenties. I've been haunted by it ever since.

As a student in the early nineties I supplemented grants and loans working as a returns clerk at a distribution plant for Sony Music. Based in glamorous Aylesbury near where I grew up, every day this enormous warehouse packed and shipped thousands of Celine Dion and Bruce Springsteen CDs to music retailers nationwide for purchase by the record-buying public (younger readers please ask mum or dad). Some of the CDs – either because they were faulty, sale or return, or by Kula Shaker – would be sent back to Aylesbury and either scrapped or returned to stock. My job was to process these returns and decide what should be salvaged and what should be recycled. As holiday jobs went – especially for a music fanatic in need of money – it was something of a boon.

The most exciting part was processing returns from the Sony sales force. Firstly, their stock was almost always 'new release', which meant being able to rifle through all the coolest new tunes available. Secondly, large portions of them carried the coveted 'Promo Use Only' sticker, meaning that even if the product was pristine in every other respect, it had to be scrapped. Those were the rules.

My, how it pained me to throw those CDs away. Hundreds of perfectly good albums by perfectly good bands headed for the scrapheap every day. It just didn't seem right. Stealing them wasn't an option of course. Aside from the fact that Sony security was tighter than a papal visit to Fort Knox, stories abounded of extraordinary rendition and water boarding for anyone caught taking so much as a stapler. So my very good school friend Thomas and I had played it safe and negotiated a weekly allowance with the manager, a quiet and thoughtful man by the name of Andy, who agreed we could each take home a handful of promo CDs at the end of the week if we worked very hard and tried our best to stop crashing the pallet trucks into the walls. Well, from that point onwards finding a promo-stickered album was like pulling an iPod out of the lucky dip at a village fête.

Imagine my joy then, when one day in September 1994 I opened one of the sales reps' submissions, pulled out a stack of Kula Shaker singles and glinting up at me from the bottom of the box was an *entire roll* of promo stickers. It was almost too much excitement to bear. Glancing furtively in both directions, I slipped it into my pocket and carried on with my work. I had found a goose that laid golden eggs.

Over the next month, I'm sorry to say that I milked that goose – if you'll pardon me while I play fast and loose with avian anatomy – for everything I could. One day, in a fit of daring uncharacteristic of a boy who had never had so much as a detention, I stickered the entire Byrds back catalogue and convinced Andy it was new release promo product destined for the scrapheap. (It was actually sale or return destined for HMV Bracknell.) High-octane thrills. But soon my conscience, the beginning of the autumn term, and fear of deportation to a country with a slipshod human rights record got the better of me. By then maybe twenty albums had been liberated. Hardly *The Italian Job*, but enough to make me feel very naughty and ever so slightly ashamed.

One of them – a debut album by a then unknown singer I had read about in the *NME* – was staring up at me from the CD wallet as I thumbed through it, Memphis-bound, on I40 east. In the time since its release by (and from) Sony in 1994, it had broken my heart, fixed it and then broken it again so many times it was hard to remember a journey, relationship or break-up soundtracked by anything else. Paris '95, summer '98, break up twenty-four, Jeff Buckley's *Grace* was a record which more than any other had scored my twenties, and I still hadn't tired of it. *Grace* is a 'break glass in case of emergency' album which goes with me almost everywhere, reassuring like the Lambert & Butler tucked behind the ear of the 40-a-day brickie; you just never know when the craving will strike.

When Manic Street Preachers first appeared in Britain's music press they were acclaimed for their music, their self belief and their manifesto of releasing one great album and then quitting. A very short, very sharp shock.

Of course there are thousands of artists who have released only one LP, but I daresay Hear'Say's first essays won't be troubling the greatest albums lists any time soon. (Equally, there are many who have made one great album and then stuffed it up by releasing a string of duffers off the back of it. The 'difficult second album' is such an oft-lamented jinx that some rookie bands even try to bottle the energy of their first sessions by recording two at once. Few succeed.) The list of great one-album artists is short. Really short. Probably only Scotty Moorhead can truly claim to have done it.

Or could claim to have done it had he (a) not died, and (b) recorded under that name. But tragically he did die, and he didn't find fame as Scott Moorhead. In the mid-seventies he changed his first name, took the surname of his biological father Tim (a folk musician who died of a heroin overdose at the fabulously unhip age of twenty-eight), and some years later seeped into the Los Angeles music scene as guitarist-for-hire Jeff Buckley. So to the distinction of being one of few artists ever to make a solitary, debut album of quality we can also add the curious footnote that Buckley is one of even fewer artists in the modern era to have remained genuinely undiscovered for the better part of a decade before gaining the recognition he briefly enjoyed.

Grace is a staggering record. It might just be the most perfect record I've ever heard. (Nick Cave's *The Boatman's Call* comes close, but then he uses the C-word in the final song and, well, you can't have a perfect album with the C-word on it, can you?) The musicianship, production, sequencing and artwork are all impeccable, but really that's so much muso flim-flam. What it comes down to is two things – the songs and the singer, and in those respects *Grace* is absolutely bulletproof. It rocks like The Deftones, and tinkles like Sigur Ros. It grooves like Queens of the Stone Age, soothes like Kate Bush.

165

And all the time it has its shapely American hand grasped firmly around your heart. Testimony to the perfectness of the record is that the greatest cover version of all time, 'Hallelujah', manages to be the centrepiece of the album without overshadowing it. (Some people will try to tell you that 'Hallelujah' isn't the greatest cover of all time. They are the same people who bought Hear'Say's debut album.) And any artist with the courage – and the voice – to pull off Benjamin Britten's 'Corpus Christi Carol' on their first record deserves every ounce and more of the critical acclaim that Jeff received for *Grace*.

After three years of touring and slowly swelling record sales, Buckley wrote songs for a second album, provisionally entitled *My Sweetheart the Drunk*. On 29 May 1997 his band flew to Memphis to start recording them with him. That evening Jeff and his friends headed to Wolf River for a drink and a swim. He stepped into the river singing Led Zeppelin's 'Whole Lotta Love' and never came back.

Wolf River was not what I had imagined when I heard that Buckley had been drinking and listening to music with friends by the banks of a Tennessee river. The vision was of moss-covered trees dipping languid limbs into a lazy, muddy swell as cicadas chirruped and birds roosted. In fact, Wolf River was apparently nothing more than the edge of Memphis which proved too wet to build on. Overshadowed by brutalist transport bridges and what looked like grain silos, it was unexceptional in almost every way – about as romantic as the name of the peninsula it skirts before being swallowed by the Mississippi: Mud Island.

A footpath ran along the river's edge about ten metres from the water. We stepped off it, clambered through thick undergrowth and over some empty whisky bottles presumably left by previous Buckley pilgrims, and made our way down to the water. First things first: a text to a mutual friend and Buckley fanatic in London to say we were on the banks of Wolf River and thinking of him. Eden Blackman might very well be the biggest Jeff Buckley fan in the world. He owns a watch made out of Jeff's leather jacket. There are thirteen in existence, and it cost more than I spend in a year on food. He was once offered five times what he paid for it by the singer in a band (I won't say who, but you've heard of them), and turned him down.

Instantly a response beeped back: 'If you can find a flower, throw it in. And don't go for a swim.'

Finding a flower in the damp, dark thicket along Wolf River wasn't easy, but after a long search I plucked a single solitary daisy from the mud and placed it into one of the discarded bottles. A few words to Eden on camera, then we tossed it in.

Joe sighed. 'This is weird.'

'It's grim, isn't it. Why would you come here to just... hang out?'

'And why would you go for a swim in *that?*'

'It's like taking a dip in the Mersey.'

Joe went silent for a few seconds. 'Makes me think he did it on purpose.'

'Don't let the Buckley estate hear you say that. His mum is adamant it wasn't suicide.'

'Well I'm not so sure.'

'Can't say I am either. You know he was wearing heavy boots at the time?'

'Really? How ironic,' said Joe.

'What do you mean?'

'They should have taken him to Boot Hill.'

'You've lost me.'

'I'll explain later. Let's get a drink.'

Jeff Buckley was a beautiful man with an angelic voice who died in a grubby waterway ill-matched to his sensitivity and dazzling talents. Pondering this thoroughly depressing thought in this thoroughly depressing place made us, well, thoroughly depressed. We were hungry, thirsty and wanted to take our minds off Jeff. So we went to Hooters. It seemed like the appropriate thing to do, being as he was such a notorious tit man.

28 OCTOBER

THE SHAWSHANK INTENTION

We drove south out of downtown Memphis to Graceland – located, appropriately, on a street named after its most famous resident: Elvis Presley Boulevard. Nothing unusual about that, you might think. Naturally the people of Memphis would want to commemorate the city's most celebrated and beloved citizen by naming a street after him. And what better than the one he had lived on? A perfectly normal thing to do when a figure as loved and revered as Elvis pops off.

But get this: it was given the name Elvis Presley Boulevard while he was still alive. This we learned – and it was news to me if it wasn't to everybody else there that day – because displayed among the exhibits of the Graceland Automobiles Museum were copies of receipts for his huge collection of cars. Name: Elvis Presley. Address: 3734 Elvis Presley Boulevard, Memphis, Tennessee.

That may not seem surprising to you, but it is to me. For one thing I'm pretty sure it wouldn't happen in Britain. We would want to know someone is one hundred per cent, categorically and certifiably dead – and therefore at no risk of going off the rails – before we named a street after them. To my knowledge, and I'll say now that I'm no authority, the only time this has ever happened was shortly after the Sarajevo Winter Olympics, when the roads of a newly-built housing estate just outside Reading were all given names relating to Great Britain's ice-dancing sweethearts Jane Torvill and Christopher Dean to commemorate their dazzling victory in the finals of the figure skating championship. Witness Bolero Close, Torvill Way, Dean Dene and so on – I've made those up, but you get the idea.

All very well, but how do we know, for instance, that they aren't going to spend the twilight of their days on a Bonnie and Clyde-style killing spree? Before you know it you've got a cluster of semis celebrating a pair of figure-skating serial killers. Best to play it safe and wait until they've popped off.

The second – and I'll admit much less far-fetched – eventuality to bear in mind when naming a street after a famous but as yet not dead resident, is that it makes life very easy for stalkers. Or does an awful lot of the leg work for them. Quite apart from taking all the fun out of it by robbing your prospective stalker of the need for proper research, privacy is an obvious issue. Then again, if you've bought a large house less than fifty yards from one of the busiest highways in Memphis and erected a set of showy gates outside it, privacy probably isn't your primary concern.

All right, I'm being a teeny bit obtuse. But it did make an impression on us. It brought home just how world-changingly, cosmos-transformingly *massive* Elvis was at the height of his career. Graceland is America's Buckingham Palace, and privacy – the 'you-don't-know-where-I-live' kind at least – is not something that rock and roll royalty expects. Having a street named after you is the preserve of the great and the good, but generally they're great, good and dead. In order to actually live on a street named after you, you have to command the kind of recognition usually reserved for actual kings and queens. (Or, if you're Jane Torvill or Christopher Dean, relocate to Reading.)

Graceland was everything I'd hoped and feared it would be. The house was gloriously tacky, large but no bigger than many detached homes in affluent suburbs all over America, and the gardens were lush and inviting.

But it was Elvis's grave we were most excited about seeing. Sure, we wanted to pay our respects to the King, but more than anything we hoped to fulfil a long-held ambition to re-enact a scene from *This is Spinal Tap*. That is, stand next to the grave, a finger in one ear, and sing some barbershop raga for the King. Joe, with his now impressive cockduster, effected a terrifyingly accurate Derek Smalls whilst I attempted a tuneless 'Heartbreak Hotel' in the style of Nigel Tufnell. Too much fucking perspective.

We jumped on a shuttle which delivered us to the second Graceland site across the road from the main house. There we were invited to show the King just how much we loved him by unburdening ourselves of our pennies in the countless gift shops. And what a bounteous panorama of opportunities so to do. Elvis sunglasses, Elvis walking canes, Elvis drinks coolers, Elvis underpants and 'Love Me Tender' boxer shorts. Elvis licence plates, Elvis radios, Elvis talking clocks ('Uh-huh, it's two-thirty'), Elvis portraits bearing no resemblance whatsoever to Elvis, the list went on. Two exhibitions, Elvis After Dark and Sincerely Elvis, apparently existed for the sole purpose of providing something to attach a gift shop to; a refreshingly short but staggeringly uninformative traipse through Elvis's interest in, say, cigarette cards would spit you out into another bewildering array of King-related retail opportunities. In the case of Sincerely Elvis, the shop was three or four times the size of the exhibition itself.

Not only that, each attraction came with its own restaurant. To our utter astonishment, the one adjoined to Elvis After Dark featured on its menu a Fried Peanut Butter and Banana Sandwich, as if to say 'Here's what finally did him in, why not try it for yourself?'

Joe looked up from his menu. 'Well, shall we?'

'No. No way. I hate peanut butter. I'll puke.'

His bottom lip folded up in disappointment, then broke into a coquettish smile. 'It's what Elvis would have wanted.'

'You go ahead if you want to. I'd rather chew tin foil than eat peanut butter.'

'But we're in this together. Aren't we?' The bottom lip again.

'Not when there's peanut butter on the menu. You're on your own now.'

Joe folded his arms and sulked like a seven-year-old deprived of dessert. 'You mean I've come halfway across

America to celebrate the birthday of a man whose music makes my ears hurt, and you can't manage one measly sandwich?'

Oh God. I was going to eat a fried peanut butter and banana sandwich. 'OK, but don't say I never do anything for you. I'm doing this for you.'

'You're doing it for Elvis.'

A waitress took our order – 'Oh, I just lerve a peanut butter and banana sandwich!' – and left us to our Dr Peppers. Minutes later she returned carrying two faux-wicker baskets containing gingham greaseproof paper, 725 calories and 39 g of fat.

I stared at it. 'There's grease dripping through the holes.'

'You'll be fine,' said Joe, taking a bite. I watched as he chewed, rested, then chewed again, then swallowed. Mopping grease from his moustache, he announced: 'Not bad. But I think you should do it in small bites.'

'Good thinking.' I held it up and inspected one corner. Just the smell made me gag. I winced and put it down again.

'Stop being so melodramatic. The King would be disappointed.'

'OK, OK, I'm doing it.' I took a bite.

'See? Not so bad.'

Not so bad. It was the most foul-tasting, stomach-turning, complexion-despoiling, cholesterol-boosting abomination I have ever forced through my reluctant cakehole. It took whole minutes to finish that first mouthful, and several small eons to finish the whole thing. But I did it. I did it for the King. And of all our efforts to get closer to our heroes, this one unquestionably made the most lasting impression.

Not only was the peanut butter appended immovably to the roof of my mouth several hours later, I was still digesting it three days afterwards. I can still smell it even now.

On the way out I overheard a husband and wife heading for the Presley planes collection:

'And that plane over there is called the Lisa Marie,' said husband. 'Ain't that neat?'

'Why, so it is,' said wife. 'Now why *did* she marry that Michael Jackson fella?'

'I really don't know. He ain't exactly marryin' material if you ask me.'

I wanted to tell them I knew exactly why she married Jacko. She was tired of being asked 'What was your daddy like?' whenever she met people. What better way to put paid to it than marrying the world's most famous oddball? Bingo – no longer is Daddy the first thing you're asked about, he's the second. Right behind 'So what's it like being married to Michael Jackson?'

Back to the car and on the road again. My turn to drive. While we're in the heart of America, with eight days and a thousand miles left to go, this seems like a good time to make a quick check on those to-do lists:

Chris:

1. Grow a formidable moustache: Lord knows he's trying.

Me:

1. Learn to love the music of Gram Parsons: Lord knows I'm trying.
2. Learn to play the ukulele: note to self – buy a ukulele.

3. Learn to play the music of Gram Parsons on the ukelele: ummm...

It wasn't supposed to be this hard. By now we should have bought a uke and I would have 'Happy Birthday' down pat. But we hadn't and I didn't.

'I've got eight days to learn an instrument. There's no way I'm going to do it.'

'You have to. One song. That's the rule.'

'Can't I pick something easier than a uke?'

'What is there that's easier than a uke?'

'They sell buckets and sticks in Walmart.'

'You'll be fine. A ukulele only has four strings. I'll teach you three chords and in three days, bingo! You're a ukuleleist. Ukulist. Uke player.'

'Can't we just drop the uke bit and play to our strengths? You do the music and I'll do the facial hair.' It felt pretty feeble confessing out loud that all I could bring to the party was the natural profusion of hair on my chin, but I was desperate.

'You sound desperate.'

'I am.'

'How desperate?'

'Sorry?'

'How desperate are you to learn the uke?'

'Pretty desperate. I've made a career out of listening to music, but I've never been able to play a note. I really want to learn, but if my efforts to date are anything to go by, I really don't think I will. Which is bloody disappointing because I'd do pretty much anything to learn an instrument.'

'Anything? You'd do anything?'

'Well, not "nosh-off-a-tramp" anything, obviously, but within reason, yes.'

An ophidian leer crept across his face. 'In that case, I've got an idea.'

Oh God. 'Do tell.'

'I think we should go to Clarksdale and sell your soul to the devil in exchange for the gift of music.'

'Sorry?'

'It worked for Robert Johnson. Why wouldn't it work for you?'

'Sounds reasonable. Which way?'

'South.'

We pointed the Grievous Angel due south towards Clarksdale – ground zero for the blues and the town with, at its centre, a rather notorious crossroads.

Clarksdale, birthplace of the blues. It was at the intersection of Highways 49 and 61 – the crossroads – that Robert Johnson supposedly sold his soul to the devil. This legend, of a pact with Beelzebub on the promise of diabolical favours, had fascinated me in all its various forms for years. It had first come to my attention, as is so often the case with cultural motifs from religious folklore, via the work of teen idol and star of *The Karate Kid*, Ralph Macchio.

Crossroads the film came out in 1986, and made quite an impression on this thirteen-year-old boy. In addition to a pubescent obsession with wanting to actually be the Karate Kid myself, a new fixation was taking over – the guitar. Specifically, getting good at it as quickly as possible and with minimum effort.

Imagine my delight then, upon learning that Macchio had made a film about precisely that. With Steve Vai in it. All I needed to do was sell my soul, sit back, and wait. Virtuoso guitar skills, money and fame would be mine, very possibly even girls into the Faustian bargain. I watched *Crossroads* somewhere in the region of seven hundred times.

Years later I learned that Jimmy Page had done the same (sold his soul that is, not watched *Crossroads* seven hundred times, though by all accounts he's a fan of Macchio's more recent TV work). So *that's* why Led Zeppelin were so good. They cheated. I wanted the adoration heaped upon my idol, but was too idle to put in the hours. Just one thing stood between me and it: I was crap at playing the guitar. There was nothing for it but to sell my soul to the devil.

So the chance of standing on the very same crossroads where Robert Johnson had signed the contract which made him the greatest, most imitated, most influential bluesman – fuck it, most influential *musician* – on earth, was not one we were about pass up. Joe needed to learn the ukulele, and fast. We were a week away from our final stop in Winter Haven, Florida, where a performance of 'Return of the Grievous Angel' on guitar and uke would mark the end of the trip. Time was running out.

The journey to Clarksdale took us through flat, featureless fields of nothingness past countless hoardings advertising, in the way American roadside signs so often do, tantalising attractions several hundred miles up ahead. Just 214 miles to Diamond Jack's casino, only 168 to The Bodyshop strip joint ('with truck parking!') and, according to a ten-foot-tall oriental lady licking her luscious lips at us all the way along I69, a mere 106 miles to Jade Spa massage parlour, also with truck parking (all that trucking must play havoc with your back).

This was the the Missisippi Delta, a flood plain between the Mississippi and Yazoo rivers whose regular submergence under the swollen waterways along its perimeter have created some of the most fertile cotton fields in the world. Cotton is a very, very thirsty crop, which is why when grown in less suitable environments it can ruin an ecosystem quicker than a Republican government. But it found an ideal home in the Mississippi Delta, as did tobacco and sugar, all simple to grow and easy to harvest provided you had enough time, energy and... what's that other thing? Oh yes, slaves.

Which is why the Mississippi Delta is a predominantly black area, and why even at the turn of the twentieth century, two generations after the abolition of slavery, two thirds of the independent farmers were black. Out of this blossomed an independent culture quite unlike any other, and along with it came a musical mix of work songs, spirituals and chants known as the blues.

Every October since 1995 a debate has rumbled to the surface of the British music media. The reason for this petty annual squabble is the MOBOs, an awards ceremony devoted to the celebration of black music in the UK. MOBO stands for 'music of black origin', and therein lies the argument: what exactly is 'music of black origin'?

'Music with roots in black culture' is the common response, which seems a perfectly laudable stab at a definition. Hip hop, for example, undoubtedly emerged from black New York in the mid-seventies, and soul can trace its lineage back to the torch singing of Billie Holliday and her peers. The same can be said of the Best Jazz, Best Reggae and Best Gospel categories of the MOBOs. But why – and this is what gets folk so hot under the collar – don't the MOBOs ever give awards for techno, or funk, or blues?

No awards ceremony can cater for all possible music genres (though Lord knows the Grammys tries) but this rather arbitrary drawing of lines has always enraged several journalists who subscribe to the belief that all music, all modern music anyway, is of black origin. The backdrop to this is Clarksdale, at the heart of the Mississippi Delta. Because it's here that modern music first drew breath, and the person who drew that breath – Robert Johnson – was black.

Today, Clarksdale looked like many other small American towns, with one significant difference. To the casual passer-by, it appeared to be closed. Every store, gas station, bank, restaurant and 'emporium' in downtown Clarksdale had apparently shut down long ago; behind every dusty window sat clusters of ageing products on sagging shelves. Even the pawn shops had gone out of business. It was like driving around the set of a twenties gangster movie during a writers' strike.

'God this is grim,' said Chris.

'It sure is.'

'The only places that are open are churches.'

First United Methodist Church passed to our right. Then a Baptist church. Then an Episcopal prayer house followed by another Methodist church. Apparently Clarksdale is a very God-fearing place.

Chris shook his head. 'Do you know what, I think I'd believe in God if I lived here.'

Silence. More churches.

We drove around, got prodigiously lost, then drove around some more before finally rolling, by means of a deserted drive-thru bank, into one of the many empty parking spaces in front of a red-brick rail shed, home of the Delta Blues Museum. Founded in 1979, it proudly claims to be the 'the state's oldest music museum', narrowly edging out the Hattiesburg Institute of Hard House by a matter of weeks.

The Delta Blues Museum is a noble attempt to do justice to a very slippery subject matter. Blues came from this very town, and blues changed popular music forever. Think of your favourite band. Now think of your favourite band's favourite bands – the artists who influenced them. Keep going and you'll likely pass through the Beatles, maybe Elvis at some point. Keep going. Eventually you'll get to Robert Johnson. Before that, either it wasn't 'popular' or it was chamber music.

But like any museum of music or hall of fame, when you try to cram a century of abstractions into a single room you're left with all the paraphernalia of music-making but none of the soul of the songs themselves. And that's what we were here for. A few guitars, a harmonica or two, some articles of clothing and several pieces of wood that were once a wall in Muddy Waters' house filled the cases and lined the walls, but in truth there wasn't much to engage the casual blues investigator.

A sign in the section devoted to Robert Johnson read: 'Johnson is said to have sold his soul to the devil at the crossroads in the centre of Clarksdale in exchange for the gift of music, although this is largely based on romantic speculation.' It also rather presumes the existence of God, the devil and indeed the soul in a saleable form. But Clarksdale, Mississippi is not a place where questioning such things is considered acceptable behaviour.

Our interest piqued but not sated, we strolled out, uncertain of how to fill time until the meeting with Ol' Horny. Across the gravel from the museum was a whitewashed weatherboard hall with twisted Venetian blinds in the windows and two broken-down sofas on the stoop. It looked like a bar, and it smelled like a bar, the perfect place to kill time while we waited for the devil. We were musical tourists in Clarksdale and we wanted a beer – preferably in a venue owned by Clarksdale's most famous denizen Morgan Freeman – and Ground Zero fitted the bill.

Up the steps, through the door and into a music venue slash pool hall slash bar where scarlet neon signs shouted the drinks and the music that made America. Long tables ran the length of the room between the stage at one end and a cluster of red baize pool tables at the other. We ordered a couple of Brooklyn lagers, ambled over to one of the pool tables and hesitantly put down a couple of dollar bills. We had only just spun the eight ball into the rack when an elderly gent in a battered trilby slipped smoothly from his bar stool and sidled over.

He winked at Chris. 'Care for a game son?'

He was so authentically old delta that Chris and I exchanged glances which said 'Is he part of the tourist entertainment?'

'Sure. But I'm not very good,' confessed Chris. As an assessment of his pool-playing abilities this is a little like Amy Winehouse describing crack as 'a little moreish'.

Our friend rolled the cue ball under his palm and placed it into the 'D'. 'Care to make it interesting?' he gummed, through ill-fitting dentures, and reached into his inside pocket. Chris raised an eyebrow in anticipation of a slick and well-practised hustle.

The face of Abraham Lincoln was rolled out onto the table edge. 'Fi' dollars?'

'Sure,' said Chris, and put down one to match.

'Or maybe a little mo'?' twinkled our friend, reaching into his pocket once more.

Would it be another five dollar bill? Or a twenty? How much was Chris willing to bet, given that losing was a near certainty unless the man lost the use of his arms in the next four seconds? Even then it would be a close match.

Onto the table flopped a packet of Detrusitol tablets – 'for the treatment of incontinence'. Wow, he must really figure he's got us scared. 'That ain't right,' he said, scooping up the pills and switching them for a fifty dollar bill.

'I can't run to that,' said Chris, sucking his teeth. 'But I'll play you for five bucks.'

'Aw, it ain't even worth chalkin' ma cue,' said a crestfallen Fast Eddie, picking up his greenbacks and sliding back to the bar.

Several games and just as many Harland victories later, we headed for the exit. Fast Eddie called after us: 'Are you comin' back? Morgan's gonna be in tonight for the show.'

'Really?' squeaked Joe. 'Morgan Freeman's going to be here? Tonight? Well then we're probably definitely coming back.'

Morgan Freeman! Get in! We skipped back to the car.

'Could our luck get any better?' said Joe, pulling out of the car park. 'We go to Joshua Tree and bump into Polly Parsons, then we get an invite to Johnny Cash's house, and now we get to hang out with Morgan Freeman at his bar in Clarksdale, Mississippi!'

'It's almost too good to be true, isn't it?'

'And the timing is perfect. On the very night we sell my soul to the devil, we raise a beer with the star of *Seven*. Seven deadly sins – that's bound to help, surely?'

'How can it not?'

We found a generic motel on the outskirts of town and checked in. Joe caught up on the World Series while I blogged, then we showered and readied ourselves for a night out with Morgan. Arriving back at Ground Zero, we found it completely devoid of customers. It was barely 7 p.m.

'How about I spank you at pool again while we wait?' said Joe.

'Go on then. If we keep going long enough I might fluke a win.'

'Care to make it interesting?'

'Oh, fuck off.'

8 p.m. rolled around and a few more people drifted in. More spanking. No Morgan.

'Another spanking?'

'No thanks. The band will be on soon. Let's get a beer and a table.'

9 p.m. Starting to fill up. Still no Morgan.

10 p.m. The band came on. By now the place was jumpin' and jivin'. Still no Morgan.

11 p.m. The door swung open. It was Fast Eddie.

Joe bowled over. 'He's not coming, is he?'

'Who?'

'Morgan.'

'Sure he is. Told me so himself.'

'When?'

'This mornin'.'

'No, I mean when is he coming in?'

'How should I know? I ain't his keeper. Stick aroun' brother. He'll be here.'

Joe slunk back to the table. 'I don't think Morgan's coming.'

'Of course he isn't. Fast Eddie's probably on the payroll. A dollar for every tourist through the door.'

'I guess he has to pay for his incontinence tablets somehow.'

'Come on, let's go. We need to be at the crossroads before midnight.'

The crossroads. I knew exactly what it would look like. A remote and dusty intersection, sepia-toned and bordered by fields of cotton stretching to the horizon, not unlike the one at the end of *The Shawkshank Redemption* where Morgan Freeman jumps down from a pick-up in search of Andy's buried treasure. Not dissimilar, in fact, to the one in *Crossroads* where Johnson waits nervously in the moonlight for the devil to show, tumbleweed drifting across his toecaps and dust swirling at his heels. We pulled up.

Two enormous blue electric guitars, floodlit and mounted twenty-five feet in the air, criss-crossed the intersection of Highways 49 and 61. We had found the right place. As if to assuage any lingering doubts, a hoarding announced in foot-high lettering beneath them that yes, this was indeed 'The Crossroads'. A Church's Chicken fast food restaurant squinted under the white lights of a petrol station on one corner of the junction. On the other was the Crossroads Furniture Warehouse. It felt a little like reserving a table in a secluded bistro and turning up at the Hard Rock Cafe.

Ever so slightly tipsy on the beers we had put away at Ground Zero, we sat and staked out the crossroads like Taggart and Rosewood tailing Axel Foley tailing Victor Maitland. Joe perched the camera on the dashboard, pointing it through the windscreen at the guitars suspended above the road. They slowly moved into focus, then out again as the camera zoomed in on Church's Chicken behind. I waved my watch in front of the lens. Time: 11.48 p.m. Place: The Crossroads.

I readjusted the viewfinder to zoom in on the guitars again. 'We need to make sure we're ready for him if he turns up. And he needs to know we're here to do business when he does.'

'How are we going to do that?'

'Well, the first thing is knowing him when we see him. We don't know what kind of car he's going to be driving, or what he's going to be wearing. Actually scratch that, we do know what he'll be wearing...'

'He'll be wearing...?'

'Prada,' I burped, confidently. 'The devils wears Prada.'

'And presumably he'll have horns, a bifurcated tail and a fork. Unless cliché is one of the seven deadly sins.'

'Good point. And when he does come, he needs to know we're in the soul-selling game.'

'We could make a sign!' squeaked Joe.

'Like a "For Sale" sign, you mean? Good idea. Have you got a pen?'

'There's one in the glovebox.'

I took it out and began writing: 'For... sale... one... soul... What do we want for it?'

185

'Well, I want the gift of music. That's the deal, right?'

I carried on writing, pen lid clenched between molars like Jack Nicholson smoking a Havana. 'Gift... of... music... or... near... est... offer... apply... with... in.' I jumped out of the car and lodged it underneath the windscreen wiper, then hopped back in. 'What time is it?'

'Eleven forty-nine, we've got ten minutes. What are the seven deadly sins?'

'Why?'

'If we commit all seven, right here right now, he might turn up. What are they?'

'Er, wrath... gluttony...'

'Gluttony – that's a good one. Are you hungry? We could get some Church's Chicken.'

'No, but if we put some chicken away that's real gluttony isn't it. One down, six to go.'

'And wrath. You were pretty fucked off when you lost at pool tonight. You're the sorest loser I've ever met.'

'I am *not* a sore loser, Joe. You're a fucking smug winner. I've never seen anyone look so fucking pleased with themselves for potting a ball.'

'I potted six balls on the spin and you turned around and said they were flukes!'

'Well they were.'

'They were six fucking *great* pots.'

'There you go, *pride*. That's two right there.'

'Whatever. Do you want me to go and get some Church's Chicken so we can do gluttony?'

'Good idea.'

'What do you want, just a chicken burger or something?'

'Just... everything. Get me everything. But hurry up, we've only got nine minutes.'

'OK, OK, you stay here and work out what the other deadly sins are.'

Joe jumped out and ran across the intersection to Church's Chicken. I was alone in the car with my thoughts, a video camera and a head full of Heineken. I monologued to pass the time.

'Absolute. Fucking. Wanker. He didn't pot those balls deliberately. They were all flukes. All of them. OK, maybe one of them was quite a good shot. But he did this other one where two balls went in at once and he tried to make out like he did it on purpose. Nobody does that on purpose. So... *pride* – right there. Wrath we've done, gluttony he's doing. Er... lust, is it? Lust is definitely one. Envy? Yeah, envy. He'll probably try and tell you I'm envious because he won the game. Or I'm envious of his ability to play pool. Well *I'll* tell *you* that he cheated. Cheating is one of the seven deadly sins. Or if it isn't it should be.'

Joe was heading back to the car with armfuls of fried chicken.

'Here he comes look, skipping across the forecourt like he's the kind of person who regularly pots two balls at once in a game of pool.'

He opened the car door and got in.

'Hi mate!' I yelped, a little too enthusiastically. 'I think I've got six out of seven.'

He handed me a box of wings. 'Great. What's avarice?'

'That's the same as gluttony isn't it?' I panted, sucking air in over a mouthful of hot chicken. 'We've done that.'

'Have you seen him yet?'

'It's only eleven fifty-five. And we need one last sin. What's the last one?'

'Shoplifting?'

'Hmmm, not sure. It's probably lying or something rubbish like that. Eleven fifty-six. He'll be along in a minute.'

'What are we going to do if he does turn up?'

'Well, I'm all right because I'm already a shit-hot guitarist.'

'True.'

'You know Steve Vai in *Crossroads*? Like that, only faster. Do you want some more chicken?'

'Ta.'

'Leg or breast?'

'You have met my wife, haven't you?'

'I'll leave the breast for you then. Hey – breasts! That's lust. So now we've done lust, we've done gluttony, we've done pride – or rather *you* did pride in a fairly fucking major way earlier on.'

'No, *you* did pride. You were too proud to admit that I'd actually spanked you at pool.'

'No, *you* did pride by being a smug bastard trying to pretend... Anyway we've been over this.'

'You had seven balls left on the table, *and* the eight ball. You cued up, missed *every single one* of them, *and* pocketed the cue ball. And I wasn't supposed to smile?'

'Maybe being shit at pool is the other deadly sin.'

'Well if it is you've got it nailed. It's two minutes until he arrives.'

And so it went on. We bickered like schoolchildren for several more minutes, waiting for Lucifer to arrive.

188

But the devil didn't show. Perhaps he doesn't like Church's Chicken. Or maybe he was hanging out with Morgan Freeman. Our brush with the Man in Black would have to wait until we reached Nashville.

29 OCTOBER

FALL OUT BOYS

What's the rarest commodity in America?

Irony? Nope. Subtlety? Nope. Environmental awareness?

No, the rarest thing in all of America is stamps. I wrote a postcard to Nicola and Noah on day six of the trip. It was now day twelve, and I had yet to find a single postage stamp. Not in hotels, not in pharmacies, not in liquor stores, coffee shops or gas stations, and not – you're going to like this – in the Post Office. We had tried three separate US Post Offices in three separate towns, but every stamp machine was out of order and the counters always closed. In Dodge I had stood in an empty postal building listening to the chatter of staff filtering through the air ducts. I shouted 'Wankers' and left. Clarksdale was similarly and infuriatingly bereft of stamps. At this rate I would be handing my wife and child a stack of postcards when I got home.

A breakfast of waffles and coffee and we were back on the road. Today we planned to traverse northern Mississippi and cross back into Tennessee by means of the Natchez Trace Parkway – a scenic, two-lane stretch of road we would pick up at Tupelo, the site of Elvis' birth, his twin brother's death and the subject of a song by Nick Cave called, fittingly, 'Tupelo'.

We drove past fields of harvested cotton – bales the size of static caravans, each one sprayed with lettering such as N-F6 or E4-E5. Either this was some form of harvesting code, or perhaps the cotton farmers of northern Mississippi were a group of sophisticated intellectuals engaged in a massive game of distance chess. Two hours of cotton, cotton and more cotton, and we arrived in the pretty conurbation that Elvis called home before Vernon Presley took the family north to Memphis.

Chris was hoping that Elvis' birthplace would be a normal house in a normal street, the only vacant abode in a run of humble but lived-in Mississippi homes, but the apparently limitless possibilities for generating money from the Presley name meant that even this tiny, two-room weatherboard 'shotgun house' had been turned into something of a theme park. In addition to Mr Presley Sr's handiwork (he apparently built it himself) was a visitors' centre, gift shop, story wall, Early Years Driving Tour and even an Assembly of God church that Elvis attended as a child, fully restored so you can experience worship just like the boy King. Lastly, a 'walk of life' – forty-two granite slabs, each one marking a year of Elvis' life – was apparently still a work in progress, as only the first eleven had anything engraved into them. Either that or the custodians of Elvis' birthplace just felt it all went downhill once he hit his teens.

The visitors' centre was closed, unfortunate as we were both in need of a 'comfort break'. So after hobbling the walk of life, crippled by our groaning bladders, there was nothing for it but to answer the call of nature in the woods behind the house, where presumably the young Elvis foraged for sticks as a child. Aware that this sort of behaviour could get us lynched in these parts – no doubt there were life-size replicas of Young Elvis Foraging Sticks available in the gift shop – we were quickly back in the car and heading for the Natchez Trace Parkway.

America is stuffed full of roads, from dirt tracks to twelve-lane superhighways and every possible permutation in between. Most are ugly utilitarian strips of blacktop transporting users from A to C without even so much as glimpsing B out of the window. The Natchez Trace Parkway is not like most roads. Two beautiful lanes stretch from Natchez, Mississippi to Nashville, Tennessee. No lorries are allowed on it, and the speed limit is 55 mph. It is impossibly quiet, and so densely populated with trees that driving it is like walking a tightrope through a forest.

We followed it for 204 miles. Imagine driving from London to Manchester with Kew Gardens licking at your windscreen all the way there. This was better. We had seen a weather report the previous day with a 'Fall Watch' feature listing the best places to see the spectacular reds, yellows and browns of the season as it crept south. According to that, by accident we were stumbling right into the heart of it. With the roof down, we trundled our way gently north with the contrast on nature's television turned up to eleven. It was an almost perfect moment.

Almost. Something was simmering between Joe and me. And it was about to boil violently to the surface. They say that sometimes it's the smallest of things that friends fall out over. In our case it couldn't have been any smaller.

Chris was driving. I blogged:

'They call it "Stockholm syndrome". Kidnap victims are deprived of human contact for so long that they fall in love with their captors. Sophie Marceau suffered from it (along with a wretched script, a five-foot love interest and the worst Bond theme ever) in *The World is Not Enough*.

It can happen quickly too. Hitherto non-violent publishing heiress Patty Hearst was famously kidnapped by the Symbionese Liberation Army in February 1974, and was robbing the Hibernia Bank in San Francisco on their behalf by mid-April.

So I had rashly assumed that a musical version of Stockholm syndrome would have taken over, and by now I would be running up to strangers and forcing them to listen to country music at gunpoint. The truth is that after almost two weeks of indoctrination I am still of the opinion that only a gun to my temple will get me through Gram's canon.

The Red Hot Chili Pepper's early work for example is widely accepted not to be their best, but in my teens I loved the image so much I listened to nothing else until I started to like it. And it worked. I imagined this would be the case with Gram, too: a couple of weeks of nothing but the Byrds and Flying Burritos and – hey presto! – I would see what all the fuss was about. Sadly 'tis not the case.

This is a fairly guilty confession, as I know that Gram is the tie that binds this trip together, and saying that his music doesn't move me feels like swearing in church. The bald fact is I don't find songs about eighteen-wheel trucks engaging. And while I know it's only one song from his canon, it's symptomatic of the problem I have with country music generally. Today is Sunday. I've got until Tuesday to get it. From here on the in-car listening will need to be like aversion therapy. Not that I'd say I'm Gramophobic, but nothing's cut through yet. And the clock is ticking...'

Things between us had reached a pretty low ebb. The pool game argument in Clarksdale and crossroads replaying of it had been light-hearted on the surface, but a definite undercurrent of 'fuck you' was flickering on both sides. We were either bickering like children or not talking at all; hardly surprising given that by now we had spent nearly two weeks with nothing but each other for company virtually twenty-four hours a day. By day we occupied the same tiny space – the increasingly Grievous Angel, now starting to resemble a pressure cooker rattling perilously eastwards – and at night we shared a hotel room, occasionally even a bed. It was beginning to take its toll. With no outlet for our frustrations other than blogs – public domain, so hardly the forum for letting off private steam – we were bottling them up with what would turn out to be disastrous consequences.

What made things worse was that all bloggings were saved in a single, steadily growing Word document on a shared computer, which meant that we both had visibility on what the other was writing. It was standard practice by now that upon switching driving duties the new occupant of the passenger seat would glance over what his driver had just written before putting fingers – or, in my case, finger – to keyboard and continuing the narrative.

We stopped on the Alabama state line to switch over. Joe took the wheel while I settled into the passenger seat and began to read. Two things struck me about his latest blog.

'You've put the apostrophe in the wrong place after Chili Peppers. It should go after the "s", not before.'

'What difference does it make? To normal people of the non-perfectionist variety, I mean.'

'It makes a big difference, Joe. How many Chili Peppers are there?'

'I'm not playing along with your silly little games.'

'How many?'

'Four.'

'Exactly, four. If the apostrophe is before the "s" it makes it one Chili Pepper. Singular.'

'And your point is?'

'My point is it's important to get this stuff right.'

'No, the point is that nobody else in the world apart from you actually cares about "this stuff". They're more worried about real things like their job or their wife or whether they've fed the cat than whether an apostrophe is in the right place. Why do you have to be so pedantic all the time?'

'It's not being pedantic. It's just doing things properly. Luckily most people know there are four members of the Red Hot Chili Peppers. But if you were writing about "my sisters' children" say, and put the apostrophe in the wrong place, you could be writing at least one sister and several children out of existence in one fell apostrophe. It's life and death stuff.'

'Now you're just being stupid.'

'No I'm not. And if you really wanted to be taken seriously as a writer you would care about it.'

'Well I don't.'

'Well you should.'

'Well I don't.'

'Well you should.'

This was going nowhere. I returned to his blog. The second thing that bothered me – and I confess that the issue of an errant apostrophe was rather clouding my judgement by now – was the admission that he still wasn't getting the music. He was feeling guilty, he said, because of the pressure he felt to love something I held so dear, to come around to the 'tie that binds this trip together', and it wasn't happening. Which is a lovely, sweet, warm-hearted thing for him to feel. It makes me feel very guilty about what I did next.

The line I objected to was how he failed to see the attraction of 'songs about eighteen-wheel trucks', and how this was symptomatic of the problem he had with the music. 'Well if you think that's all it is,' I seethed silently in the passenger seat, 'then you're clearly not trying hard enough. You of all people are supposed to be open-minded about music – *all* music. It's your job. And what's Johnny Cash if he isn't country? After everything we've done together, the miles we've travelled, the times we've shared – Christ, this was *your* idea – and you're not even trying!'

So I opened a new document (this was my most serious crime, now we had *secrets*) and, quietly smouldering while Joe kept his eye on the road, started typing. Vitriol and sarcasm tumbled over the keyboard. I fumed about his unwillingness to make an effort, raged about his lazy dismissal of Gram's music as being for 'truckers and cowboys'. I didn't want him to post the blog – really I didn't – but if he did, I would be ready. I would immediately post a watertight defence and win the day. Closing the laptop, I felt better for my private little spleen-venting session.

The sun slouched out of view to the west and immediately the scenery changed, like a *Super Mario Kart* race track reset from 'country' to 'city'. We were spat out into unpretty Nashville, where we would meet Jack Fripp, the Cash Cabin guy that Shilah had put us in contact with. Chris had arranged a meeting place.

'Where shall we meet?'

'At the waffle house.'

'Great – what's it called?'

'The Waffle House?'

'Yeah, what's the name of it?'

'Just Waffle House.'

We rolled into the car park with five minutes to spare.

Peering through the grubby windows we saw brown booths and menus wilting forlornly on chipped Formica tables. The enormous waffle-shaped sign twenty foot above us told cars on all four highways around us that this was indeed 'Waffle House'.

As we waited for our man, something about the phrase 'Waffle House in Nashville' nagged at me. It wasn't a lyric or a movie quote or an old advert, but deep at the back of my memory, somewhere amidst a thousand stand-up routines learned whilst making in-flight comedy programmes in the nineties, those four words were reverberating.

'Does the phrase "Waffle House in Nashville" mean anything to you?' I asked Chris.

'Other than that it's where we're standing?'

'Yes.'

Chris looked confused. 'Well, no.'

And then it came to me. Of *course*.

At one time we had even considered going via his home town of Houston as he fitted the brief of the trip – being both rock and roll, massively influential and, importantly, dead.

But we hadn't. And yet it seemed that in a manner of speaking he had found us.

'Got it!' I barked.

'Go on then.'

'It's Bill.'

'Drummond?' said Chris.

'Nope.'

'Clinton?'

'Nope.'

'Er... Oddie?'

'Hicks.'

'Really?'

'Pretty sure, yeah. You know how he used to talk about reading a book in a restaurant and the waitress comes over and says "What you reading for?"?'

Almost as though he we were holding it in his hand, Chris continued the script: '... and the trucker in the next booth comes over and says "Lookee here – looks like we got ourselves a *reader*."'

'Exactly. That was in a Waffle House in Nashville.'

'This one?'

'Maybe not. But then again, maybe.'

The only person who could confirm whether or not this was the exact Waffle House died of pancreatic cancer in 1994. We stood on the cooling tarmac drinking in exhaust-flavoured air, smiles creasing our faces and toying with the satisfying thought that maybe, just maybe, we were standing right in the middle of a routine by the greatest stand-up comic of all time – Bill Hicks. Bill, and I use the world advisedly, fucking Hicks.

Our Nashville contact, Jack Fripp, worked with the man now at the helm of the studio since the demise of the Man in Black, Johnny's son John Carter Cash. A telephone conversation with Jack the day before had begun with a check of my credentials. Evidently there were people trying to get hold of him that he was in no hurry to speak to – debt collectors, attorneys, nothing serious I'm sure – and he wanted to be sure I wasn't one of them. This and the fact he possessed a voice not unlike the growl of a grizzly on a Harley Davidson created an image in my mind of a giant, rugged bear of a man. The kind of guy you don't fuck with.

So when a Harley roared into the car park of our Waffle House meeting point and deposited a bearded Hell's Angel, leather-clad and sporting bear tattoos across biceps bigger than both my legs combined, he wasn't difficult to spot. He pushed the door open, stepped inside and paused to scan the restaurant.

'Hey, Jack,' piped a waitress. 'What can I get ya?'

'Hey, Tiffany. Get me a bacon double patty melt, a side of grits and a coffee, black and strong.' He winked. 'You sure look purty today. You seen two English guys come through here?'

Tiffany flicked her thickly mascaraed eyelashes in our direction. Bear man padded over.

'Which one of you is Chris?'

'Er, hello Jack,' I simpered, standing up. 'That's me. How do you do?'

My hand felt puny as it shook – and disappeared into – his wrecking ball of a fist. Noting a thicket of goatee dangling several inches below his Desperate Dan jaw, I felt suddenly and excruciatingly aware of the feeble excuse for a horseshoe moustache perched sheepishly on my upper lip. 'This is Joe.'

He smiled broadly. 'Great to meet you. Shilah told me all about you guys. I've been lookin' forward to showin' you around. Tiffany – get these gentlemen somethin' to eat, would you darlin'?'

I felt a sudden, inexplicable warmth towards the man, a mixture of relief and gratitude for not being the big nasty monster I supposed him to be. It was a feeling I last experienced at the age of eight when feared school bully Duncan Farnley spared me a punching because he fancied my sister.

As he worked his way through several plates of fried food and half a dozen refills of coffee, Jack told us all about himself. With the immediate candour so typical of Americans but frightening to most Brits upon meeting them for the first time, he told us *everything*.

His life, he said, fell loosely into two phases: 'drugs' and 'post-drugs'. Drugs Jack, whom he referred to in the third person, had been a lying, cheating, womanising drunk. The Jack sat before us now was addicted, he assured us, to nothing stronger than Starbucks Doubleshot. He smiled readily and often, and was disarmingly eager to please. The zeal with which he opened up every detail of his chequered life story – the drug dependency, the string of failed relationships, the issues with his kids – was terrifying and weirdly reassuring at the same time, like being pinned down by a St Bernard and licked to within an inch of your life. By day he sold cleaning products to businesses in the area, and by night he worked as a talent scout for John Carter Junior's production company.

'You're gonna *love* the cabin,' he smiled, wiping ketchup from his beard. 'Oh and John Carter's gonna be there. He wants to meet you.'

Get. In.

Get. The fuck. In!

The visit to the Cash estate in Hendersonville, just to the north of downtown Nashville, was planned for Monday night. Today was Sunday, so we had time for a get-to-know-you night out with Jack. But first we needed to go back to the hotel, freshen up and post the day's bloggings to the website. I let Joe have first dibs on the computer, waiting to see if he would post the blog about Gram Parsons being music for truckers.

'All yours mate,' he said, clicking 'post' and standing up from the dresser. 'I'm gonna jump in the shower. Have a read.'

I sat down and scanned his latest posting. Stockholm Syndrome... swearing in church... there it was: 'I just don't find songs about eighteen-wheel trucks engaging.' Absolute... fucking... fucker.

201

The shower clunked into action in the bathroom. Then singing:

'… Billboards and truckstops passed by the Grievous Angel…'

Christ, he was even singing it in the shower!

'… Twenty thousand ro-oh-oads I went down, down, down…'

Bit rich, don't you think mister? Blogging that you don't get it and then singing it in the shower?

'… And they all led me straight back ho-oh-ome to yoooou…'

Don't like trucker music, huh? This'll show him.

I pulled up my secret blog:

'A common argument levelled against country music often runs along the lines of "I just don't find songs about eighteen-wheel trucks engaging." That's a fair point. I wouldn't find that interesting either. I have no interest whatsoever in heavy-goods vehicles. In fact vehicles generally just aren't my thing. Music of any genre with an exclusively automotive theme isn't likely to float the boat of anyone but the most ardent petrolhead.

So what's the appeal of these songs then? Darned if I can work it out. But I'll give it go.

"Return of the Grievous Angel" by Gram Parsons, for example, does appear to reference articulated transportation of some sort: "Billboards and truckstops passed by the Grievous Angel." HGV fans hold your hands aloft and sing hallelujah – this is the song for you!

But wait a minute – what's this line here at the end? "Twenty thousand roads I went down, down, down, and they all the led me straight back home to you." It jars somehow with the other lyrics in this eulogy to eighteen-wheeler heaven. What on earth could it refer to? Some allusion to loneliness and longing perhaps, to the feeling of coming home to a loved one after a long time apart, possibly on the road.

But if that's the case, all this other stuff about truck stops and billboards just doesn't make sense. Maybe, just maybe, there's another level of meaning in the song – what the literary boffins refer to rather impenetrably as "metaphor". Can it be that all this talk of long journeys is in fact a clever means of illustrating some other, more deeply felt emotion than a love of trucking?

I'm just not sure. If it were, surely that – along with the beautiful melody, fine harmony and instrumentation – would make it a pretty wonderful song? If in fact the song weren't actually about trucking at all, but about – I don't know – that sense of comfort human beings derive from knowing there's someone out there who will always represent home, who will always be there no matter how far your travels take you away from them, well, what a wonderful song that would be. Anyone on a long journey, far away from their loved ones, would find it incredibly comforting I'm sure. [This line was a particularly cheap shot, given how much Joe was missing Nic and Noah.]

"Grievous Angel" is no more a song about trucking than "Wichita Lineman" is a song about the wonders of telecommunication, or "A Man Needs a Maid" about Neil Young's inability to look after himself without home help. It can be a little hard to tease these things out sometimes, but if you really try – I mean really try – you'll get there in the end.'

I was about to hit 'post' when Joe emerged from the bathroom amid plumes of steam.

The moment I stepped out of the shower Chris closed the laptop. Which meant he was doing something on the computer that he didn't want me to see. Which for most men would be porn, but for Chris would most likely be pedantry.

'What are you up to?'

'Nothing,' he protested, hands caught in the cookie jar.

'Let me see.'

'It's nothing, really.'

This called for more aggressive tactics. I loosened the towel and started to dry myself in what, for the sake of decency, I'll describe as 'a distracting manner'.

'Is it for the website?'

'Maybe.'

The elusiveness pointed either to guilt or embarrassment or both. Irritated, I adopted the 'parent talking to infant' voice. 'Was it about the itty-bitty apostrophe?'

This was intended to annoy Chris into telling me what he'd been typing. It was only half successful.

'It isn't actually. But I still think you should care more about grammar if you want to be taken seriously as a writer.'

'And you should care more about being less of a condescending wanker.'

By now I was completely dry and had to stop towelling for fear of looking like I was rubbing myself over punctuation. Neither of us was going to let this descend into a playground fight over the computer, so as the shirt and trousers went on I tried silence as my next tactic. He opened the laptop. 'Have a read if you want.'

I read the blog. Something about me being too intellectually feeble to appreciate the majesty of the things that he liked. 'What the fuck's this?'

'Just letting off a little steam. I'm pissed off with you.'

'Well that makes two of us.'

'Don't be so hard on yourself,' sneered Chris.

'No, *I'm* pissed off with *you*. Wanker.'

Silence.

'I called you a wanker.'

'We need to meet Jack,' said Chris, ignoring my attempt to initiate an air-clearing slanging match, and with that we went to the car and drove in silence to meet Jack.

Jack took us first to the Texas Roadhouse for dinner – 'They do great steaks there, and I'm kinda sweet on one of the waitresses' – and on into downtown Nashville to take in a few clubs. He wanted a 'second look' at a band he was considering for recommendation to John Carter.

We ducked into one of the numerous music venues on Broadway. Silk & Saddle – a troupe of three girls on fiddle and mandolin, accompanied on guitar by a teenage boy curiously endowed with the facial hair of a middle-aged professional beard-wearer – played bluegrass to a raucous and appreciative crowd. The mandolin player had the bored and studied nonchalance of a Victoria Beckham or Paris Hilton down pat. She was also possessed of a figure that either of them would be happy showing off to the paparazzi on the Croisette in Cannes. That she was happy to give us a good look at it in a pair of barely-there hot pants and a skin tight, cropped leather jacket, was an unexpected treat. She'll go far.

At Tootsies, a little further along Broadway, we went into an upstairs room where a younger, fatter version of Tim McGraw belted out country standards and twangy versions of rock and pop favourites. (Perhaps he was attempting to emulate the career of Ronan Keating in reverse – millions of record sales based on the simple formula of removing the twang from tried and tested country hits and then flogging them to an unsuspecting British public.) Fat Tim's set included, to the delight of a gaggle of middle-aged Winconsonian women vacationing without their husbands for the first time in centuries, a rousing interpretation of Def Leppard's 'Pour Some Sugar on Me'. This he delivered from the top of the bar, allowing the Witches of Wisconsin to position themselves beneath – and be photographed uproariously pointing at – the singer's bulging appendage immediately above their heads. When he returned to the stage to join his band, they turned their attention to Jack (possibly Joe and I looked a little unattainable), who promptly suggested it was about time for him to be in bed, and we left.

It was a relief to have spent the evening watching live music. It lessened the need for conversation, which in turn disguised the fact that Joe and I, as polite and effusive with Jack as he was with us, had barely exchanged a word all evening. Perhaps that, and not the Witches of Wisconsin, was why Jack couldn't wait to leave. A night on the town in Nashville watching country music with two petulant Englishmen, one of whom hates Nashville and country music, both of whom hate each other, possibly wasn't his idea of a fun night out.

As ridiculous as the blog showdown had been, it felt as serious as a fist fight. OK, so we didn't come to blows. We're not come-to-blows types. When Joe gets riled he's more apt to dent inanimate objects than people – the Radio 1 music library still bears the toecap-shaped scars of the time he was nanoseconds off the beat segueing two records during a Jo Whiley comfort break – and I apparently turn into a brooding, sulky teenager more prone to private bursts of anguish than flying fists of fury.

And it was the first time, beyond the refereed confines of the Radio 1 playlist meeting, that Joe and I had had a proper, meaningful disagreement about something. That it should happen three years and several thousand miles into a journey aimed at deepening our friendship was one part ironic to three parts catastrophic. Right now our relationship couldn't have been any deeper; it appeared to be several feet below ground under a headstone marked 'Bromance is dead'.

30 OCTOBER

A BOY NAMED JOHN

I was still pretty narked with Chris, and also a little frustrated with myself. Not about punctuation, but about music, specifically my inability to play a note. The only hope of fixing this was to actually buy an instrument, which in turn meant confronting, head-on, a long held prejudice.

I believe that you should never, ever trust a man carrying an acoustic guitar. A man carrying an acoustic guitar is only ever a millisecond away from whipping it out and playing it at you. Another thing that life has taught me is that when said gent pulls out said six-string, the chances are he's about to play some Bob cocking Marley.

Nothing against the man personally, it's just that I've lost count of the number of beaches or hostel fireplaces I've sat around whilst some tool with an educated accent, dust in his ringlets and faux-ethnicity henna'd all over his wiry frame shits on the 'Re-bastard-demption Song'. And the girls sat around, oh how they love it. Why wouldn't they? They're on holiday without Daddy for the first time since they wintered in Klosters and he nipped off to Paris for two days to nail the au pair, and this lad in front of them is actually playing music and singing! So Peter Total-Fucking-Tosh gets laid whilst my friends and I (all right, yes, just me) sit on the periphery of the group, scowling.

Which is the reason that, when we devised this trip and decided that we should sing a song at the end of it, I elected to try and master the ukulele. It was all part of the quest. That and the whole figuring out American music thing.

Somewhere in the world Gavin Rossdale was celebrating his birthday. Singer and guitarist for Bush, Rossdale fronts a band which had the same problem as me, but in reverse. For five years in the mid-nineties they hurtled around North America selling out arenas and guesting on innumerable TV shows, but in the UK they just didn't connect. Worse, they were held as something of a joke. For a band formed within drumstick-throwing distance of the BBC's Television Centre, their inability to get a slot on British TV must have been painful. Gavin understood the lyrics, the riffs, the poses and the quotes that America wanted, but to his frustration the Brits didn't think much of Bush, if they thought of them at all.

I have nothing whatsoever in common with Gavin Rossdale, but at that moment I could appreciate his predicament. By this point we had travelled two thousand miles, crossed mountains and canyons, rivers and plains and all to a soundtrack that felt like homework. There is an ocean between Britain and America, physically and musically, and there was still seemingly nothing the tufty-lipped man to my right could do to bridge it.

But back to the ukulele, or (phonetically) *ooh-koo-lay-lay*. That's how it's pronounced you know. It was, oddly, the Chili Peppers' Anthony Kiedis who corrected me on my pronunciation, citing that it was the only instrument he had managed to master to any significant degree. Having as few strings as it's credibly possible to have, as well as being portable and favoured by the singer in one of my favourite bands, this was clearly the instrument for me.

In my youth, various instruments were foisted upon me by parents eager that my mind and soul be nourished by the healing benefits of music-making. The piano clearly had too many notes and pedals for my eight-year-old mind. Three subsequent years of learning the flute still didn't get me to a level where I could take an exam. (When even your music teacher accepts that after thirty-six months of practice it would be taking the piss to make anyone other than themselves listen to your toils, then you know that this isn't the instrument – and possibly not the art form – for you.)

A couple of years pointlessly learning bass guitar further endorsed my world view of music being a discipline for geeks, nerds and, fundamentally, show-offs. I say the bass was pointless as this was the age at which many are forming bands, jamming, covering their favourite songs and exploiting the rare opportunity of being both parent-tauntingly loud and parent-pleasingly musical.

The key to it was the forming of a band. Sadly, my school year was sorely lacking in the diverse musical skills required to do this. Of one hundred and twenty students, there were but three lead guitarists, one bass player (me), and a particle-physicist-cum-piano-prodigy who knew Bach but not It Bites.

So, enamoured as I was of the musical stylings of Iron Maiden, I spent two years practising the playing style of Steve Harris alone in my bedroom. With no one else to rehearse with, my efforts were wasted. When I realised that signing up for design and technology classes meant being able to play for hours with welding equipment and weapons-grade petroleum products, the bass guitar and musical ambitions were consigned to the cupboard.

Fast-forward eighteen years and I resolved to have another bash by buying a ukulele. The plan had been to pick one up in Los Angeles to allow for maximum rehearsal time, but we never made it into a music shop. Same story in Denver; same again in Memphis. So on meeting Jack at the Waffle House, Chris had asked him to recommend somewhere we could purchase a reasonably-priced uke and guitar. When he said 'Guitar Center', I feared another embarrassing replay of yesterday's waffled arrangements – 'What's it called?', 'Just Guitar Center' – but by now we were wise to the naming conventions. We arrived late in the afternoon.

Just as the Waffle House serves up more than waffles, at Guitar Center you can get more – much more – than guitars. From the outside it looked like B&Q. On the inside an infinite world of musical possibility hung on the walls, stood on stands, was stacked and racked in enormous rooms, each dedicated to a particular instrument. In the electric guitar room a colour wheel of Gibsons, Fenders, Gretschs and Washburns covered every available inch of wall. The drum room resembled a percussion laboratory filled with every conceivable size, weight and colour of drum, stand and cymbal.

There weren't, it's fair to say, a lot of ladies in the shop.

We were here to buy a ukulele, about which I knew very little, but Chris owned a couple and had enough knowledge, he thought, to tell good from bad. Entering the store, he glided straight past the 'stringed folk instruments' section as though on a tractor-beam and walked to the glass door of a wood-panelled 'Acoustic Room' where... he fell in love.

She was three feet tall with a curvaceous body and perfect complexion, and her name was Martin. She was, with wearisome inevitability, a guitar. Without blinking, he picked her up and started to strum. I apparently was no longer in the room. For the next ninety minutes I tried out a range of fiddly little four-strings on my own before deciding to splash out a whole $100 on a beautiful Mitchell specimen, light tan in colour with pearlescent ivory trim around the body and sound hole. Pleased with my purchase, I flicked through a book of chords while Chris continued to pick and pluck in his soundproof booth. This was a serious infatuation. Or a thinly-disguised ploy to avoid talking to me.

After two hours of strumming, two minutes of negotiation with salesman Dave 'Mad Dog' McGruin, and *two thousand* dollars later, he left the room. That's five times what I paid for my first car. For about $1,950 less he could have got a blow job. Back at the hotel, several more hours of picking, stroking and cooing ensued, until I prised her from his loving arms and suggested it was time to meet Jack for the Cash Cabin visit.

Ever since I was a child there has been an inextricable connection in my brain between old men, country music and the musty smell of alcohol and grooming products.

When I was a boy, my grandparents would visit often for Sunday lunch. At around midday my granddad would disappear to the pub to play dominoes and drink several gallons of pale ale while my mum prepared a roast. After lunch he would retire to the living room to let it go down. Sitting bolt upright in his favourite armchair, he would open the newspaper, turn to the sports section, and fall asleep. His head would slump backwards, hoisting his capacious nose towards the ceiling to reveal arched, cavernous nostrils above his now gaping mouth like darkened church windows over an open portico. He slept for most of the afternoon until, stirring sometime around 5 p.m., he would wake up with a start and brusquely inform my nan that it was time to go home.

But not without leaving a small gift to remember him by. Over the course of several visits, a thin, shiny layer of hair lacquer would accumulate on the back of the armchair, which combined with the alcoholic sweat to create a musty odour capable of outlasting several hot washes. Each time I sat in that chair to eat my crumpets and watch *The Dukes of Hazzard*, scenes of law breakin', bonnet slidin' and car chasin' became ever more intimately associated in my mind with the whiff of granddad, the twang of banjo and the saw of fiddle.

I'm convinced I have *The Dukes of Hazzard* – specifically Daisy Duke, if I'm absolutely honest – to thank for my love of outlaw country. Waylon Jennings narrated the show and sang the theme tune ('The Good Ol' Boys', which told of modern day Robin Hoods out to straighten curves and flatten hills while evadin' the law in the General Lee). The combination of fast cars, exhilarating stunts and Catherine Bach in denim hot pants was impossible to resist. To this day I can sing every word of the theme tune and even now found myself fighting an impulse to slide across the bonnet of the Grievous Angel every time Joe and I switched driving duty.

I had no idea who Waylon Jennings was back then, and didn't find out until well into my twenties; liking country music as a teenager was as likely to attract the girls as a bout of halitosis. But later I learned from classroom music mentors – and they're running record labels now, so they must be right, right? – that it was fine to like country as long as it wasn't Garth Brooks or Billy Ray Cyrus. There was a band of men – Waylon, Willie Nelson, Merle Haggard, Kris Kristofferson and later Gram among them – being called 'outlaw country', and that sounded fine by me.

But Waylon's Nashville flatmate and partner in crime was the greatest outlaw of them all: Johnny Cash. Johnny's hell raisin' – part real life, part carefully cultivated image (drink, drugs and starting forest fires, yes, prison never) – meant he always had an uneasy relationship with the cosy Nashville establishment. At opposite ends of his career he received both a ban from the Grand Ole Opry and induction into the Country Music Hall of Fame, like a stubborn, greasy stain on the back of the Nashville armchair which people eventually came to love. By the time I woke up to him, which wasn't until his reinvention by Rubin as hip, countercultural icon, he was an old man. I have a constant, lingering regret that we didn't have a chance to get better acquainted while he was still alive.

In 1994 Johnny Cash performed at the Glastonbury Festival in what is regularly cited as one of the greatest performances the festival had ever seen. His features were starting to swell and sag as his years of amphetamine use took their toll. In his regulation black he was, even on television, utterly compelling, and if I were granted one wish by the musical genie and allowed to travel in time to see just one performance, it would be that one.

He played classics 'Ring of Fire' and 'Folsom Prison Blues'; he played the greatest comedy song every written, 'A Boy Named Sue', and a handful of newer songs from his latest album. The next day I went to Parrot Records in Canterbury and bought a copy, entitled *American Recordings*. Along with subsequent albums *Unchained*, *Solitary Man*, *The Man Comes Around* and *A Hundred Highways*, it rounds off a canon of albums which are the greatest last act in rock and roll history. They are a triumph of performance, production and song, but most of all they are recordings of soul – and Cash Cabin is not only where it happened, but what made it possible.

Jack had told us to meet him at a gas station on a road leading north out of Nashville towards Hendersonville, the location of the Cash estate. Being as the main road to Hendersonville is called Johnny Cash Parkway, there seems little point in being secretive here. A crisp moon hovered in the graphite-black night sky above the gas station. Jack was already there. We drew up alongside as he wound down the window of his small, battered hatchback.

'Follow me.'

With a throaty cough from his exhaust, he eased off. After half a mile we turned into a small residential street lined with squat, newly-built houses like the treeless suburbs of *Edward Scissorhands*. After another few minutes the road dead-ended at a cul-de-sac in front of two enormous, black, wrought-iron gates.

Jack buzzed the intercom. Nothing. Chris and I looked at each other. Maybe this wasn't going to happen after all. In fact, hadn't it been ridiculous to imagine even for a second that it would? Who was this guy we were tailing, and where was he taking us?

He buzzed again. Still nothing. Maybe he was a fantasist or obsessive or con artist or murderer. Perhaps our names were about to be added to a list of recent 'disappearances' in the area. Nashville police would find two dismembered heads in the Hendersonville countryside and wonder why two apparently respectable, otherwise judicious English professionals would grow bad facial hair, meet a large, scary man in a Nashville Waffle House and freely follow him to the scene of their own horrific demise.

A third buzz, then Jack's thumb appeared out of the car window and the gates opened to reveal a narrow tarmac drive leading away with broad sweeps of grass on either side. Veering right, we made out a huge, floodlit castle of a home on the passenger side. That, presumably, would be the Cash family home and Jack, then, was not a serial killer. Double thumbs.

The headlights flashed through tall, densely-packed trees as the road wound through the estate. The house disappeared over our shoulders to the right as we continued into the blackness down a shallow slope. Jack stopped. We were there – wherever there was. We stepped out into stillness and listened to the sounds of the woods all around: the rustle and flutter of wildlife in the nearby nature reserve, the bray of deer, the hoot of owls.

Somewhere off to the left was the faint orange glow of lights behind curtains, which we presumed to be the cabin. Looking back up the hill, we could see the mega-home of the Cash Family, gothic and imposing.

We waited for a few minutes, then Jack made a call on his mobile phone – to check where John was. Maybe this wasn't going to happen after all.

Jack snapped his phone shut. 'He says he's not feeling too good.'

Shit.

'But he's putting the kids to bed and then he'll drive down.'

'Ace,' I said.

Somewhere in the woods a deer brayed. Up at the house a pair of headlights flicked on. They floated towards us, and a few moments later a silver Mercedes crackled to a halt on the gravel in front of us. Out stepped a sturdily-built man wearing a beaten-up cap and a mustard-coloured corduroy shirt.

'Hey Jack,' he said.

'Hey John. I'd like you to meet Chris and Joe.'

'Hey guys,' said John with a wave of his right hand. With the other he held a handkerchief to his nose. 'Excuse me. I got a real bad cold.'

'Pleased to meet you,' we replied in unison, and both tried to shake his hand at once.

'You too. You wanna see the cabin?'

'Very much so,' I said, 'very much so indeed.'

Johnny and June built the Cash Cabin in 1978 as a place to get away from it all whilst remaining within the grounds of their 240-acre Hendersonville estate. Big and solid, a little larger than the average terraced house, it was modelled on the home in Poor Valley, Virginia (seriously) in which June Carter was raised. Made of wood and stone masonry, it has a raised front porch of the kind where you might expect to see John Walton relaxing after a day chopping lumber. Recording equipment was installed in 1993, and for the rest of his life Johnny was able to record albums without leaving his own back yard.

It was the smell that hit me when we walked in: musty and lived in. Not an exact match for Eau de Smithwicks, Brylcreem *et* Crumpets, but not far off. It was the smell of old men and country music, the whiff of granddad and Hazzard County. And what caught my eye first wasn't the guitars, the cabling, microphones or state-of-the-art recording equipment – though they were all there in abundance – but the mug tree on the kitchen table, the chintzy lampshade in the hall, the brush and poker by the fireplace, the kitsch seventies table and chairs. Straight ahead as we entered the main space was a tallboy covered with crocheted linen, on top of which sat a carved wooden mirror and a cluster of family photos including a smiling Johnny and June, both sporting fabulous bouffant hair.

I've spent a lot of time in a lot of studios, some of historical note, most not. For the best part they are large, airless spaces with faders and flashing lights. Cash Cabin made other studios look like caravans. Not because of its size – it was smaller than most – and not because of the equipment; there was no excess of 'outboard' (as hardware is known in production circles, with electricity being known as 'juice', and new equipment being called 'kit').

What set it apart was the atmosphere. The vibe. The feel. There was more magic in the Cash Cabin than in Abbey Road, Air Studios and Rak put together. Stuffed animal heads looked on from the walls, interspersed between tastefully chosen pictures from Johnny's life. In the kitchen he stood with June backstage at a show – her beaming with pride and affection, him still looking dangerous twenty years and forty pounds after he gave up amphetamines and starting forest fires. Above the tallboy a black and white portrait of him as an old man looked stately and ghostly, like he was watching us from down the ages. Y'all behave now.

Johnny had died exactly three years earlier. As there is no book of etiquette on how to behave when being shown around the famous home studio of a recently deceased legend by said legend's only son, Chris and I stood frozen in front of Johnny's portrait, unsure what to say. I'm not sure I was even breathing. John Carter, tall and broad with a splendid auburn goatee and chunky sideburns, a light Tennessee accent and a gentle manner, clearly sensed the nerves.

'Feel free to take a look around. Take some pictures if you like.' Then he and Jack went into the control room to power up.

From the Persian rug on the oak floor of the main performance room, we shuffled through the open-plan, diner-style kitchen into the piano room, not daring to touch the keys of Johnny's 1896 Steinway, guarded by a deer head on the wall above.

In a small living space a photograph of Bob Dylan – from the artwork of *Nashville Skyline* – sat in the fireplace, lit by a deer-antler chandelier. We photographed the carpets, the walls, the ceiling. This was Johnny's special place and there was no detail too trifling for our admiration. Returning to the mixing room we found Jack and John attending to a Mac, mixing desk and twenty-four channel thingummyjigs nestled among the hand-hewn woodwork.

It seemed intrusive to ask about Johnny, but this desk was where five of my favourite artist's best albums were recorded by my favourite producer, and I wanted to hear about it from John.

'So this place was special to your dad?'

'Absolutely. Dad spent a *lot* of time here – that's his chair right there.' He pointed at one of two sumptuous black leather chairs pulled up to the console.

'And whose is the other?'

'Usually the producer's.'

'Rick Rubin's then?

'Yup. Take a seat. You want to hear a couple of tunes I've been working on?'

We sat and listened to some of his latest productions, John in his daddy's chair, me in Rick Rubin's, proud as a five-year-old invited to the cockpit of a jumbo jet. And for once in my life, I didn't screw it up. Not like the time I told Damon Albarn he needed to improve his pitch. (I was talking about football, he thought I was talking about his singing.) Or the time I hung up on the lead singer of Wales' biggest heavy rock band Lost Prophets because I didn't think he sounded Welsh enough. Or the time I accidentally told Cher she looked like a witch.

No, this time I held it together. We talked about music, John's fascination with medieval English legends, the books of Julian Cope, his taste for the films of Werner Herzog and how his cold was getting bad.

After a while I left Chris, Jack and John talking and spent a few moments alone in each room, quality time with the memory of the Man in Black. I felt like my team had won. To the right of the kitchen was a vocal booth, fashioned from wood and with bark still peeling in places. Above it John had framed an A3 piece of paper from his dad. Written on it in a shaky hand were the chords for the first verse of 'I Walk the Line', and underneath the words:

I keep a close watch on this heart of mine
I keep my eyes wide open all the time
I keep the ends out for the tie that binds
Because you're mine I walk the line

Happy 10th Birthday John. Love from Dad.

If you can read that without welling up then you're tougher than I was that night. I returned to the control room. John thanked us for coming, posed for a photograph and headed back to the house to tend to his cold. We followed Jack in convoy onto the freeway in silence, thrilled and exhausted. Chris held out his hand. We shook. Nothing else needed to be said.

31 OCTOBER

RETURN OF THE BODY SNATCHERS

I got up and checked the website for responses to our request for company from a few days previously. Joe and I had made up, but we needed other people around us – and soon – if we were to reach Winter Haven without falling out completely.

There was a handful of replies. One in particular stood out, from a cyberfriend of long-standing, Annie Rich. Real name Courtney, she had been by far the most enthusiastic and helpful of our online pals since we had set up the website earlier in the year. A lifelong Gram fanatic (her online moniker comes from the opening line of 'Grievous Angel' – 'Won't you scratch my itch, sweet Annie Rich?'), we had made a loose arrangement to meet up at the end of the journey as she had grown up in Gram's home town of Waycross. These days Charleston was home, several hours to the north in South Carolina, but she planned to drive down and show us around Waycross, the penultimate stop before Winter Haven.

There were several reasons why I was excited about meeting her. Firstly, her email expressing interest in being involved in our silly project revealed a passion hitherto unencountered in anyone not directly associated with the GP story. Secondly, her name was very nearly an anagram of 'country'. And finally, judging from her profile picture, she was unspeakably pretty.

```
Date: 30 Oct, 10.43 p.m.
From: Annie Rich


Chris & Joe,


I would absolutely love it if you guys could
make it to Charleston! I realize it may not
be possible (It's a 7.5 hour drive from
Nashville), but I thought I would just throw
this sample itinerary your way... do with it
what you will:


* Come to Charleston on Wednesday or Thursday
(stay with me, of course).
* Go with me and friends on Thursday night to
the Charleston County Fair to see the Charlie
Daniels Band. These events combined will be
an unparalleled 'Southern' experience that I
promise you will enjoy. If nothing else it
will be some of the best people-watching you
have ever experienced in your life.
* Then on Friday morning we'll get up and go
to Waycross, etc.
```

Either way I also wanted to try to talk y'all
into staying an extra day in Waycross. Hope
you're enjoying the ride so far!

As ever,
Courtney

I shouted to Joe, who was in the bathroom, shaving. 'Mate?'

'Yes, m'colleague?'

'Who's Charlie Daniels?'

'Who's Charlie Daniels?'

'Yes, who's Charlie Daniels?'

The top of his head emerged at the doorframe. 'You don't know who Charlie Daniels is?'

'No! Who the fuck is he?!'

'Why do you want to know?'

'Courtney's invited us to the Charleston County Fair and he's playing. Do we want to see Charlie Daniels?'

Joe sprang with both feet into the hallway. Wearing nothing but underpants, a smear of shaving foam down his right cheek and a grin that would frighten small children, he began hopping from one foot to the other. Then, half singing, half rapping in his best Southern drawl, he broke into song:

'The devil went down to Georgia, he was lookin' for a soul to steal...' – a doh-si-doh to the bed – '... he was in a bind 'cause he was way behind and he was willin' to make a deal...' – a drum fill on the bedside table – 'when he came across this young man sawin' on a fiddle and playing it hot, the devil jumped up on a hickory stump and said "Boy, let me tell you what"...'

The performance continued, punctuated with stabs to the air with the razor, across the bed to the window.

'Fire on the mountain, run boys, run! The chicken's in the House of the Rising Sun!' – he circled back past the foot of the bed – 'Chicken in the bread pan pickin' out dough. Granny will your dog bite, no child no...' – and with a final swipe of Gillette past my nose, he ended the performance, jazz hands aloft, on one knee in front of the mirror.

'Very nice,' I applauded. 'But who the fuck is Charlie fucking Daniels?'

'He did "The Devil Went Down to Georgia". That was "The Devil Went Down to Georgia".'

And off he popped to clean his teeth.

You'll recall that Joe is highly adept at memorising quotations as well as given to sudden bouts of rhetorical flourish in everyday speech. It's high impact stuff. Dropping a precisely fitting bon mot into social intercourse impresses at any dinner party, and the effort he puts in – if he puts any in at all – certainly pays off.

But tell me this. What possible benefit could there be in memorising, start to finish, the lyrics of 'The Devil Went Down to Georgia' by Charlie Daniels? Two possible explanations sprang to mind. The first is that he'd figured it would make a good party piece for an audience of one in his pants at a Nashville motel should the opportunity ever arise. Possibly he wasn't planning on that audience being me, but he saw his chance and he went for it. Or maybe – and this was my strong suspicion – he liked country music more than he was letting on and he'd just given himself away in the most spectacular fashion.

In September 1979, before MTV, before *The Tube* and not long after my bedtime was extended to half past seven, there were but two weekly rituals in our house. The first was a regular Saturday night cowering as Tom Baker did battle with the terrifying contents of a far-flung interplanetary props cupboard, and the second was *Top of the Pops*. Nowadays, of course, *Top of the Pops* is a byword for everything that is predictable and lacklustre in music telly, but in 1979 when programming only started in the mid-afternoon and concluded barely seven hours later with the national anthem, 'The Pops' wasn't just 'The Tops', it was 'The Nuts'.

For a young lad from Marlow Bottom, the added excitement came from a weekly row with my sister as to which was the best record in the chart that week. We each chose a song at the start of the show, sat down, crossed our fingers and hoped that our song was highest. If it was, you officially had the better music taste, and a weekend of crowing and smug condescension was yours.

One such Thursday in September 1979, my sister and I sat alert on the sofa and observed that very ritual. My sister had chosen 'Video Killed the Radio Star' by Buggles with its showy video featuring musical genius Trevor Horn in spectacles best described as 'wanker glasses'. I, meanwhile, had plumped for a curious hoedown of a tune by a man who looked like the missing sibling of Jesse Duke and Colonel Sanders, and whose bearded band fashioned a curious fire-and-brimstone tale of soul-selling in the style of the Muppets' house band The Electric Mayhem Orchestra.

The numbers got smaller and the hits got bigger until we got to number fourteen, when my behatted heroes appeared on the screen. Gutted. Worse still, as the show went on Buggles still didn't appear. Eventually, at 7.26 p.m. the inevitable announcement came: Buggles was the nation's favourite, pick of the pops, top of the heap, the UK's official number one. This was a disaster. My music taste was fourteen points worse than my sister's, my weekend ruined. I'd like to say I retired to my room in the manner of *Shawshank*'s Andy Dufresne and lay back with the sound of Charlie Daniels in my ears, but I suspect I probably just pinched my sister on the leg and ran up to my room to draw on the walls.

The words of 'The Devil Went Down to Georgia' stayed with me though, and throughout that autumn whenever it came on the radio I ran to the speakers and strived to learn its bizarre narrative by heart. The song tells the story of the Devil running low on souls. So he heads to Georgia where he challenges Johnny, a gifted local fiddle-playing lad, to a musical duel. If Johnny plays the best he gets a gold fiddle. If Ol' Horny wins, he gets the boy's soul. If I had only applied myself to school as much as I did to learning those lyrics, my report might have been a little different that year ('a little better, still too many animal noises').

I replicated every inflection and twang of Charlie Daniels' vocal until I could recite the entire thing. Bloody annoying for my family of course, and – as I discovered when an almost chemical memory burst out of me – bloody annoying for Chris too. Because at that moment I sang him the entire song. Hadn't done it for almost three decades but, like a TV ad you watched too often, I could remember the whole thing. It was like speaking in tongues. Weird seventies country and western tongues.

Chris understood this to mean 'Yes, Joe would like to see the Charlie Daniels Band.' He understood correctly.

'Safe to say you're a fan then?' I hollered, chickening out of taking him to task on the country music thing. This was not the time to be bringing up so thorny an issue as the one that had very nearly seen us end the drive in separate cars.

'Hwftwntly.'

'Come again?'

A mouthful of toothpaste landed in the sink. 'Definitely.'

'And there's a kind of symmetry to the "deal with the devil" thing, isn't there?'

'So there is. Maybe it's a sign.'

'Shall we go to Charleston then?'

'Absolutely. We've got a few days to kill, haven't we? Now that we're not going to New Orleans.' New Orleans, where Gram's remains were buried – or what remained of his remains following the Joshua Tree flambéing – had been dropped from the itinerary. After Wichita, bang in the centre of the lower forty-eight states, we had originally planned to dogleg south through Oklahoma and Texas into Louisiana, picking our way along the Gulf of Mexico into Georgia and finally Florida. But when the Cash Cabin visit became a serious possibility, we had re-routed east through Nashville. Even for a journey tracing one man's life from grave to cradle, two graves was possibly overdoing it.

'OK. Great idea,' I said.

And that's exactly how it happened. It was Joe's idea to go to Charleston. To see the Charlie Daniels Band.

But before we went to Charleston so that Joe could see the Charlie Daniels Band, we had a lunch date. Our unexpected detour through Nashville had presented the opportunity of rendezvousing with a very singular septuagenarian by the name of Mr Mangler.

Phil 'Road Mangler' Kaufman – Gram's road manager, best friend and unequivocally the 'go-to guy' if you ever need a dead country-rock musician barbecued – is a man who very nearly defies description. I hesitate to use the phrase 'larger than life', generally reserved these days for wearers of wacky ties, to describe a man who has lived a life more eventful, more packed with mirth, melodrama and misadventure than a Don Simpson high-concept action movie. Phil Kaufman has more skeletons in his closet than most so-called larger-than-life characters have ties in theirs. So no, that won't do. He's a seventy-one-year-old rogue with a mischievous grandfatherly charm, but 'loveable rogue' doesn't do him justice either; it speaks of schoolboy scrapes and Oliver Twist, and there is nothing schoolboy about the scrapes this gentleman has had to extricate himself from. His life story reads like a Hunter S. Thompson novel or Hollywood film script. His life story *is* a Hollywood film script.

Kaufman's first career was, by his own admission, a profession not wisely chosen. Twice he smuggled large quantities of marijuana into the US from Mexico, and twice he got caught. His next move, facing the near certainty of five to twenty years in prison, was to jump bail and head to Europe under an assumed identity, borrowing the splendidly apt name of his friend Harold True, and keeping a low profile by appearing in a number of films shot in Spain. Following another of his cross-border shopping trips, this time to Morocco, he headed north, pausing long enough in Paris to get caught up in student riots before winding up in a Swedish prison on the biggest drug-smuggling charge ever seen in the country at that time. He passed the days either attempting to escape or reading – and then consuming – some very mind-blowing letters from LSD guru Dick Alpert.

Later extradited back to the US, he did time in nine separate prisons, notably Springfield (where he delivered contraband to Vito 'Don Vito' Genovese) and Terminal Island, where he met and accidentally kick-started the music career of one Charles Manson. Phil Kaufman, as you're probably starting to work out for yourself, is a man with a tendency to fall in with the wrong crowd.

Have you ever opened the newspaper, scanned a report naming the savage murderesses of a Hollywood film actress under instructions from a charismatic cult leader, and thought 'Goodness, I've had sex with every one of those women?' No? Nor, so far as I can recall, have I. Phil Kaufman has. Having met the soon-to-be-released Manson – an aspiring musician – in prison, Phil put him in touch with some Beach Boys contacts in LA and unknowingly fell in with just about the wrongest crowd on the planet.

Once released from prison himself, he found Manson's hippie harem to be a uniquely satisfying way of reacquainting himself with the pleasures of life on the outside. Which is how he came to be on first-name terms with Charlie and his peace-and-love-commune-turned-racist-murderous-cult the Manson Family, bagging that most dubious of honours, the production credit on Manson's failed solo album *Lie*, into the bargain. (To this day Kaufman's least prized possession is the copyright in all of Manson's recorded music.) The La Bianca couple, inexplicably and brutally murdered by the Manson Family the day after the Sharon Tate killings, lived next door to a house where the Family had attended a party the previous year – the home of none other than one Harold True.

Possibly it was this that inspired a change of career. Kaufman, with his unrivalled capacity for picking the unlikeliest of company, became 'executive nanny' to the Rolling Stones in LA. In town in 1968 to record *Beggar's Banquet*, the Stones were in need of an LA driver/fixer; Kaufman, whose reputation for minding difficult characters preceded him, was the only man for the job. (The title was given to him, like a knighthood, by Mick Jagger because he catered to their noses and kept their needs clean. Sorry – catered to their needs and kept their noses clean.) And so began an illustrious career 'moving people, not equipment'.

On the road with Frank Zappa he inspired the title of a track on *Joe's Garage* by screaming the eternal question 'Why Does it Hurt When I Pee?' from the tour bus toilet. He once told Ray Charles that his shirt clashed with his trousers. He organised his own benefit concert when he was diagnosed with cancer. In England he lived with a woman for a year before discovering she was a prostitute. And he has your name tattooed on his butt. (This is absolutely true – he really does have 'your name' inked onto his rear.)

So Phil Kaufman has been many things in his life: drug smuggler, convict, record producer, road manager, executive nanny, film producer, stuntman, film extra, short order cook, spot welder, encyclopaedia salesman. But history will not remember him for any of these things. Kaufman will be remembered solely for one drunken, defining moment in September 1973 when, to borrow one of his own well-worn maxims, he put the 'fun' in funeral by stealing and then burning Gram Parsons' body at Cap Rock in the Mojave Desert. And we were about to get a lesson in corpse-burning from him.

We met at Brown's Diner on Blair Boulevard in Hillsboro West End, purveyor of burgers, beer, bravado and grease to Nashville's music crowd. Phil had raved about Brown's in his emails, asserting that no rock and roll road trip would be complete without a visit to Nashville's most famous music and burger joint. And who were we to argue: Phil had been road managing for forty years, so if anyone knew where to get a decent burger, it was probably him.

We arrived to find that the legendary Brown's consisted of two trailers spliced together and propped up on breeze blocks on a raised bank of grass behind a petrol station. With a flat, felt roof, it resembled one of those temporary school classrooms that never get pulled down and after ten years start to sag like a shoebox left in the rain; only the smell of grease and the words 'Bud Light' glowing blue neon in the window diluted the feeling that we were arriving for an afternoon of double maths.

I had learned a little of what to expect of Phil during our first telephone conversation. Back when the trip was planned as a documentary, I had tracked him down to his favourite Nashville haunt and made arrangements with the barman to call back the next day when Phil would be in at his usual time. I called at the allotted hour: 'You'd better make it quick; it's nearly time for my afternoon wank.' I cut to the chase. Would he fly out to Joshua Tree and show us exactly how and where he did the deed? Sure he would. My heart leapt – what a scoop! He named his price. My heart sank. It was several times our meagre budget for the entire programme. When you carve out a living as 'the guy that burned Gram Parsons', I suppose you have to make the opportunities count when they come along.

So the chance of catching up in Nashville for no more than the cost of a burger was not one we were about to pass up. We went in and scanned the room for likely body snatchers. More neon buzzed from the imitation wood-panelled walls; lone diners perched on high stools at the bar, bantering under the drone of baseball commentary on TV screens above them. One customer, in a John Deere cap and matching green T-shirt, alternated between mouthfuls of chilli dog and puffs on a cigarette.

We spotted Phil sitting alone at a shelf table running along the window near the 'musician's entrance'. (Brown's has two entrances. One leads to the Emerald Room, where 'ordinary people' enjoy their burgers, while the musicians enter via their own door at the rear.) The trademark moustache, a little greyer than in the photos we'd seen but unmistakably Kaufman, wiggled as he winked and welcomed us over. A red baseball cap with the name of his team – the Nashville Sounds, named for the city's music pedigree – and a white T-shirt emblazoned with the Triumph logo, said 'I'm Phil. I like music, baseball and motorbikes – OK?'

'Phil Kaufman?' I ventured, walking over.

'Guilty as charged. You must be Chris.'

'Yes sir,' I said, shaking his hand. 'Great to meet you. This is Joe.'

Harland stepped forward and shook Phil's hand while I chastised myself for calling him 'sir'.

'Take a seat,' said Phil. 'I'll order burgers. You gotta have a Brown's burger. They're the best in town. Say, where did you boys park?'

'At Harris Teeter across the road,' said Joe. 'Why?'

'Shame. You could have parked out back under the kitchen extractor fan and opened the hood for a free lube job. How do you like Nashville?'

'Love it,' I said. 'Jack Fripp took us to Tootsies last night. Pretty cool place.'

'Man, I love that place. Great for playing elbow tit.'

'What's elbow tit?' I asked.

Phil looked surprised. 'You never played elbow tit?'

'No. What are the rules?'

I really asked Phil Kaufman what the rules of elbow tit are. Joe rescued me, offering up the story about the Gram-related card exchange that inspired our little rock and roll odyssey. Tag-teaming between stories like animated children telling granddad what they got for Christmas, we told him about LA and Laurel Canyon, meeting Polly in Joshua Tree, the 'Wichita Lineman' experience, Jeff Buckley and Elvis in Memphis, selling our souls on the Crossroads, Johnny Cash and the cabin studio.

'So you're commemorating dead rock stars?' said Phil, finally getting a word in.

'More like celebrating them,' I replied. 'We're on our way to Winter Haven for Gram's sixtieth birthday. We're hoping to throw a party. Are you doing anything to celebrate?'

'Celebrate what? He's still dead, ain't he?'

He was right, of course. Polly had thought it was a great idea, what we were doing for Dad. Phil thought it was the most ridiculous thing he'd ever heard.

'Shame we couldn't get it together to fly you out to Joshua Tree,' I said. 'It would have been great to have you as tour guide at Cap Rock.'

'You went out there, did you?'

'We did. Sat under Cap Rock and raised a beer to Gram, right on the spot where you smoked him,' said Joe.

'Under the rock, where all the dedications are?'

'Yep,' we chorused proudly, like boy scouts expecting their Grampire badges.

'I didn't do it there.'

Joe affected a fabulous double take. 'Sorry?'

'We dumped it by the side of the road.'

'You didn't do it under Cap Rock?'

'*Near* Cap Rock, not under it. The coffin was too heavy, so we just slid it out of the hearse by the side of the road. We were drunk, and we needed somewhere to turn the hearse around.'

'Where did you get the hearse from?' I asked.

'Michael Martin, a friend of Gram's. His girlfriend Dale drove a hearse. She and Margaret were with Gram when he died.'

'Margaret?'

'Margaret Fisher! Jeez, you guys didn't do your research, did you?! You need to read my book. It was Margaret who stuck the ice cubes up his ass to try to revive him.'

'And you chose Cap Rock because it was Gram's favourite place, right?'

'Nope.'

I choked on a French fry. 'Er... oh.'

'In fact I don't think he ever went there.'

I glanced at Joe. 'Ri-ight.'

Cap Rock has always occupied a kind of mythical place in my mind. Every book and magazine article I have ever read about Gram describes him sat on top of a rock in the Mojave Desert, tripping and stargazing with Keith Richards. It's where friends go to get deeper into – or further out of – their minds. It's where one man set another's spirit free. So top of my list of places to be at one with the world isn't Stonehenge or Uluru. It's Cap Rock that holds special significance.

'It's funny,' Phil went on. 'To this day people think Cap Rock has some special significance, like it's a sacred place or something. We were just too drunk to carry on. Gram loved the desert, don't get me wrong, and he wanted to be cremated out there. But Cap Rock didn't mean shit to him.'

I felt like Dorothy Gale. We had followed the yellow brick road, but ended up in the wrong place. I hesitated as I framed my next question, half fearing another disappointing answer, half afraid of causing offence. 'So... Did you open the coffin?'

'Yep.'

'What did he look like?'

'He was naked and had surgical tape all over his chest from the autopsy. I said "Hey Gram, what's that on your chest?" and then flicked him on the nose. We used to do that to each other all the time.'

'Then?'

'Then I doused him in gas and sent him up in smoke. We watched the body burn for a while – his ashes went into the air just like he wanted – then hit the road. There wasn't much of him left when we were finished.'

We chatted a while longer, Mangler one-liners tumbling over the repartee ('That was a couple of years after Gram stopped smoking', 'John went to Penn State and I went to State Pen') but he had to split. He wanted to get one more round of golf in before the frost arrived, and then he was going back on the road with Etta James. We walked outside together.

'Wait there. I've got something for you,' he said, disappearing across the car park to his Harley. When he returned he was carrying a book, which he handed to me: it was his autobiography, *Road Mangler Deluxe*. 'I'll sign it for you.'

'Would you? That would be fantastic,' I said.

Taking a pen from inside his leather jacket, he wrote a dedication on the title page, forward dating it to Gram's sixtieth birthday, the final day of our journey. 'That'll be a dollar for the book, and nineteen for the signature.'

I gave him the money. We'd had our twenty dollars' worth.

Later, in the car as we neared Knoxville, I noticed that the price on the back cover of the book had been struck through with a black marker pen. I rubbed it with my thumb to see what was underneath. $16.50.

Manners, we are told, are what separate us from the apes. This manifests itself in many ways, including the genteel way that the British advertise their products: 'Try this – it's great!' is as close as we get to outright declarations of fabulousness. That evening, as I sat in our Knoxville motel room flicking through TV channels and chewing on jerky, it seemed to me that American commerce is a little more ruthlessly competitive:

'Ovaltine is three times as nutritious as Nesquik and tastes nicer too.'

'Advil is twice as effective as Tylenol.'

'Buy a Ford truck – only fags drive Toyotas.'

This isn't surprising of course. Americans have always been a little more direct than us when it comes to selling. What *was* novel though, was that this confrontational method had apparently moved over into political advertising too. There was some election or other taking place in the next few days, although quite what it was actually for we had no idea. A blizzard of names and an avalanche of possible offices swept past the car windows on signage attached to every house, mailbox and bumper in all Tennessee, but the party political broadcasts on television seemed to dispense with this essential information in order to maximise the time spent rubbishing their competitors.

Harold Ford Jr was a Democrat incumbent and was faring particularly badly in this televisual slanging match. 'Harold Ford supports gay marriage and wants to put contraceptive pills in high schools,' we learned in one ad break. The next advert warned that 'Harold Ford Jr says he's a qualified lawyer, but he didn't even pass the bar exam.' The next sternly informed us that 'Harold Ford diverted state funds to pay for the legal defence of a Los Angeles pornographer.'

The next advert was Harold Ford Jr himself staring pleadingly from the screen beseeching us 'not to believe the lies they're telling about me – I don't support gay marriage and I don't want to put the pill in schools'. (That he didn't deny the other claims suggested either he *was* a porn-loving legal charlatan or his Chief Advisor on Name-Calling wasn't keeping him fully briefed.) What became distressingly clear was that there was absolutely no fact-checking going on. Apparently it was fine to accuse your opponent of anything on telly as long he is given the chance of buying his own ad space to refute all the lies.

With three days to go until the elections I was hoping the race would get even tighter so we could see what how far this game of 'diss' would go. 'Harold Ford left a floater in my toilet', 'Bob Corker is a paedophile'. With no one to arbitrate then we might get what we all really wanted – two candidates standing at lecterns in a nationally televised, sixty-minute game of 'your mum'.

I NOVEMBER

A DATE WITH THE NIGHT

Trapezoid Tennessee is an almost perfect parallelogram. The northernmost borders of Mississippi, Alabama and Georgia to the south form a perfectly flat line running west to east, on top of which sits Tennessee like a deck of cards laid flat and squished east towards the Atlantic. Stopping them from spilling into North Carolina are the Great Smoky Mountains, in the shadow of which sat our next planned overnight stay, Asheville, due east of Nashville just across the state border. We had chosen carefully. Among the city's long and impressive list of accolades were several that held a very obvious appeal, if not for two music obsessives on the look-out for rock and roll high drama, then definitely for elderly vegetarians looking to reinvent themselves.

Chief among these distinctions was Asheville's appearance in the 'Top 50 Most Alive Places to Be', as voted by everyone's favourite magazine for the over-fifties, *Modern Maturity*, a poll presumably intended to signal to the world that, for its healthy but ageing readership, being alive is still very much on the agenda. Three years later *Modern Maturity*, having changed its named to *AARP Magazine* – incidentally the highest circulation publication in the world – voted Asheville one of the 'Best Places to Reinvent Your Life'. (My favourite publication for the older market, spotted in the racks of a Nashville supermarket, was *Prevention* magazine, presumably offering information and advice to readers committed to stopping things from happening.)

What's more, PETA had named Asheville the most vegetarian-friendly small city in America which, though Joe and I are both meat eaters, appealed for the simple reason that a road diet of burgers, beef jerky, Dr Pepper, burgers and beef jerky was starting to take its toll on our complexions. Lastly, and most importantly, *Rolling Stone* magazine had voted Asheville, with its reputation for alternative and bohemian living, the 'New Freak Capital' of the US. It sounded like our kind of place.

The plan had been to make Asheville our final stop before Charleston, where we would meet Courtney, see Charlie Daniels and, crucially for the coast-to-coast aspect of the undertaking, dip our toes in the Atlantic.

But by 10 p.m. we had found ourselves 120 miles short of Asheville and in need of sleep, electing instead to check into a Knoxville 'MicroLodge'. Unsurprisingly given the name, it was cramped, utilitarian and depressing, but clean and – importantly at this stage, as the guitar purchase had put something of a dent in my finances – cheap. Cheaper in fact than the Firebird Motel in Dodge City with its unique ceiling hook facilities, and attractive therefore despite the repeated assurances of the twenty-something receptionist – apparently paid on commission – that he would 'hook us up' if we chose MicroLodge over Days Inn across the road. ('Hooking us up' turned out, much to our undisguised relief, to translate roughly as 'meet and exceed both price and service expectations vis-à-vis our chosen lodgings'.)

We were glad, the following day, for having stopped early in Knoxville. Had we pushed on, the Smokies might have skulked by unnoticed in the dark, denying us the display of morning mountain fog they take their name from, and to which we were now treated. Whisps of morning mist – warm air from the Gulf of Mexico cooling in the upper elevations of Appalachia – rose between the highest trees like a forest fire. Lower down a thick fog flooded the spaces between interlocking mountain ridges receding into the distance like a theatre set.

I40 carried us through Pigeon River Gorge into North Carolina and south on to Asheville. Parking on College Street, we noted a bumper sticker on a Buick in front petitioning to 'Keep Asheville Weird'. As if on cue, two bearded drunks, huddled over a chessboard on a bench in the square opposite, raised their beer cans and grinned toothless gums as we stepped out of the car. We found a table at nearby Maybelle's Diner, where we lunched outside on the street under crisp autumn sunshine. I called Courtney between courses to make final arrangements for our rendezvous later that afternoon. A satellite delay of several seconds rendered conversation virtually impossible, made worse by the fact I was vainly trying to relay directions to Joe as we spoke.

'Make a left onto East Bay Street,' shouted Courtney into my right ear, 'then a right onto Calhoun.'

'Left. East Bay Street. Right. Calhoun,' I repeated.

'Right,' said Courtney.

'Was that a left or a right onto East Bay?' whispered Joe.

'Left.'

'No, *right* onto Calhoun,' crackled the voice in my right ear.

'Sorry Courtney, I was talking to Joe.'

Silence, then Joe – 'Definitely left *onto* East Bay, not off it?' – and Courtney – 'Oh OK, bit of a delay on the line!' – at the same time.

And so on.

Maybelle's – all gingham tablecloths on rustic pine tables – was friendly, wholesome and family-run, just the place for two men starved for weeks of greens and keen to savour the curious offerings of America's freak capital. Not only was it the only restaurant in the entire country apparently able to resist the temptation of drowning a perfectly healthy salad in Thousand Calorie Dressing, our waitress also added another trophy to the city's growing list of distinctions.

Chatting to her as she cleared our empty plates, we asked about the city's reputation for weirdness. She was young with asymmetric hair, horn-rimmed specs and a voluminous flowery blouse which clashed with a tiny checked apron tied around her waist.

'Asheville ain't so weird,' she said, pausing to rescue her gum from behind a molar. 'If you ask me it gets kind of a bad press.'

'Why do you think that is?' I enquired.

'I really don't know. It sure is a shame though. There's more to Asheville than freaks.'

'Such as…?'

'Well let me tell you this,' she pronounced, wagging an index finger emphatically. 'Asheville has the highest percentage of people in the whole of North America who want to be pirates.'

'Excuse me?' I said.

'Pretty cool, huh?' And with that she disappeared into the kitchen, leaving us to contemplate this latest credit while a semi-naked street drinker shouted chess moves at passers-by. Asheville had given us precisely one hour of its time, but in that short window had proved itself to be freakish, vegetarian friendly and, *Modern Maturity* readers will be reassured to learn, very much alive. We pressed on to Charleston.

As we neared the coast I asked Joe, busily blogging in the passenger seat, to find the directions he had taken down over lunch. He reached into his pocket and handed me a small piece of yellow card.

'This is Phil Kaufman's business card,' I said, offering it back to him.

'Turn it over.'

There was a scrawl of red pen on the reverse. 'You've written directions to Charleston on the back of Phil Kaufman's business card?!'

'Er, actually I ran out of space on the back.'

On the front, in thick pen obscuring Phil's name and job title – 'Road Mangler & Executive Nanny' – were the words 'Right again into Starbucks'.

'Christ, Joe!'

'What?'

'We must have collected hundreds of scraps of paper in the last two weeks – maps, tickets, postcards, hotel bills – and you've scribbled all over the business card of the one man without whom it would very likely never have happened?'

'Er...'

'Look! You've even written over his job title! There is no one else in the *entire world* with the title 'Road Mangler & Executive Nanny'. Mick *Jagger* gave it to him for crying out loud!'

'Right. Yes. Sorry.'

After a fashion we arrived at our scheduled meeting place. Courtney had suggested we meet at a Starbucks in downtown Charleston, presumably the safest place she could think of to meet us, if there is such a thing as a safe place for a lone woman to meet two strange men she has met on the Internet. She worked at a day spa nearby and would meet us straight after work around six, assuming there were no dramas closing up. Don't worry, I had told her, we were in no hurry. We ordered moccachinos and waited.

And waited.

And waited.

'You have to wonder,' I mumbled through a lemon and poppy seed muffin, 'what sort of girl agrees to meet up with two blokes off the Internet and lets them stay at her house for three days.'

'Hopefully a very nice girl.'

'Doesn't it strike you as a little weird?'

'What are you worried about? That she's the leader of a country music death cult out to feed us to the 'gators in the swamp?'

'Well I wasn't, but I am now.'

'Don't worry, no alligator could ever get its mouth around your noggin anyway,' laughed Chris. (I have a large head.)

'Thanks. That thought will cheer me up as you slip down 'gator gullet to the strains of Dolly Parton. What does she look like?'

'Blonde. Big tits,' said Chris.

'Really?'

'Come on, you must know what Dolly Parton looks like.'

'No, Courtney.'

'Oh. Pretty, if her profile picture's anything to by.'

This could be a problem then, because profile pictures lie. Social networking brings much joy and pleasure to many people (along with lashings of recrimination, resumption of old relationships, reconfirmation of youthful prejudices and rekindling of old dreams), but the single most depressing aspect of them, for me at least, is the profile picture.

The question is, which photo do you use? How do you find something that says 'Screw you, I'm fine now' to the ex you still haven't forgiven for shagging Carl Rigby, but that won't frighten your silver-surfing grandmother when she sees a picture of you with your tongue in a stripper's ear? And then there are the colleagues, bosses, old friends, new friends and friends of friends who might – as we all do – make up their mind about you based on eighty-by-eighty pixels they've found on MyFace.

Perhaps go for that one of you engaged in some extreme and impressive pursuit like bungee jumping? Fine, but in real life you had better be more outward-bound than Bear Grylls or people will feel a tad misled. Which leaves us with what? In the pub with friends? Too smug. A cute animal? Too wacky. A photoshop of you with Obama? Too needy. A snap with your children? Too twee. Reading a book? Too pretentious. Rarely has the phrase 'You can't please all of the people all of the time' been so apt. Which leads us to one simple conclusion: you cannot possibly tell what someone is going to look like from their profile picture.

Chris was getting agitated. 'Where the hell is she? She's nearly an hour and a half late.'

'Probably sharpening her knives.'

'Well she'd better get a move on or we're checking into a hotel.'

'Perhaps you should call and ask her to sharpen her knives more quickly.'

She walked in. Even prettier than her picture, and no knives. Things were looking up. As were we: Courtney was a tall, slender gazelle of a woman, and in three-inch heels – her, not us – we found ourselves rocking onto the balls of our feet to make eye contact. She had long, dark hair pulled up in pins revealing a high forehead and wide eyes, like a brunette version of a seventies Olivia Newton-John.

'Hey guys,' said the perfect American smile. 'Sorry I'm late. My boss kept me late after work and then I had to walk the dog and then I couldn't find anything to wear and…'

'Absolutely no problem at all,' said Chris, perking up suddenly, and it wasn't the seven moccachinos kicking in. Courtney was, in the absence of any other word for it, hot. I did what mates are supposed to do at times like this and let him lead.

'Charleston looks beautiful. What do you suggest we do while we're here?'

'Well it kinda depends on what you're into, but I was thinking maybe we could have something to eat at this nice Italian place called Il Cortile del Re, then go to the Music Farm to see the

Secret Machines, then AC's for a drink and then tomorrow go to the Coastal Carolina Fair to see Charlie Daniels and then see the Slackers play after that... Maybe?'

'Sounds like you've got it all figured out! Perfect.'

We went outside. Chris opened the driver's door – 'Jump in the back would you Joe, let the lady ride up front' – and Courtney directed us into the heart of Old Charleston.

'Thanks for putting us up,' smiled Chris, pulling out of the car park.

'You're so welcome. I've been looking forward to meeting you guys. Your blogs are great.'

'Thanks,' I said. 'I've got to ask you though – weren't you just a little bit nervous about meeting two strangers from another country and inviting them to stay in your house?'

'Not really.'

'Joe thought you might be the leader of a country-rock death cult who feeds tourists to alligators,' said Chris.

Courtney turned to the back seat to look at me, wearing an expression of slight confusion. 'Well I'm not a cult leader if that's any help.'

'Good. I'm glad that's settled,' I said.

'And I love meeting new people. I did this Global Freeloading thing a while back. It's like a network of people around the world who offer up their spare room or couch in exchange for free accommodation wherever and whenever they need it. It was pretty cool.'

Well that made a bit more sense. Shades of hippy free love maybe, but she was clearly just a nice person. Phew.

'And reading the stuff on your website I knew you weren't going to be weirdos. You can tell a lot from the way someone writes. In fact, being that I'm a girl and you're two guys, shouldn't I be the one with the serial killer concerns?'

She had a point, but I didn't want to ruin Chris' cool by admitting we were cowardly lime suckers who couldn't stash a body in the trunk even if we wanted to. Primarily because Chris would lock the keys in with the victim.

Charleston's age and pedigree were visible even in the dark. The houses were stately, well preserved and deeply varnished, with brightly-polished brass fittings on every door. Furls and detailing, elaborate drainpipes, columns and lintels on every building in the carefully preserved downtown spoke confidently of the city's 400-year heritage.

We arrived at Il Cortile del Re in the antique district and had a glass of wine at the bar while we waited for a table.

'I guess I was a *little* nervous about meeting you guys,' said Courtney. 'You've met some cool people in the last few weeks.'

'Like who?' I said nonchalantly, as if my life were just one long series of rock and roll encounters.

'Well Phil Kaufman's pretty cool.'

'I guess,' I conceded, reluctantly. Lacking the fascination that Chris and Courtney both had for the Cap Rock cremation story, I found it hard to see Phil as anything more than a slightly barmy old man we had a burger with.

'What was he like?'

'Short, fat, big moustache.'

'What did you talk about?'

'We talked about Gram, Polly, the body-snatching incident obviously. And how he likes to play elbow tit.'

'What's elbow tit?'

'Some sort of game that men play in bars.'

'I see. What are the rules?'

Courtney and Chris were going to get on just fine.

The next stop on Miss Connor's impressive itinerary was an agricultural equipment store turned live music venue by the name of Music Farm, where Texan space-rock three piece The Secret Machines were due to play. Our hostess generously bought both our tickets, as well as smoothing things over with security when at first they refused entry to Chris, whose steadfast refusal to assent to American social norms by carrying ID now threatened everybody's noses in the effort to spite his own face. Finally making it inside the venue, we bought a round of beers and waited for the band to come on.

Even in the absence of performers our eyes were fixed on the stage. We had very little choice in the matter because the stage was absolutely monstrous, and right in the centre of the room. A circular riser twenty feet in diameter was littered with amps, guitars and cables. Scaffolding poles around the circumference rose high into the air, on top of which sat a vast aluminium wheel festooned with lighting gimbals and strobes. It dominated the dancefloor, leaving barely any room for fans so that most of the audience were forced to stand, like us, at the bar.

How was the gig? Well, the band were ear-splittingly loud, the light show synapse-snappingly bright, and I fell asleep standing up.

Which is a something of an achievement even for a borderline narcoleptic like Harland. Not only did he fall asleep standing up while The Secret Machines – a band generally acknowledged as being one of the rockingest rock bands in rock music – assaulted our senses just metres from where he slumbered, he did so without spilling a drop of his beer. This was one tired fellow.

In his defence, I should tell you a little about how Charleston 'rolls'. The southern European influence is writ large all over town, not least in its approach to going out. Just as we Brits are draining the dregs from the last pint of the evening and heading home to fall asleep on top of our wives, the Spanish and Italians are readying themselves for a big night out. The same is true of nightlife in Charleston, where 11 p.m. is when most people start getting ready to go out. Any band still playing after 11 p.m. in London will very likely find themselves in trouble with the rozzers. Any band taking to the stage *before* 11 p.m. in Charleston will very likely be playing to the sound engineer and bar staff.

Which is why, when The Secret Machines struck the final chord of their final song and left the stage, it was getting really rather late for a man of Joe's delicate constitution. It's also the reason, when Courtney woke him up and suggested going to AC's, that a look of horror came over his poor little face when it became obvious that AC's was a bar and not some quaint Charlestonian euphemism for bedtime.

But Joe, as you will have gathered by now, is a man of resolve and resources. At AC's we took a booth near the pool tables and were joined variously and intermittently by Courtney's friends in between games. Energised by his power nap, a shot of bourbon and a steady stream of American people to tell stories to, Joe valiantly went in search of – and found – a mighty second wind behind AC's generously proportioned and well-appointed bar. Tales were told and anecdotes recounted.

Out came the one about The KLF burning a million pounds of their own money, Bill Drummond's travails trying to sell a Richard Long photograph for $20,000 (and how thirty, dollar-sized pieces of it ended up hanging on my living room wall), even the one about his mum being a professional chocolate taster who counsels anorexics in her spare time. His audience was enraptured and he was playing to it, pulling out only his choicest yarns and spinning them out with hilarious asides and amusing bonus content. He was the funniest, most engaging person on earth.

As designated driver and seemingly the only sober person in the entire place, I was the least funny, least engaging person in the room. I was having precisely no fun at all and confess I was making very little effort to have more.

Courtney and her friends all had names like characters from *The O.C.* – all Jacks, Joshes, Tiffanys and Cary Anns. The boys were in regulation skinny jeans, Chelsea boots and short-sleeved check shirts, tattooed of forearm and styled of fringe. The girls were regulation impossibly attractive. They were young, cool, beautiful and hanging on Joe's every word. If this was an episode of *The O.C.,* then I was Season One Seth failing to get with the cool kids. Or worse, I was Joe Harland scowling by a campfire in Thailand while Peter Total-Fucking-Tosh impresses the girls with 'Re-bastard-demption Song'. Tomorrow it would be my turn to have a few drinks and let my hair down. I would have to be very, *very* funny indeed. Either that or get my guitar out.

2 NOVEMBER

THE DEVIL WENT DOWN
TO CHARLESTON

I was having a lovely dream about flying a Harrier jump jet. Piloting a jump jet is not easy, especially when your co-pilot leans in close and licks your face with her tongue.

Another lick. I woke up to a chilly Charleston morning on a blow-up bed apparently determined to tip me onto the floorboards of a wooden house warped into a Riddler's lair by years of barometer-shattering humidity. Chris was asleep on the sofa, Courtney had left for work, and her dog, a sturdy but friendly Weimaraner by the name of Lily, seemed to want to go somewhere. Presuming that she needed the doggie toilet I took her downstairs, opened the front door and watched in horror as she whipped by my right leg and ran into the road.

'Car!' was all I could squeak as a red Nissan, sun-bleached pink, raced towards her.

Ohshitohshitohshitohshit. I'm going to have to tell our generous host that we're grateful for your hospitality, we've enjoyed your company, and we've killed your beautiful pedigree dog. (And while we're getting it out there, Chris is thinking about playing his guitar at you.) The car braked, the bonnet dipped, the rear springs rose, and with a nonchalance which said 'I know what I'm doing, you plum,' Lily skipped out of the way with so little time to spare that she left a sliver of drool on the bumper.

I ran over, unsure whether to chastise or kiss her. She must have thought I was going for the full snog, because she glanced left and ran like only big dogs can, out of sight in this city I didn't know.

Nononononono!

I ran in the direction she had, looking for evidence of four-legged intrusion – upturned bins, startled children, that sort of thing. Nothing. I walked around, practising the conversation in my head. It was an improvement on the first scenario, but not a big one.

'Hi Courtney – there's good news and bad news.'

'What's the good news?'

'I didn't kill your dog.'

'And the bad?'

'I lost her. Do you fancy a go on my mate Chris?'

After nearly an hour of searching I slunk dejectedly home. There I would tell Chris what I'd done and we would get in the car and go, leaving a note of apology on the door. I walked into the living room. Chris was snuggled up on the sofa with Lily watching the Weather Channel.

'Been for a run?' he asked.

'Er, yeah, sort of.'

'It's going to be a beautiful day. Breakfast?'

'Yes please.'

Lily looked up at me with a mischievous glint in her eye, and growled a little growl that sounded disquietingly like a laugh. We jumped in the car and drove into historic downtown Charleston.

Charleston had existed for precisely 111 years longer than our West Coast jump-off point, but Los Angeles had done an awful lot of catching up in the 225 years since, growing to three times the size of its older cousin and a whopping thirty-two times the population. While LA generates $800 billion every year for the American economy, exporting Californian culture to every corner of the world, Charleston subsists largely on tourist dollars, being one of few American cities with a history longer than the sideboard in grandma's front room.

All of which makes Charleston sound rather slow, which is precisely and gratifyingly what it is. Los Angeles, like its puffed-up Muscle Beach body-builders straining to press another ten pounds for the passing crowds, is a city with a point to prove. Charleston, by contrast, strolls past in deck shoes, khaki slacks and a seersucker blazer, oozing old money confidence and eccentric society charm. LA is the Eagles; a supergroup formed for the express purpose of shifting albums by the squillion. Charleston is Ella Fitzgerald and Louis Armstrong singing 'Summertime' to an audience of twenty in a sweaty downtown jazz club. And LA is still in a hurry to get somewhere; Charleston arrived long ago and is relaxing on the porch with the papers and a gin and tonic.

What a pleasure it was then, after a week overnighting in cheerless hotels outside dreary, identikit towns, to know we had at least one full day to explore an ancient, beautiful city which time had forgotten, to borrow the opening line of DuBose Heyward's *Porgy*, upon which Charleston folk opera *Porgy and Bess* is based. What cheer, after a string of Nowherevilles with no-go downtowns overrun with banks or robbers, at the thought of a lazy amble among the densely-packed antebellum houses of the Charleston peninsula. What novelty, accustomed as we now were to driving from hotel to restaurant across one highway and two enormous car parks, in ditching the car and exploring on foot. And what an unexpected relief to step off the music trail for a while and enjoy a place simply for what it was, and not for who recorded, overdosed, sold their soul or bought their groceries there.

Courtney had left a hand-drawn map to get us started. We followed it the length of Rutledge Avenue, which delivered us onto the Battery, the southernmost tip of the peninsula where, as Charleston carriage tour operators love to joke, 'the Ashley and Cooper rivers meet to form the Atlantic.' This is where Charleston's most prestigious homes can be found – palatial, plantation-style white villas whose double and triple-height verandas, elaborate column work and immaculate gardens trumpet the city's colonial past and place it so strikingly at variance with virtually every other city in North America.

We parked the car, breakfasted on pancakes, and then walked them off in the sunshine along Broad Street and the surrounding network of lanes and boulevards. Being narrow, occasionally curved or – just as uncharacteristically for America – named after people, places or wars rather than numbers, they were pleasingly conducive to getting lost, which we delighted in doing for a couple of hours.

Further from the Battery the houses were smaller but every bit as pretty. An eighteenth-century frontage tax imposed by the British Crown resulted in the Charleston crush of tall, narrow properties whose deep porches run perpendicular to the street, creating a tantalising sense of mystique as well as frequent opportunities to peer into people's front rooms as we walked by.

Joe's perpetual quest for stamps took us to the imposing main post office, which a friendly Charlestonian dog walker directed us to on Meeting and Broad. (The American convention of dropping the words 'street', 'road', 'boulevard' and so on was hardly new to us, but I still found myself occasionally double-taking when asking for directions and apparently being told the state of play in an American football game: 'It's on 3rd and Long.' 'That's great, but where's the train station?') The opulent interior of the post office made The Wolseley look understated. High coffered ceilings above marble columns on brass attic bases echoed the squeak of trainer on marble floor. Post office boxes, decorated with elaborate brass trim and mounted into carved mahogany, took up every inch of wall.

I had a look around and took pictures while Joe went in search of stamps. Browsing a postcard carousel, I picked one out listing the South Carolina state symbols. State motto: '*Dum spiro spero*.' ('While I breathe, I hope.')

State bird: Carolina wren. State dance: the Shag (and not, disappointingly, the Charleston). Further down they read less like state symbols than a ten-year-old listing his favourite things. State reptile: loggerhead sea turtle; state insect: Carolina mantis; state snack: boiled peanuts. I half expected to see a favourite colour or state Pokémon. South Carolina even had a state hospitality beverage (tea).

We later discovered that twenty-six other states had a favoured hospitality beverage and, to our utter astonishment, that Nebraska's was Kool-Aid. We also learned there were such things as state soils, state crafts, state swords and state 'prepared foods' such as muffins, doughnuts, desserts and cookies. Oklahoma even had several of its own state 'menu items', including barbecued pork, chicken fried steak and biscuits with gravy. ('Well if Texas gets chilli con carne then I'm having chicken fried steak and barbecued pork.')

Further along Broad Street was Berlin's clothing store, which had been decking out the city's gentlemen folk since 1883, and where Courtney had worked to pay her way through college.

Charleston fashion is as vibrant and unique as its architecture. A more flamboyant, Southern take on the traditional American preppy look, it combines linen and seersucker jackets with button-down shirts and chinos in a rainbow of pastels to match the weathered hues of the city's street frontages. Nantucket Reds, showy trousers by most standards, are embroidered all over with sporting marlins, sailing boats, ducks or criss-crossed tennis racquets, worn just above the ankle over slip-ons ('weejuns') or boat shoes, always without socks. True eccentrics mark themselves out with a bow tie. I was tempted to make a purchase, but fancied that this kind of flair, against the dreary backdrop of London, would look less sartorially eccentric than consummately unhinged.

We returned to Courtney's apartment. We had some rehearsing to do.

After two weeks of dedication, hard work and sheer grind, the moustache was in fine form. The same could not be said for my musical skills. The failed attempt to put me on the Satanic fast track left me no option but to learn to play the bloody ukulele properly. This meant practice, and practising a musical instrument is not something I was cut out for. I quickly regress into a despondent teenager if I'm not playing note-perfect Chopin within the first hundred seconds, with a tendency to throw said instrument into a corner, forever to gather dust.

But Chris was confident he could do what previous music teachers Miss Shepherd (piano), Miss Tysen (flute), Mr Michaels (recorder) and Mr Spears (bass) had failed to do. He really believed he could teach me a song. We sat in the sun on the twisted beams of Courtney's sloping back porch, ukulele and guitar in hand.

'We're going to learn a Gram Parsons song,' said Chris.

'OK.'

'It's very easy.'

'It'll need to be.' Petulance rising.

'"Grievous Angel" has only got five chords: G, C, D, A and B-minor. I've transposed it to make it easier on the uke. This is a G.' He held down three of the strings and strummed lightly, effortlessly conjuring the sound of a warm luau. 'Now you have a go.'

Looked easy enough. Fingers go here, here and here.

'Like this?'

'Yep.'

Ker-thumpf. It sounded like a sausage being dragged over chicken wire.

'I told you I couldn't do it!' I huffed triumphantly, like a child determined he'll never ride his bike without stabilisers.

'Try again.'

Sausage on chicken wire once more.

'And again.'

Sausage on violin.

'And again.'

Fingers on violin.

'And again.'

Fingers on ukulele!

'There you go!'

Wow. Check out Christopher Miyagi. It wasn't Chopin, but it was, for the first time in my life, a proper chord. The other chords quickly followed and before an hour was up, I could play all the bits necessary for 'Grievous Angel'. I couldn't play them in time, at the right speed, or in the right order, but I had all the components, and that was a start.

Another hour and we'd have nailed it. But my student had achieved a lot in his first session, and he really needed to put in some hours waxing the car and sanding the floor of the *dojo* before moving up a grade. Besides, there was a Martin D-35 acoustic guitar calling to be taken out of her case and strummed. While Joe perfected his B-minor, I set about the task of getting to know my latest clinch.

It's very hard to explain to someone who doesn't play guitar precisely what it feels like to pick up an instrument as beautifully crafted as a Martin D-35. I can only say that it's a little like falling in love. Though I had spent two hours trying her out – yes, *her* – at Guitar Center before finally getting my wallet out, in reality it was a fait accompli from the first note. Love at first sight.

Yes, it had been an impulse purchase, but she was more than just a holiday romance. For one thing I would have to seriously improve my playing if we were to have any kind of future together, and that would take time. Seven Lemonheads songs and a few Gram covers were hardly worthy of a $2,000 guitar. With the sun on my face, I picked out the chords of 'The Outdoor Type' and pictured blissfully happy times ahead.

'"The Outdoor Type", I love that song,' said a voice behind the porch door. Courtney was home.

'Hey, how was work?' I chirped, putting down the guitar.

'Don't stop,' she said, joining us on the porch. 'It's nice. Work was OK. Did you go downtown?'

'We did,' said Joe. 'It's stunning. Easily the most beautiful city of the trip so far.'

'Isn't it? I'm very lucky to live here.'

I finished playing. 'You most certainly are.'

Courtney's eyes widened suddenly. Perhaps it was my guitar playing. 'Oh my – the trash! Let me take it out. I can't believe you've been out here with the stinky garbage all this time. I'm so embarrassed.'

'Hadn't noticed!' said Joe.

'Hey, I need to walk Lily,' said Courtney. 'She hasn't been out today.' Joe and I looked at each other. Yes she had. 'Wanna go to the beach?'

'Sounds great,' said Joe. 'Let's go.'

We jumped in the car and headed for Folly Beach, overlooking the Atlantic just outside Charleston, where Courtney could walk Lily and we could dip our toes in an aquatic bookend. We were travelling coast to coast for a multitude of reasons, the first being that if you hire a car in America and have more than two weeks to kill, then driving from one side of the country to the other is really the only thing to do with it. There is of course the $500 financial deterrent levied by all car hire companies called the 'One-Way Drop-Off Fee', but other than that... well there's no reason not to is there? No one ever fundraises by pogo-sticking from John O'Groats to Wolverhampton. You can't regale your drinking friends with stories of the time you walked from Lands End to Paignton. And Route 66 may be remembered as the quintessential rock and roll highway, but one of the reasons it has disappeared from America's travelling agenda in recent years is that it runs, not as many believe from LA to New York, but from LA to Chicago. From the Pacific, 2,488 miles all the way to... a lake. That ain't coast to coast. It isn't Kerouac. All the way west to all the way east is the only option.

And all the way east was where we were. What with the sand fleas, the dead horseshoe crabs and the sun setting in the west when we were looking east, Folly Beach wasn't the bromantic conclusion we'd had in mind, but at least there were no syringes in the surf. Job done, time for some Charlie Daniels.

A strobing lava flow of brake light snaked ahead of us into the blackness of the South Carolina night. Red lights turning from dim to bright and back again, the shunt and chug of cars making their way slowly to the Coastal Carolina Fair.

'See – I told you Charlie Daniels was popular,' I boasted.

Chris was in the back seat. 'I don't think they're *all* here for Charlie… Are they?'

'No, they're here for some classic Southern entertainment,' Courtney jumped in. 'And maybe a bit of Charlie.'

We sniggered. Because we're childish.

To pass the time, and to get us in the mood, I put *Charlie Daniels' Super Hits* on the car stereo. Charlie sticks to a well-worn and successful formula: over fast and furious country hoedowns he layers densely-packed, staccato rhyming, delivered exactly halfway between singing and rapping, with a nursery rhyme simplicity which is easily imitated by a car full of excited children on their way to a funfair. Charlie is especially good fun, of course, when singing about selling his soul to the devil.

But not so awesome when he's singing about beating up gays. Track eight, 'Uneasy Rider '88', appeared to be some sort of queer-bashing anthem. This was a particular surprise to us, as I imagine it was to many of Charlie's fans when in 1988 he decided to re-record his 1973 novelty hit 'Uneasy Rider' (about being attacked for having long hair and liberal attitudes at a Mississippi bar), but with lyrics updated for more enlightened times. And what better subject than beating up on some ho-mo-sex-y'alls that came onto him and a buddy when they stopped at the Cloud Nine Bar & Grill.

Chris poked his head between the head rests. 'And this is the guy we're queuing up to see?'

'Oh yes,' said Courtney.

'Do you think he'll play "Uneasy Rider '88?"'

'Maybe. And what's worse is it'll probably be one of his biggest crowd pleasers all night. This is the South, don't forget.'

The Coastal Carolina Fair takes place during the first week of November in Exchange Park, ten miles outside Charleston. Run by the National Exchange Club, and lighting up the South Carolina social calendar since 1957, it is an altogether different experience to the fairs that pitch up with their tombolas and coconut shies on village greens around Britain every summer. At a British fair there might, if you're very lucky, be a Medium Wheel to delight the kiddies and shake up their elder siblings' alcopops. In South Carolina, as so often when it comes to comparisons between Britain and America, they just do it bigger. There are the regulation haunted houses, bumper cars and merry-go-rounds. Then there are towers, coasters, flumes, motorbikes, chair-lifts, even helicopter rides if the vertiginous thrills of the Mega Drop aren't sufficiently vertiginous or thrilling. Sweets in a jar it ain't.

We parked in the long grass and made our way into the fairground. Exchange Park also plays host to events such as the Land of the Sky Gun Show and the Low Country Coin Show, but the Coastal Fair is the jewel in the calendar. Over the course of a week, 200,000 people come to get their annual fill of thrills, spills and snack foods so high in saturated fat and so devoid of nourishment that they can cause obesity and malnutrition at the same time.

A family of four with matching paunches went through the gates ahead of us, dwarfed by the enormous chicken legs they were cramming into their greedy faces.

'Jeez Courtney,' I marvelled, gesturing towards the Squatzenheimers. 'How big are your chickens?'

'They're not chicken legs, look.' She pointed to a nearby food stall with a red and yellow sign shouting 'Donnie's BBQ Turkey Legs'.

'Is that a thanksgiving thing, or greed thing?'

'Neither – turkey legs are pretty popular. You gonna try one?'

'Think I'll skip that. I sort of have a policy of not eating anything wider than my own neck.'

The best thing about Donnie's was that all the servers wore a 'BBQ Turkey Leg Tour' T-shirt. And when one of them turned around to heave another bucket of limbs from the back of the shack, it revealed a month-long list of the fairs, rallies and rodeos that Donnie and Team Turkey would be appearing at. They were the rockstars of fast food.

'Do you think they get groupies?' I wondered.

'Probably,' said Chris. 'Really fat ones.'

Never has the American credo 'the same, but bigger' been so artery-cloggingly apt as when applied to fairground snack foods. Take funnel cake, guaranteed to quicken your pulse even if the turkey legs or Haunted House don't. Perhaps, as I have, you have stood in line for doughnuts at a funfair or music festival and watched transfixed as small, perfectly formed rings of batter plop gratifyingly from a hop into four sizzling rows of four below. Now imagine all sixteen of them deposited in a single swoop through a similar funnel the size of an industrial hoover attachment, brandished by a toothless redneck tracing repeated, overlapping pentagrams approximately the size of your head. The resulting criss-cross of batter resembles a bird's nest just large enough to accommodate an American bald eagle. Garnish with icing sugar, or – if your fancy takes you – strawberries and whipped cream, and you have in your hands that quintessentially American delicacy, funnel cake.

The search for novel ways to get fried dough into your face has become something of an art form in America. If funnel cake doesn't do it for you, there are always elephant ears, doughboys, beaver tails, frying saucers, whale tails – all variations on a theme – to get your cholesterol rising. Or my favourite – the corn dog, which is a frankfurter coated in cornbread batter and deep fried on a wooden stick, thereby obviating the need for a bread roll and leaving a spare hand to hold either your tummy or the side of a rollercoaster. All of them are perfect fodder for throwing up over yourself later when your insides have been hoisted and dropped, flipped and flopped by a succession of stomach-churning fairground rides: cheap, tasty, and double the fun as you enjoy them in both directions. Those resourceful Americans think of everything.

No rides for us just yet however. We were running late for Charlie's scheduled stage time of 7.30 p.m., trotting briskly to the 2,000-capacity grass and concrete amphitheatre. We arrived to find the great man, still favouring the beard of Jesse Duke and the fashion sense of Colonel Sanders, cantering through a set of middle-of-the-road country to the polite applause of the assembled masses. When a brief between-song chat about his key seventies album *Fire on the Mountain* drew rapturous cheers, it was obvious that, like me, everybody was waiting for just one tune. Sure enough, as his allotted hour drew to an end, Charlie and his group of mild-mannered demons channelled for Ol' Horny and served up an impressive medley of his hit, 'The Devil Went Down to Georgia'. Standing on tiptoe on the grassy periphery stood a man with a stupid great grin on his face as he shouted along to every word. Reader, that man was me.

By now we were rolling four deep – me, Chris, Courtney and her friend Jack, a Stroke-a-like about town who looked like he could comfortably front any US indie band from the last five years. Which is to say his style and demeanour said 'Whatever you're into, I was into it before you.' He described himself as a metrosexual redneck, which is such a splendid and accurate description that I'll not try to better it.

We headed back to the funfair. Briefly tempted by the MTV Fun House (sadly not a life-size replica of Chris' office, just a regular fun house festooned with bad likenesses of Britney Spears and Michael Jackson), we passed the Big Drop (self-explanatory), the Big Wheel (ditto) the Really Big Wheel (really ditto), and dozens of others before arriving at the Scrambler.

Chris magnanimously suggested he escort Courtney, leaving me to cosy up behind them with Jack.

'Y'know, I'm not a big fan of fairgrounds,' he drawled as we waited for the thing to start.

'Why's that?'

'Well, my daddy told me he used to come here as a kid and help set these up.'

'And?'

'He said that once they finished building all the rides, there was always a big pile of bolts left over that they couldn't figure out what to do with.'

And with that the music started and we were catapulted into a series of figure eights like a Kaleidosketch on G-force ten. We span. We squished. We shared a modicum of DNA. We panicked because a small part of us believed the story about the bolts. Getting off, we held our stomachs and went in search of snack foods made out of fried dough.

Now let me ask you, what's the worst job you've ever had? Abattoir assistant? Head of bedpans at an old folks' home? Whatever it is, at the Coastal Fair we saw something that tops it.

Past the food stalls lurked a collection of what can only be described as freak shows. There was 'The World's Smallest Horse' (overheard from one visitor: 'Dude, that shit was a pony.'), 'The World's Smallest Woman', and lastly but most intriguingly an attraction promising, in ghoulish font above the entrance, 'The Head of a Real Girl with the Body of an Ugly Snake'. Alongside this was a painting of an armless brunette boasting scaly breasts, a long curly tail and a remarkable resemblance to Celine Dion.

Pride stopped me from going in. Jack had no such scruples. Two minutes later he came out, laughing and holding his stomach, saying it wasn't real. Disappointed, we went on our way.

An hour later we passed again. This time the intrigue gnawed at me. I went in. In a large wire cage sat a bed of straw. On the straw was a table, and on top of that – specifically poking through it – was the head of a girl with a snakeskin ruff and a stuffed snake's body attached to her neck. She was trying hard to smile, but rolled her eyes as people paraded past asking 'Are you really a snake?' or 'What do you eat?' Some buffoon barked 'It's fake!' – you don't say – and walked out. I followed.

I'm sure that poor lady didn't plan on a career as an ugly snake girl. Surely she had other plans for her life, her education, her career. But no, for fair reasons or foul her passport, if she had one, said 'Occupation: ugly snake girl'. If your job sucks, you can always dream of moving on. If it isn't quite as exciting as you'd hoped, you can at least take pride in doing a dull job well. No such luck for ugly snake girl. I suppose she could always do some moonlighting as a Celine Dion look-a-like.

She wasn't real, so it wasn't a genuine freak show, but I still felt a pang of guilt at the exploitation of the poor love. Moments later Jack practically fell out of the tent, wiping tears of laughter from his eyes. He said the head belonged to a different girl to the one he saw earlier. He was still chuckling about this in a Charleston bar four hours later.

3 NOVEMBER

PIANO MEN

Dūs'ter, *noun* **1.** cloth for dusting furniture etc.
Dūs'ter scāle, *noun* **1.** standard of measurement by which to judge magnificence or intensity of a gentleman's cockduster moustache, ranging from 'Prince' (discernible) to 'Leatherman' (formidable).

My to-do list had but one entry on it – grow a formidable moustache – and it was not going well.

I had last had a complete shave the day before flying to LA. Bearded Joe had handed down the moustache directive on the flight. Thanks m'colleague. On day six – through Joshua Tree and Grand Canyon to Monument Valley – I shaved the horseshoe in for the first time. Joe, who of course had started way past 'discernible' and was by then approaching 'respectable', didn't notice.

Five days and six states later – through the Rockies and across the seemingly endless Kansas plains, over the Mississippi Delta and into Tennessee – I had another go. Definite signs of life this time – rather as though a slug had crawled across my face while I slept, and after briefly contemplating my nostrils, turned for home.

By Charleston, on the East Coast, I had begun to elicit a few looks from people, possibly because of what they imagined to be an unfortunate birthmark, but at least it was attracting attention. Joe's moustache was definitely admirable if not actually formidable by now. That he seemed to have skipped the moustachioed rock god stage – difficult to pull off when you're carrying a ukulele – and was now careering headlong into Village People territory, was a consolation, as I also appeared to have all the camp of Leatherman without any of the attendant bushiness.

And there was another problem.

Have you ever had choose between friends? Pick bridesmaids or a best man maybe, or godparents to your children. Or worse – the most deserving recipient of your free introductory gym membership. It's a horrible position to find yourself in.

So when, a few days before setting off, Joe had said 'I've got tons on, you pick the music for the car,' I was more than a little aware of the pressure to bring the right people along for the ride. The trust placed in me was akin to a bride letting her future husband take care of the wedding invitations while she got on with ordering the flowers. It was a huge vote of confidence, but a tremendous responsibility, and in the end the trust turned out to be entirely misplaced. Barring a handful of old friends whom I knew could be relied upon not to make a scene – Neil Young, Jeff Buckley, Johnny Cash – my guest list featured several total strangers who either failed to bring anything to the party or, in Gram's case, threatened to spoil it altogether.

The thinking was this. I wanted, over the course of three-and-a-bit weeks and 4,500 miles, for us jointly to discover one record which would become the 'signature' album of the trip. The soundtrack to a road movie which years later would recall the people, places, scenes and faces to far greater effect than any photo album, scrapbook or journal. Tried and tested 'old familiars' never work – they are already laden with nostalgia for other times and other places. We needed blank disks on which to save the raw data of new experience.

It had worked once before. On a trip in New Zealand a few years previously, Nada Surf's just-released *Let Go* had turned out to be the perfect complement to the remote and dusty roads of the South Island, becoming a daily fixture on the car stereo and a near obsession both for me and fellow traveller Hannah. To this day the opening chords of 'Blizzard of '77' deliver me onto the shores of Lake Tekapo more instantly than the Starship Enterprise transporter. Five seconds of 'Killian's Red' and I'm listing through the unsettling green tussock of Lindis Pass amid minor progressions in the late afternoon of autumn 2003. I ration the number of times I listen to it for fear of overwriting those memories with new ones. I wanted Joe and me to have a *Let Go* of our own.

And I came close. In fact our *Let Go* almost ended up being *The Letting Go*, Bonnie 'Prince' Billy's new album of gothic Americana whose 'Cursed Sleep' ('cursed eyes never closing') was apt but effective during the first unsleeping nights of the trip. But once sleep finally arrived it seemed to have served its purpose, both for me the insomniac and Joe the victim of it. Thomas Dybdahl's plaintive *One Day You'll Dance For Me, New York City* had perfectly scored the drive back from Cap Rock through a twilit Joshua Tree National Park, and received further spins over the next week before the scratched CDR fell foul of a temperamental CD player. The Shins' latest album, *Wincing the Night Away*, failed to float Joe's boat to anything like the extent it floated mine.

In short, I failed. I did not feel good about this. Quite apart from the personal disappointment, there was the professional embarrassment. That a man paid by MTV to programme music for an audience of millions was apparently unable to cater adequately for an audience of two, was ever so slightly shameful.

Rewind to Denver, ten days and six states earlier, where we had stopped at Radio Shack to buy a new wireless card for the laptop. Joe had suggested we pick up some new tunes for the car.

'It's weird isn't it,' he said, picking a CD from the rack, 'how some American artists translate in the UK and some don't? Phish are massive here.'

'Never heard of them.'

'Exactly. Hardly anyone in the UK has. They're a jam band.'

'God I hate jam bands. There's nothing more depressing than a bunch of bearded goons noodling on guitars for four hours while a crowd of stoners try to convince themselves they're having a good time.'

Joe returned the CD to the rack and moved along the aisle to M. 'And Dave Matthews couldn't get arrested in London.'

Dave Matthews, American readers will not need telling, is the purveyor of the dreariest, most soulless adult-oriented rock ever committed to tape. He's huge in America.

In the autumn of 2001 Dave, his manager or his record label decided it was time the UK knew about him. They lined up a series of TV performances too lowly for consideration in the States, as well as a 'teaser' campaign around London and other major cities. Huge posters all over town, in bold black type on a white background, asked one simple question: 'Who is Dave Matthews?' The answer would be revealed when his newest album, *The Space Between*, topped the December charts. Eye-watering amounts of money, time and effort were expended by the label's marketing and promotions departments to make sure this happened.

Sure enough, in December *The Space Between* ripped a hole on the Top 40, roaring in at... 35. On the morning the chart position came in, the poster outside Radio 1, which for a fortnight had been demanding to know just who Dave Matthews was, finally bore the answer, handwritten in thick black marker pen underneath: 'That's showbiz.'

Joe moved along the racks, reaching J. 'Billy Joel's done well though, for a man with unfortunate initials and dubious taste in wives.'

More invective began to form in my head, then stopped when it reached my mouth. 'Er, I quite like Billy Joel.'

Joe flashed a look at me, eyes wide and ears unbelieving. Then his face dropped, and with a sideways glance to make sure no one was listening, he said, 'Actually, so do I.'

'Shall we?'

'We can't. Can we?'

I shrugged a conciliatory shrug. 'Who's gonna know?'

'OK, but don't breathe a word about this to *anyone*.'

We skulked to the counter, an illicit double CD hidden under computer accessories like a copy of *Razzle* between the pages of *The Sunday Times*.

And that's how two men, one responsible for filling ten channels of music television every day with the coolest new videos, the other for specialist programmes on the UK's hippest national radio station, came to be cruising south along the east coast of America between Charleston and Savannah, harmonising to Billy Joel's 'She's Always a Woman', in what has since become known as 'the least heterosexual moment of the trip by a Kansas mile'. Picture Thelma and Louise doing Max and Paddy doing the *Minder* theme on *Phoenix Nights*, with added camp. Between the Rockies and the eastern seaboard the performance had been fine tuned, lyrics learned and harmonies honed. Joe would solo in the bridge when my baritone wouldn't reach the high notes – 'Oh, she takes care of her-say-ee-yelf' – then I would join in again on the hummed refrains. Occasionally a piano trill would be tapped out with fingers on the dashboard.

It's also how the signature album of the 'Live Fast, Die Young Tour' – the one record which most readily evokes the spirit of a journey to the heart of rock and roll America – came disturbingly and harmoniously to be *Billy Joel: The Ultimate Collection*.

Say what you like about Billy – and I'm sure you will – his strike rate is impressive. Yes, he's written some howlers, but for every 'Uptown Girl' there's an 'Allentown', a 'Movin' Out', an 'Honesty' and fourteen more at least as good. He has released whole albums of howlers in fact. But for every *River of Dreams* there's a *52nd Street*, a *Turnstiles* and a *Piano Man*. (My favourite, *The Stranger*, doesn't make it onto that list, perfect but for final track 'Everybody Has a Dream', apparently rescued from Andrew Lloyd Webber's 'too schmaltzy for Broadway' rejects pile.)

Perhaps when you're looking for music that two people can agree on, somewhere around the bottom of the barrel you hit Billy Joel. Maybe he's lowest common denominator, or maybe he has an everyman quality we can all identify with. Maybe we leapt on him because he was something – anything – we could agree on when we really, really needed to agree on something. (Even down to which songs to skip on the CD and which ones to turn up. All of CD one – the seventies – got the thumbs up. But in 1983 Billy Joel went spectacularly off the boil with *An Innocent Man*, which Sony had conveniently lumped in with *Storm Front* and *River of Dreams*-era dross, meaning we could skip straight to 'Allentown' when the CD reverted inexplicably to the early eighties.)

Or maybe Billy Joel is just great road music. He certainly isn't 'Live Fast, Die Young' music, as so far he has done neither. All I know is that joining in with the steel mill noises in the intro of 'Allentown' – ooh, sssh, aah! – at full volume whilst cruising at 70 mph in an open-top car is about as much fun as a man can have behind the wheel with a clean licence and a clear conscience.

A blue sign passing on our right welcomed us to Georgia: 'We're Glad Georgia's On Your Mind.' That's nice, isn't it? Makes British road signs seem so perfunctory and impersonal by comparison. A sign announcing that you are entering Yorkshire or Wales or Little Guffing might give you a stiff welcome before demanding that you drive carefully, respect your elders or stop biting your nails. American road signs, like Americans themselves I suppose, are a good deal more chatty and voluble. There are very few countries I can think of where you're welcomed across borders by Ray Charles. (I hope his estate gets royalties.) With miles of straight roads and endless rows of pine trees ahead, we fought the boredom by looking out for the Georgia state bird (brown thrasher), state reptile (gopher tortoise) and state shell (knobbed whelk).

Driving in convoy along the Georgia coastline, Courtney led the way to Waycross – her home town and Gram's – oblivious to our ooshing, aahing and air-drumming behind. We broke the journey in charming Savannah, whose pretty shaded squares under oak trees hung with Spanish moss offered the perfect spot for lunch. One square in particular was on Joe's list of must-sees – Chippewa Square, where the opening sequence of *Forrest Gump* was filmed. Evidently there was a certain bench which needed sitting on, but frankly I was irked by the intrusion of such family-friendly references onto our outlaw itinerary.

Sitting on a bench in the square – not *the* bench, which we later learned was a fibreglass prop since relocated to the Savannah Visitors' Centre – I suggested to Joe that this was about as far away from misadventure as it was possible to get.

'I suppose,' he said, 'but Nic and Noah would never forgive me if I came to Savannah and didn't get a snap of Daddy on the Forrest bench.'

'Fair enough. Hardly rock and roll America though, is it?'

'Well if it helps, John Lennon's in the movie.'

'Thanks, it does. Lennon's the ultimate rock death, isn't he? Assassination in America scores double points.'

Courtney changed the subject to more pressing matters. 'Who's hungry?'

'Starving,' I said.

'Famished,' said Joe.

Courtney stood up. 'Great. I'll get us some lunch.' We watched as she crossed the square and disappeared into a coffee house.

'What's the catch?' said Joe after a few minutes.

'How do you mean?'

'With Courtney. There must be a catch. She's hot, hospitable and not mental.'

'I know. Regular little Southern belle, ain't she?' I said, reviewing the photos on my camera.

'I'd almost say Scarlett O'Hara, but she's far too nice.'

I turned the camera off. 'Yep. We've definitely lucked out there.'

Courtney strode back across the square with armfuls of sandwiches and canned drinks. 'I just bought a random selection. Hope that's OK.'

I shuffled along the bench to make space. '*More* than OK. What have we done to deserve this? You've been so kind to us the past few days Courtney. I hope we can pay you back some time.'

'No need,' she said, sitting down. 'You're in the South, don't forget. It's what we do.'

'Well I'm very glad we are,' said Joe.

'Me too,' I said.

Courtney smiled. 'I'm glad you're here too. Now, we've got a BLT, a Reuben and a turkey club. Who wants what?'

Joe beat me to it. 'Frankly my dear, I don't give a damn.'

Back on I95, we continued south for another fifty miles to Brunswick and then west again, inland on Highway 82 towards Waycross.

We cruised along pale tarmac, the wooded roadsides interrupted only by firebreaks offering brief glimpses deep into the forests, and by weather-worn hoardings offering local produce far up ahead. Maybe as a Brit I am too used to living in a country where you're never more than ninety miles from the sea, but marketing local honey to passing trade from a hundred miles out seemed, well, optimistic.

Woods turned to fields, which turned to farms, which turned to occasional houses. The red lights on the first traffic signal we'd encountered in two hundred miles told us that we were somewhere: Waycross. Chris and I turned to each other with a single eyebrow raised in the internationally accepted facial expression of 'Is this it?'

We had known in advance that the town wasn't what you'd call remarkable. It had no monuments of renown, no intriguing history in which to immerse ourselves, no cinematic landmarks at which to gawp. No battles were fought there nor agreements signed. What we hadn't bargained for was Waycross being so fantastically not-remarkable that it had a pretty good claim on the title of 'Most Unremarkable Place on Earth'. There were the requisite US town features like fast food outlets squaring off across road junctions, gas stations doing likewise, a church here, a motel there.

But like the city in which our trip had started – Los Angeles – it appeared to have no discernible centre; just an enormous, sprawling suburb with no obvious beginning or end. Also like LA, we appeared to be in a land where you build out, not up. If I stood on tiptoe I could see Florida.

Would anyone care to guess how Waycross got its name? Yes madam, you at the back in the red shirt. No, good guess, but it's not because the town planner had a short temper. You sir? Correct! There are two huge rail*ways* in Ware County, Georgia, and the centre of the town is where they *cross*, hence Way-cross. Which is the third most interesting thing about Waycross after its famous sons Burt Reynolds and Gram Parsons. It's a pretty steep drop-off on the interesting scale after Burt to be fair.

It was in this town that one John A. Snively founded a crate manufacturing plant supplying his citrus company in neighbouring Florida, a business so successful that at its peak it was responsible for a third of all citrus grown there. He later fathered Avis, who married a man called Cecil, who in turn fathered a boy called Ingram, later known as Gram, the town's second most famous resident.

For the Gram Parsons fan there is just about enough of interest to keep you in town for an hour or two. I was ready to keep on driving. Chris, however, had other plans. Between him, Courtney and her mum they had booked us in for a Gram Parsons tour the following morning. Which meant an evening in the town that never wakes.

If you've ever wondered where the phrase 'up the Suwannee' comes from (meaning 'gone wrong', 'broken' or 'knackered'), then wonder no more. The Suwannee River rises in the Okefenokee Swamp just outside Waycross. It is probably, if you're looking for one, the closest thing there is to a real-world location for Shit Creek, and we had just arrived.

4 NOVEMBER

A HOSTEL ENVIRONMENT

In November 2003 Emmylou Harris played a string of dates at Hammersmith Apollo in London. Her record label, knowing I was a Gram devotee and correctly assuming I was similarly in thrall to the lady whose career he kick-started, invited me to see the show. (Gram is generally acknowledged as having discovered Emmylou: he hired her as an unknown to sing harmony on solo albums *GP* and *Grievous Angel*, and she regularly credits her success to him even today.) After the gig, which included Gram songs and a dedication to her road manager – one Phil Kaufman – Emmylou's radio plugger asked if I would like to come backstage and meet her. I thought about it for a moment – wow, a private audience with the high queen of Cosmic American Music, a once-in-a-lifetime opportunity of rubbing shoulders with a bona fide music legend, and one with a direct line to Gram to boot – and then politely declined.

You see, they say you should never meet your heroes. Many people sensibly follow this advice out of a genuine and understandable fear that they will be disappointed. For me it's down to the very strong likelihood I will perform a special party trick which I apparently reserve for the people I admire most. That is, stand mute and immobile for upwards of thirty seconds before finally blurting out something simultaneously so banal and creepy it renders the hero in question utterly speechless themselves. This had last happened upon meeting Stephen Malkmus of legendary lo-fi indie rockers Pavement when, despite best efforts to find an intelligent conversation-starter – the fantastic show they had just played perhaps, the beautiful venue – I heard myself complimenting him on his trousers. If I did meet Emmylou, there existed the very real possibility I would embarrass both her and me by admiring her teeth or trying to touch her hair.

But even supposing I had met Emmylou and managed by some miracle not to make a tit of myself, the short distance from front of house to dressing room would have brought me no closer to Gram's music. To do that – to find his Wichita County line, his 'Our House', his Tupelo – had necessitated a journey of several thousand miles to a one-horse town in southern Georgia called Waycross.

More than any of the songwriters on our itinerary, Gram wrote about home – getting away from it, missing it, coming back to it. But it was a concept he had a complicated relationship with; it represented everything he loved and despised about his southern roots – family, security and integrity on the one hand, racism, religious fervour and small-town values on the other. And while Waycross was the setting for a happy, comfortable childhood, it also held painful memories, not least the suicide of his father in 1958.

The Georgia sun glinted on the puddles in the car park of the Pinecrest Motel as grumpy grey clouds blew eastwards. Courtney had arrived early and explained what was in store. I could only work out that it involved two fellas named Billy Ray Herrin and Dave Griffin, a van and a long list of places I had neither heard of nor cared about.

A splash of tyres announced the arrival of our tour guides. Judging by their wheels, we were about to be shown around Waycross by the A-Team, which frankly was at least as diverting as the prospect of touristing in a one-horse town. The doors swung open, but sadly no Hannibal or Face.

'Hi guys, I'm Billy Ray,' said Billy Ray.

'And I'm Dave,' said Dave. 'Good to meet y'all.'

Dave was tall and slim with thinning grey hair to his shoulders and a neatly trimmed beard. Wearing cowboy boots, jeans, a smart jacket and round, Lennon-style sunglasses, he had the look of a retired rock star. Billy Ray was also grey of beard, but shorter and more solidly built, sporting a beaten-up baseball cap and mirrored sports sunglasses. We shook hands and exchanged smiles.

'Thanks for showing us around,' enthused Chris, 'do you do this often?'

'Seems like we do it more now than ever,' said Billy Ray, his melodic, Southern drawl by far the most pronounced of any we had encountered so far. With an impressive economy of lip movement, he swished rounded vowels and retroflexed Rs around his palate like mouthwash. 'New folks are discoverin' Gram all the time. The BBC made a documentary a while back, which Dave and me helped on, and there are four biographies out, so there's always folks comin' through. If someone's in town and wants to know about Gram, then we try to show 'em around if we can find the time.'

'And how much time do you have today?' I wondered, nervously.

'Oh, we got plenty.'

Dave jumped in the driver's seat while Billy Ray slid open the side door of the van to reveal a plush, carpeted interior with coach-style seating and a bewildering array of cup-holders. We climbed in.

'We'll drive around town some,' said Dave, 'take y'all to some of the hot spots, then finish up at Gram's house on Suwannee Drive.'

'So how are you guys connected to Gram?' asked Chris.

'Well I first started gettin' into Gram's music just before he died,' said Billy Ray, 'then in '74 I opened a record store named Sin City Records, after the song on *Gilded Palace of Sin*. I had to change the name because the nice folks of Waycross objected. I been spreadin' the word about Gram's music pretty much ever since.'

'Then in '98,' said Dave, jumping in, 'I figured we should do somethin' to celebrate Gram's music. So we started the Gram Parsons Guitar Pull. It started out in my back yard, just friends jammin', and now it's an annual festival.' We pulled out of the motel car park onto Memorial Drive. 'That's the Jacksonville Highway right there. Keep going ten miles and you reach the Okefenokee Swamp.'

'Okefenokee!' I blurted. 'I love that word. Oh-kee-fen-oh-kee. I could say it all day long. OH-*kee*-fen-OH-*kee*...'

'It's Native American,' said Billy Ray. 'Seminole. It means "land of the trembling earth".'

Dave looked up at me in the rear-view mirror. 'You ever listen to the words of "A Song for You"?'

'A Song for You' is a naked, heartfelt ballad on *GP* about shifting sands, troubled times and uncertain futures. Emmylou sings harmony – as on most of Gram's solo recordings; her voice appears almost to carry Gram, who sings each line as though the emotional effort required to deliver it might desert him at any moment. By any measure it's a bit of a heart-render.

Dave sang the first line: 'Oh, my land...' In his glorious Southern drawl, the word 'land' had three distinct syllables over three separate notes – 'lay-ee-und.'

I quoted the next line: 'Trembles and it shakes, 'til every tree is loose...'

'You got it,' said Dave. 'That's the Okefenokee Swamp.'

'Well I never,' I said. 'I always wondered what that meant.'

The Okefenokee is the largest black-water swamp in North America – half a million acres of cypress and mangrove trees stood in boggy wetland which straddle the Georgia–Florida state line. Plant life grows in peat beds which float on the mirror-black water and undulate with the movement of the wind and wildlife. It literally trembles and shakes.

'I thought maybe the shaking earth thing was tremors in southern California,' I said. 'When he lived in LA.'

'Could be,' said Billy Ray. 'I guess I always read it more as a symbol of his home life – his daddy killin' himself, his mama's drinkin'.'

Waycross or California, it seemed Gram's roots were never set in solid ground. We were barely out of the car park and already a favourite song spoke to me more directly than it had before. This was a good start.

Courtney leaned forward in her seat. 'It's pretty cool, the swamp. There are 'gators all over. We could take a drive out there later.' The Okefenokee also teems with animal life, much of it – alligators, bears, snakes and mosquitoes – of the kind that turns tourists into lunch.

'I can hardly wait,' said Joe. 'Perhaps we should pick up some 'gator repellent on the way though, just to be safe.'

It is a common observation that natives never 'tourist' in their own cities. A Liverpudlian rarely goes anywhere more Beatley than John Lennon Airport, and for most Londoners the only connection to the city's significance-swollen past is a vague awareness that the streets they're shopping on have been there for, like, ages. But visitors come from far and wide to splash about in the rich cultural waters we residents stride through unawares. I couldn't help feeling, as our Waycross tour wound on, that a morning cruising around a town so geographically and culturally irrelevant even its inhabitants weren't sure they lived in it, was rather perverse and perhaps utterly pointless.

Billy Ray turned in his seat. 'So whereabouts are you guys from exactly?'

'London,' I said.

'D'you like it thur'?'

'Yeah, I guess so.'

The chubby Michelins on the B-Team van clicked across rusting rail tracks, and I wondered what I could offer Dave and Billy Ray by way of diversion if they ever came to visit me in Hammersmith. There's the stained-glass West Bromwich Albion crest over the doorway of a house that once belonged to Adrian Chiles, but what else? In Waycross I began regretting the lack of attention I had paid to the bits of the capital that really mean something – the breadcrumbs of modern music and film that lead a trail to the present day. As we criss-crossed the town I ran through my daily journey to work in my head.

Walk to Hammersmith – home of the Apollo, immortalised by Motorhead on the album *No Sleep 'Til Hammersmith* and one of the few truly great music venues left in London. Then Goldhawk Road and Shepherds Bush Market, where Ray Winstone got bested at fisticuffs for once in *Quadrophenia*. On to Wood Lane – the home of BBC Television Centre, star of the opening credits to *Going Live*, several attempts to break the world record for a very large number of tap dancers tap-dancing near each other, and a place where every year you can see newsreaders 'dancing like you've never seen them before!' on *Children in Need*.

Turning away from the swamp towards the centre of Waycross, we drove along a five-lane highway past a Huddle House, a Cypress Creek Steakhouse and a Wendy's fast food restaurant. Every commercial premises that wasn't an eatery was a gas station or car parts specialist. Arriving in what looked like a downtown area, Dave pulled up and pointed across an intersection towards a large white painted church on the opposite corner. Looking like a cross between a mosque and a university campus building, it bore a sign which read: 'Grace Episcopal Church'.

Dave smiled. 'Mean anything to you?'

It didn't at first. Then a lyric lit up in my brain; an image of a preacher talking to a crowd. It was from '$1000 Wedding', another Parsons ballad from his last record *Grievous Angel*. It tells the story of a young man left waiting at the altar for a bride that never comes. (We never find out why, only that she 'went away'.) The song vacillates between acrimony and resignation, rising to a swell as drink-fuelled recriminations ensue, then ebbing to sober reflection as the protagonist recognises the 'old lies' on his friends' faces. In the final bridge, a Reverend Dr William Brace is preaching to a congregation; a crescendo of guitar, drums and steel rises once more with his tales of fire and brimstone, before the song finally descends to a sombre, funereal close.

I have listened to '$1,000 Wedding' at least as many times as 'Wichita Lineman', very probably more. One of Gram's most portentous songs, definitely his most accomplished, it is an obliquely narrated tale that manages to avoid the bathos and triteness that so many country storytellers fall foul of. It makes me wonder what Gram could have achieved as a songwriter if he hadn't ballsed it up so magnificently in 1973.

'"$1,000 Wedding"?' I ventured.

'Yip,' said Dave. 'That's where Gram's family went to church in the forties and fifties.'

'His daddy's funeral took place here,' said Billy Ray. 'Reverend Dr William Brace was the priest. Gram remembered what he said and put it into the song.'

Another eerily visceral experience of a favourite song. But unlike the Wichita County line, Grace Episcopal Church looked nothing like the one in my imagination. They were two very separate places in my head, and I found it impossible to overwrite one with the other. The church we now looked at was real but imaginary, a little like when you try to describe the familiar setting of a dream and find yourself saying '... except it didn't look anything like the one in real life.'

I was still in my head too. Continuing my internal commute, at Westbourne Park I could jump out for a pint at a pub that starred as the Mother Black Cap in *Withnail and I*. Then it's Latimer Road in the heart of Portobello, home of Hugh Grant's famous blue front door in *Notting Hill*, of Michael Caine's flat in *The Italian Job*, and the excellent Sarm West Studios where the Band Aid song was recorded.

Then it's Edgware Road (The Blue Lamp, Pete Doherty's regular cell), Paddington (*A Hard Day's Night*, *The Long Good Friday*), Baker Street (Holmes, Holmes and more Holmes) and lastly, up to street level near the bottom of Regents Park (everything from *Harry Potter* to *American Werewolf in London* to *Brief Encounter*), a brisk walk along the edge of Park Crescent, where Hitchcock's Hannay left his cart and horse in *The 39 Steps*, and I'm at my desk.

Dave drove us across town to Cherokee Heights – the affluent, leafy suburb of Waycross where Gram had grown up. Wide, tended lawns swept down onto straight boulevards in front of mostly single-storey brick and weatherboard homes. Eighty-foot pine trees, branchless below house height but with a proliferation of dense, spiky foliage above, dusted the roofs with needles and shaded the gardens like a gazebo.

Immediately another Parsons song popped into my head – 'Hickory Wind' from the Byrds' album *Sweetheart of the Rodeo,* and re-recorded 'as live' for *Grievous Angel.* It's another ballad about yearning for home, nostalgia for a place that no longer exists. The opening line describes the 'many tall pines' of Gram's childhood surroundings, the oak tree he climbed and the 'hickory wind' that transports him there from far away, setting them in successive verses against less wholesome images such as the 'riches and pleasures' that later life has brought.

'Gives a whole new meaning to "pining for home",' said Joe.

Courtney laughed. 'Although the lyrics say the pines are in South Carolina.'

'Poetic licence,' I replied. 'Georgia doesn't scan.'

We pulled up on Suwannee Drive, where Gram lived for the first twelve years of his life.

'And right here is where Gram's house was originally built,' said Billy Ray. 'So in a manner of speaking it's where he grew up.'

Courtney went quiet for a moment, and then sprang bolt upright in her seat, grabbing the arm rests with both hands. 'Oh my God!'

'What?' I said.

'Really?!' squeaked Courtney.

'What?' yelped Joe.

Courtney's eyes widened. 'Gram grew up... here?'

'Sure,' said Billy Ray. 'Right there on the corner.'

'On this plot, anyway,' added Dave. 'A developer moved the original building in the sixties. To another plot out of town.'

Courtney looked confused. 'But I've driven up and down Suwannee Drive a hundred times looking for Gram's old address, and it doesn't exist. There isn't a 1600 Suwannee Drive.'

'That's because they moved the old house across town,' said Billy Ray.

'And when they built the new one,' Dave went on, 'the front door faced the other way. So this house' – he gestured to the one we were parked in front of – 'is on Seminole Trail, not Suwannee Drive.'

Courtney's jaw dropped. 'I used to live in that house.'

Joe and I gasped simultaneously. 'Really?'

'Yeah. My mom and I moved back here from Charleston after she divorced my dad. I lived in that house for three years.'

Even Joe had to admit that things just got interesting. Courtney was about as big a fan of Gram Parsons as it was possible to be. And she had just found out that in addition to sharing his home town and given surname, she had grown up on the very same patch of earth as him. The Gram trail had led straight to her own front door.

I shook my head in disbelief. 'Wow Courtney, that's incredible!'

'I know!' said Courtney.

'Darn,' said Dave.

'Crikey,' said Joe.

'Well I'll be,' said Billy Ray.

We took in several more hot spots on the Gram trail – the house where he was conceived, the factory his dad managed and the railway station where Gram last saw him alive – then thanked our Waycross tour guides and bid our farewells.

It was hard saying goodbye to Courtney. Our Southern belle had gone out of her way to give us a taste of Southern hospitality, and we – me especially – had grown fond of her in the short time we'd been together. Which is a roundabout way of saying I had developed something of a schoolboy crush and was going to miss her. Not least because she knew all the Emmylou Harris harmony parts on *GP* and *Grievous Angel* and Joe didn't.

But we had a road trip to finish. Today was 4 November. Tomorrow would be Gram's birthday – his sixtieth – and we planned to be celebrating it 224 miles to the south in his birthplace of Winter Haven, Florida. Then we would return the Grievous Angel to Dollar Car Rental at Orlando airport and fly home, job done.

So where else to spend our final night than Gram's Place, a music-themed hostel in Tampa run by Parsons fanatic and self-confessed oddball Mark Holland. We had arranged on the phone for Mark to give us a guided tour of the hostel for our video tapes. It would be a rare pleasure, he said, to celebrate Gram's birthday with people who had actually heard of him, as most of his guests hadn't and frankly weren't interested. He was sorry we wouldn't be able to stay in the Gilded Palace of Tin, a converted tool shed taking its name from the Burrito Brothers album, on account of its being occupied by a guest of long-standing from New Zealand, but he could offer us the Country Room instead. We drove south from Waycross, skirting the Okefenokee Swamp and crossing into Florida at Folkston.

We barely noticed Tampa as we approached it in the late afternoon; its unremarkable skyline might have been any major metropolis in North America. Carried by a criss-cross of flyovers, underpasses and feeder roads into a homogenous beige townscape, we regretted, for the first time in over 4,000 miles, not relenting to Dollar Car Rental's sustained sales pitch for satellite navigation. In short, we got spectacularly lost.

After an unplanned detour of nearly an hour through an area of Tampa apparently full to brimming with opportunities for gift purchases of guns and crack for our loved ones back home, we finally pulled up outside Gram's Place. Situated in Tampa Heights, an older residential neighbourhood with faded stately charm, it slouched behind a tall wooden fence on the corner of a shaded intersection facing a large, open cemetery.

Entering the compound through a rickety gate, we found hostel owner Mark sat behind an outdoor bar overlooking a decked jacuzzi area. Built to resemble a Hawaiian tiki bar, it had a slatted wooden counter and high stools under a porch hung with beads, flags, wind chimes and salvaged street signs. Beach music blared from speakers propped up on shelves behind the bar.

'Hey guys! Glad you could make it. I thought you weren't coming!'

'We had a little trouble finding you,' said Joe through gritted teeth.

'Seen a little of sunny Tampa, huh?' He smiled. Podgy cheeks swelled under his sports sunglasses. 'Well I'm sure glad you found me. I've been looking forward to hanging out with you.'

As we shook hands, Mark gripped my elbow enthusiastically with his free hand. The childlike grin, bright shirt and hearty welcome felt less like a hello than a Care Bear Holiday Hug. The staff at the Four Seasons in LA were trained to make us feel like they had been waiting all their lives for us to check in. Mark seemed almost as though he had. 'Hey – I'll give you the guided tour!'

Gram's Place is an exceptional guest house even by the occasionally wacky standards of the international hostelling circuit. It is a conjoining of two neighbouring properties – a forties cottage with private rooms and a larger bungalow next door with dorms and shared living spaces. Mark had transformed it into a kind of roots music theme park, each dorm decked out according to a different genre – the Jazz Room, the Blues Room – and every wall covered with instruments, photographs, album sleeves and other assorted memorabilia.

Joe rolled camera while I stepped into the role of interviewer and prospective guest, Mark playing the part of gregarious host with gusto. 'This is the Parsons Pub,' he began, with a wide sweep of his arm. 'It's BYOB. That means "bring your own bottle". We have satellite XM radio and a jukebox with over 400 CDs. The music plays 24/7 at Gram's Place. I consider it a major disaster if the power goes down for even five minutes.'

'What happens then?'

'I get the guitar out. And you don't want that! Let's go inside.'

He led us across the decking and into the main house. Turning right and up some steps, he unlocked the door to our room.

'This is the Country Room, where you guys are staying.' Metal bunk beds faced each other across a small dorm decorated with photographs, album sleeves and 45s tacked to the walls. A banjo was propped up one corner next to a hand basin. 'You'll be sharing with Jimmie Rodgers, Hank Williams, Merle Haggard and Patsy Cline.' A stubby finger pointed out each of their pictures. 'I put these here to educate people. I want them to know that Barf Brooks and Billy Ray Virus are not country music.'

'Very nice.' I applauded.

'Well, I just think it's horrible that people know who Billy Ray Virus is but they don't know who Jimmie Rogers is. It's an atrocity.'

'And what about Gram?' I said. 'I guess if people don't know about him when they arrive, they will when they leave, right?'

'Not true. Most people don't know who he is when they come, don't know when they leave. Most don't care. And that's fine. People just like Gram's Place because it's got this funky, bohemian thing, whatever you call all this. Some people call it Markitechture.' He winked behind the sunglasses, still clamped tightly to his face even indoors. 'This place is the childhood fort you always wanted to build as a kid but your parents would never let you. Follow me.'

We passed through a darkened living area cluttered with sagging furniture and musical instruments. A piano stood in one corner surrounded by several acoustic guitars, making Joe's camerawork visibly shake at the thought of an evening jamming Gram numbers. Then Mark led us through a fifties-style communal kitchen before finally taking us back outside to Parsons' Pub.

'This side of the hostel is named Little Montreal,' Mark went on. 'That's why you see a lot of French stuff here.'

I stopped and read some of the signs. 'What's the connection with Montreal?'

'Just that I go there a lot and I love it. I like to be in a country where everything is misspelled. Makes me feel like I'm out of the United States. It's what I really liked about Holland, everything was misspelled.'

'Why does that make you feel better?' I asked, resisting the temptation to point out that the words weren't so much 'misspelled' as 'in another language'.

'Because I don't know what the fuck it says! It makes me feel like I'm on another planet.'

The swearing threw me off momentarily. Coming from this cuddly, boyish personality, it was like Barney Rubble breaking character and swearing at the kids. I pressed him further. 'Why does it feel better to be on another planet?'

'Because I *am* from another planet! I'm from planet Pluto. And I can prove it to you, right here.' Edging back and looking up, he pointed to a sign under the eaves of the porch: 'Bienvenue Planet Pluto.' 'I figured out a long time ago that I'm an alien from another planet. I just don't fit into that place on the other side of the fence. I don't really belong here. I'm not interested in war, I'm not interested in capitalism, corporations or religion. In fact there's really nothing on this planet that interests me other than music and having fun.'

'So everything you need is here?' I asked, getting caught up in the idea of Gram's Place as a kind of Neverland that Mark had created around himself in order to pretend that the 'real' world didn't exist.

He sidestepped me. 'Well I'm just doing the best I can living in a place called Tampa. I'd much rather live in Canada or Europe. I envy you guys that live over there, I really do. I'm not happy in America. We have a dictator for president, we have the illusion of elections and a fascist police state. We live in the Divided States of Illusions.' His face dropped, then suddenly lit up again. 'Hey, let me show you Little Amsterdam!'

Skipping three yards to the left, he announced: 'Now we're in Little Amsterdam.' A lime-green, European-style telephone booth stood by the fence next to a tall rubber plant, Dutch flags hanging on bunting above.

'Where does your fascination with Holland come from?' I asked.

'Well, my last name is Holland. So I figure why not?' This was the answer I was most – and least – expecting. That you happen to share a name with a country is both the best and worst reason for crossing an ocean to see it. But then who I was I to talk – I had just crossed a continent as a birthday present to a man most people have never heard of. 'Up here is the Crow's Nest,' said Mark. 'It's like a Huck Finn, Robinson Crusoe kind of thing. Go on up.'

We followed a staircase up onto a network of wooden walkways which wove between the buildings and led onto a lookout platform at the top of the hostel. Looking down over both properties I pressed on with the interview. 'How long has it taken to get this place to where it is now?'

'Twenty-nine years. That's my whole life. I was a young man when I came here. Actually it's all illegal. The city is making me re-zone.'

'What does "re-zone" mean?'

Barney Rubble broke character again. 'It's another term for extortion and bullshit. The government makes you buy products and services that you don't want, need or get. And if you don't buy them you become a criminal.'

'I'm still not sure I know what you mean?' I said, guessing he was talking about taxes, but I wanted to hear his own interpretation.

'It's all about "You have a wallet, and we want that wallet from your pocket into our pocket". That's what re-zoning means.'

This was getting a little heavy. I changed the subject. 'Do you manage to make a comfortable living out of Gram's Place?'

'Well I don't get a pay cheque, but it pays the bills. I don't do this for money though, I do it because it's a passion. I just like to share the music. It's called Gram's Place but it's not about Gram so much as what he stood for – sharing music.'

Gram's Place seemed to me like an unruly younger brother to the Alley rehearsal space in LA. Like the Alley, it had the look and feel of a film set. Take the Lost Boys' hideout in Spielberg's *Hook*, swap piracy for music, stick it in Tampa and you're there. Nothing matched; not the doors, nor the furniture or the rooms. But it had been put together with massive personal drive and care. Yet like a child's train set it seemed once a room or area was finished it was left to gather dust while Mark took his excitement to another part of the house. It was a schizophrenic, manic environment, the closest I've ever come to walking around the inside of a man's head. Gram's Place was the physical manifestation of the mind of Mark Holland: musical, eccentric, passionate, sprawling and slightly troubled, with hidden corners holding unexpected oddments and idiosyncrasies. It was utterly unique.

While Joe blogged, I chatted to Mark some more in his office. We talked about his interest in Gram, how in 1980 he had started the Gram Parsons Foundation to 'share, perpetuate and educate', and how he had shot the first ever television documentary made about him, *The Legend of the Grievous Angel*.

He asked if I wanted to jam a couple of songs on guitar, but I made excuses, saying Joe and I needed to find somewhere to eat, maybe later. I feel bad about that. Mark's passion for music was unquestionable, his belief in its unifying power admirable. That he seemed to invest all of his energies in it to the exclusion of everything else however, made me uncomfortable – perhaps this was what it meant to cross the line from fan to fanatic? Gram's Place was a lively musical playground, but one run by a boyish character who resented paying taxes and felt persecuted by the authorities. That he rejected all of the trappings of 'the world beyond the fence' made Gram's Place seem less welcoming to me, not more.

And frankly I was feeling nervous about how all this reflected on me. Hadn't I just driven 4,500 miles across America to celebrate the birthday of a man most people have never heard of, much less care about? Hadn't I crossed the line myself?

Two thoughts consoled me. The first was that Shilah, Polly Parsons' best friend and partner in crime, had mentioned in Joshua Tree that she had met plenty of Grampires in her time and could confirm – bless her – that we were categorically not Grampires ourselves. Phew.

The second thought was that the whole thing was Joe's idea anyway. Weirdo.

5 NOVEMBER

EXIT MUSIC

Strum, strum, strummity… shit. Strummity… shit. Strummity… shit!

Today we would end the journey by commemorating the life of a man rated eighty-seventh most influential artist of all time by *Rolling Stone* magazine. And there in the Country Room of Gram's Place I was proving beyond all doubt that I was something like ten billion places behind him. Strum, strum, strummity… shit.

I had planned by now not only to have mastered my chosen instrument, but also to have acquired a deep appreciation of the style of music I was to perform. I hadn't. With my extravagant ukulele purchase, I was the snowboarder who hits the slopes in a bank loan's worth of Puffa-wear and then sits on the chairlift the wrong way round. 'All the gear, and no idea' or, as they say in West London, 'all the kit, and still shit'.

There were just sixty miles between Tampa and Winter Haven. It was late morning and I had until some time after lunch to learn an instrument and to love these songs. I could have lied, told Chris that I got it, trucking songs are great, now play the one about the car. But that wouldn't have been right, and I'd still be shit at the ukulele. I just needed more... time.

But Chris was in a hurry to get going. Mark appeared to have found a new best friend and was reluctant to let him leave before they had made beautiful music together. I jumped in the passenger seat, waving goodbye from the topless Grievous Angel. Chris prised his hand from Mark's, threw the bags in the boot and slammed it shut. Then he climbed into the driver's seat and reached for the ignition. 'Have you got the key?'

'No, you've got it.'

'Ha ha. There's no time for this, I want to get out of here.'

'I haven't got the key!'

'Where the fuck is it then?' said Chris, starting to panic.

'It would appear,' I smiled, 'that you have performed your party trick again, would it not?'

'Check your pockets.'

'I haven't got it!'

Pockets were emptied, ashtrays opened and slammed shut, seats pulled forward and pushed back. He'd done it again. And this time he had really outdone himself. This time there was no Dollar Rental lot attendant on hand to help us out, just a man who would much rather we stayed for several more weeks. We returned to Gram's Place. Chris buzzed.

'Oh, hi guys,' said Mark, confused to be seeing us again so soon. 'Everything OK?'

'Do you know of any locksmiths? We, er... I... appear to have locked the car keys in the trunk.'

303

'Oh man, bummer! There's a place around the corner on MLK. I'll go give him a call.'

We waited. Chris fumed.

'He'll be here in a couple of hours,' said Mark, emerging from his office. 'Just enough time for a drink. Lucky Parsons Pub never closes!'

It was a long two hours.

Finally a portly Samoan locksmith rolled up armed with keys, a can of lube, a knife, small rubber truncheon and a flinty determination to see it through. We would soon be on our way. He was a cuddly chap; by the time he'd waddled across the road he was sweating and licking his top lip like a bull dog. After twenty minutes of squeezing, turning, wrenching, twisting and lifting, his orange work shirt was sodden, and we were still stood on the pavement.

'You guys' – huff, puff – 'have got two options.' Deep breath, sucking of teeth. 'You can drill out the lock and pay for a new trunk at the airport. Or you can stay here and wait for the rental company to send out their own guy. But I doubt they'll come out today.'

Noooooooo!

Then a thought appeared to flicker across his sweaty brow. 'Or, there's one last thing I can try.'

This sounded good. It was dangerously close to Michael Caine and his 'great idea' at the end of *The Italian Job*, but we were desperate. The 'last thing' in fact involved simply pulling out the moulded back seats of the Grievous Angel and beating the shit out of the thick fabric wall that separates the boot from the car. A car drove past and slowed to take a look. It probably did look strange: three guys casually watching a fat man beat up a car.

Huff, puff. 'We're in!' The titanic struggle had created a small hole in the lining approximately the size of a coffee cup. 'Only I can't get my arm through.'

This called for the weediest person present. I stepped forward, climbed into the rear seatwell and fed my right arm through the hole like a vet delivering a calf. There was a bag – no – move across, what's that? Oh, guitar case. Carry on, what's this? Metallic, jangly… yes!

We repaired the car as best we could, threw fifty dollars at the locksmith and, restating our goodbyes to Mark, hit the road for the final time.

With less than five hours until the return of the Grievous Angel to Dollar Car Rental, less than two until 'Return of the Grievous Angel' performed on guitar and ukulele in Gram's birthplace of Winter Haven, two men drove east along US570, Gram Parsons on repeat, punctuated by the sporadic, clumsy chords of a ukulele being impatiently abused.

In the late afternoon we arrived in Winter Haven, a sprawl of retirement community chic squeezed into the gaps between the Chain of Lakes which fleck the central Florida landscape like droplets of spilt milk. The lakes, as if to emphasise to the old folks of America that 'this is the place for you', had names like Henry, Alfred, Mabel, Maude and Bess. Or they promised lazy Sunday afternoons on Hammock Lake or Lake Easy. The hygiene-conscious octogenarian could even live on Lake Sanitary. As we drove through, expansive pools opened up suddenly to our left and right like inland seas. For us, as for many of the people living there, Winter Haven was the end of the line.

Had we found the spirit of rock and roll America? Certainly not here. But we had found it in a cosy cabin in Nashville and a tiny motel room in Joshua Tree. We had shaken its hand at the Cash studio and re-enacted westerns with it on a real-life movie set in Pioneertown. We had tasted the loneliness of the 'Wichita Lineman', the sinful excess of a Church's Chicken economy bucket on the crossroads in Clarksdale, the peanut butter and banana sandwich that finished off the King. And in a way, though it pre-dated anything that could be called rock and roll by about 160 million years, we had seen the true birthplace of American music in Monument Valley, the original Wild West.

Had Joe learned to love the music of Gram Parsons? No. Did I think he would? Not really, but it would have been nice. Isn't it natural to want your friends to share the things that are important to you? And he tried. But that bit of the experiment was doomed to failure from the start. A month-long immersion in all things Parsons was as likely to succeed in making Joe like Gram as a Dave Matthews poster campaign.

And of all people I should have known this. A good part of my career has been spent making playlist choices based on the persistent overtures of record label promotions departments. Of the thousands of new artists presented to me by radio pluggers as the next big thing, the ones I remember – the ones whose careers I am proudest of having a hand in starting – are the ones I discovered myself. That's part of being in love with music – discovering it for yourself. When it's shoved down your throat it becomes as palatable as a plate of funnel cake on a Scrambler.

And Joe's outlaw heroes were all from the silver screen – Butch Cassidy, The Magnificent Seven – while mine were from the grooves of a longplayer. He had Cliff Michelmore to thank for his memories and I had Waylon Jennings (OK, Daisy Duke). He had no nostalgia for country, I had none for westerns, and we never would. But it had been fun trying.

The trees hung still in the breezeless air as we drove around Winter Haven looking for a suitable place to complete the quest. The town centre looked like every other pedestrian precinct in every other town in America. We carried on. Winter Haven hospital, where Gram had entered the world, just looked like a mall. The crossroads in the centre of town was the regulation rainbow of traffic lights and fast food outlets; performing in the car park of Popeye's Chicken & Biscuits didn't seem right. We drove back along East Lake Howard Drive where, reaching out over a lake turned golden by the setting sun, we spotted a jetty.

'That's the place,' said Chris with convincing finality.

We parked and walked out onto the water, Chris' guitar casting a moody silhouette on the wooden planks. Two kids were fishing by the water's edge. Seagulls wheeled above.

'Right,' said Chris, 'can you remember the chords?'

'Yes.'

'Can you remember the order?'

'Not so much.'

'Well, let's give it a go.'

'Won't you scratch my itch, sweet Annie Rich
And welcome me back to town...'

I really wish I could say I gave a faultless performance. I wish I could say I got all the notes right, that I hit the strings more often and with more conviction.

'Billboards and truck stops passed by the Grievous Angel
Now I know just what I have to do…'

I wish I'd been able to give Gram a more fitting tribute than I did. Even if his music hadn't moved me, I had come to realise from talking to the people we'd met on the trip that this guy meant a lot to them. He had spoken to them, changed their lives, inspired them. And here I was butchering his sixtieth birthday tribute so badly that it was starting to look deliberate.

'I remember something you once told me
And I'll be damned if it did not come true…'

Did Chris think I had brought him all this way and screwed up the punchline just to make a point? I hoped not. And most of all I hoped that a musician who died five months after I was born, who lived fast and died young, wherever his soul may be, didn't think I was taking the piss.

'Twenty thousand roads I went down, down, down
And they all led me straight back home to you.'

We sat in silence for a few minutes and watched the sun set over the lake.

I was the first to speak. 'You know, I think I might keep the cockduster. I've grown to like it.'

'You should. It suits you,' said Chris, stroking his.

'Gonna keep yours?'

He thought for a moment. 'I don't think so. It's just not me. It's uncomfortable, slightly stupid and makes me feel a bit self-conscious.'

Silence for a few seconds. 'That's exactly how I feel about country music.'

EPILOGUE I

TWO YEARS LATER

I was driving along the Uxbridge Road in West London when it happened. I switched radio stations and a familiar, swooping pedal steel lit up the dial on Radio 2. As it did, a great big stupid smile spread across my face.

As the song played, credits rolled in my head. The credits to a film about two guys who drove across America looking for the soul of American music and ended up unsure of whether they had found it.

The credits scrolled upwards on the right-hand side of the screen while bleached-out highlights of the movie played on the left. As the tune played on, soundless visual highlights flickered by, each one ending in a brief freeze-frame before fading into the next. Laurel Canyon. Punk Rock Mike. Joshua Tree. Monument Valley. Wichita County line. Wolf River. The Crossroads. Cash Cabin. Courtney. Charlie Daniels. Billy Joel.

And for the first time in my life, 'Return of the Grievous Angel' by Gram Parsons made me happy. Not because the singing was soulful, or because Emmylou's harmonies were perfect, or because the lyrics were so sweetly metaphorical. It was because it took me back in time to a silly experiment which seemed to have failed, but which, I realised now as my Converse tapped the footwell and my lips sang silently along, in its own small way was a success.

Twenty thousand roads I went down, down, down
And they all led me straight back home to you.

Indeed they do, Mr Price. Indeed they do.

EPILOGUE 2

TWO YEARS AND SEVERAL MONTHS LATER

All of which meant I had rather failed to keep up my end of the bargain. There had been just one entry on my to-do list and my moustache, just entering the realms of barely discernible when it was time to fly home, had remained on American soil. There was a balance that needed redressing.

Have a look at the photo of us on the back cover. That's me on the right. It took several months, but if that's not a formidable moustache, then frankly I don't know what is.

missingparsons.com

ACKNOWLEDGEMENTS

Chris and Joe would like to thank the following people:

Each other for the journey.
Mark Lewis and Martin Toher from B-Unique for their encouragement (and the loan of the camera).
Mike McCormack at Universal Music Publishing for 'reaching out' like only he can.
Thomas Eagle at thomaseagle.com for making us look so good.
Nicola Di Tullio for not letting us chicken out.
Noah Harland for letting Joe go.
Mardi Caught at Sony Music, formerly of MTV, for letting Chris go.
Andy Parfitt and Ben Cooper at Radio 1 for going along with it all.
Mike Davies for the gift of Tito's Tacos.
Stacey Dee for the invaluable motel advice.
Terra Naomi for the excellent vibes and the baseball bat for protection.
Paul Fox for reaching the parts of LA that other managers can't reach.
Matthew and Brett at Moving Talking for keeping it rolling.
Margo and Yvo Kwee for keeping the spirit alive in Joshua Tree.
Polly Parsons for liking what we do.

Shilah 'The Fixer' Morrow for making so many things happen.

Mary Patton for the tour of Pioneertown.

Barber Judi for the number 17s.

John Carter Cash for opening his doors and letting us see the magic.

Phil 'Road Mangler' Kaufman for helping Gram stop smoking.

Courtney Connor, the perfect Southern belle, for more than we can possibly list here.

Lily the Weimaraner for being warm on a cold night.

Josh who doesn't bang dudes for his perfect smile.

Jack the metrosexual redneck for cosying up on the Scrambler.

Dianne Hayman for the best Southern hospitality ever.

Dave Griffin and Billy Ray Herrin for the definitive Waycross experience.

Mark Holland for showing us what it means to be a true fanatic.*

Liz and Zack Gowen for a wonderful send-off.

Simon Kilshaw for his production chops and song-writing.

Carol and Graham Parker for the writing retreat.

Andy Hipkiss at Triple A Media for being an agent of progress.

Diane Banks at Diane Banks Associates for finding a book amongst the ramblings.

Jennifer Barclay, Dave Pearson and all at Summersdale for their support and advice.

James Dean Bradfield, Zane Lowe and Huw Stephens for their kind words.

ACKNOWLEDGEMENTS

Friends, fans and followers of Missing Parsons for your comments, messages and friendship, in particular undisputed 'Most Helpful Parsons' Jane Arthy, Scott Black, Richie Auriemma, Matt Bridges, Julie Jackson and Cozmicfolkfan Amable.

Johnny Cash, Glen Campbell, Jimmy Webb, Neil Young, Mike Nesmith, Elvis Presley, Billy Joel, Robert Johnson, Jeff Buckley, Red Hot Chili Peppers, U2 and Charlie Daniels for their music and inspiration.

And lastly, but most importantly, **Ingram Cecil Connor III**. We hope you would have approved.

***A special note about Mark Holland:** Almost exactly one year to the day after our visit to Gram's Place, we were saddened to learn that Mark Holland had died. It was Gram Parsons' birthday. It was difficult writing the Tampa leg of the trip; we didn't want to eulogise, any more than say uncharitable things about a man who was no longer with us. In the end we could only write it as we saw it on the day. Rest in peace, Mark.

thecalmzone.net

For more information about Live Fast, Die Young, including how to purchase the Missing Parsons soundtrack, please visit missingparsons.com.

'A PITHY THROBBER OF A BOOK'
Chris Stewart, author of *Driving Over Lemons*

good vibrations

COAST TO COAST BY HARLEY

TOM CUNLIFFE

GOOD VIBRATIONS
Coast to Coast by Harley

Tom Cunliffe

ISBN: 978 1 84024 113 6   Paperback   £7.99

'*A motorcycle the size of Roz's Betty Boop would have been beyond the dreams of the craziest pack leader at the Ace Café on London's North Circular Road in the monochrome days of rockers, Nortons, Bonnevilles and Marianne Faithfull, when 'good' was middle class, 'bad' misunderstood and the motorcycle offered stark hope to a generation of inarticulate searchers.*'

Tom Cunliffe and his wife Roz take life in the saddle and on to the American highways and byways astride the quintessential 'dream machine' – the Harley-Davidson.

Bikes Betty Boop and Black Madonna are chrome steeds for an extensive road-trip: from Maryland on the East Coast to San Francisco on the West (and then back again), they thunder their way over the sun-beaten plains, through scorching Death Valley, neon Las Vegas, the deep South and everywhere in between.

With flashbacks to the sixties, the eclectic assortment of moonshiners, bikers hard and not-so-hard, cowhands, Sioux Indians, strippers, Bible-bashers, war veterans, Southern gents and the occasional alligator delivers a unique insight into the diversity of the USA.

An easy-riding peepshow into today's America through British eyes and between the handlebars of the great Harley-Davidson.

'*Good tomes for bikers are few and far between, but Tom Cunliffe's account of an epic trip deserves to battle for bookshelf space with Zen and the Art of Motorcycle Maintenance*'
SUNDAY EXPRESS

LOST
IN THE
JUNGLE

A HARROWING
TRUE STORY OF
ADVENTURE
AND
SURVIVAL

YOSSI GHINSBERG

LOST IN THE JUNGLE

A Harrowing True Story of Adventure and Survival

Yossi Ghinsberg

ISBN: 978 1 84024 672 8   Paperback   £7.99

'*I heard the rustle again, too close and too real to ignore. I clutched the flashlight, stuck my head out of the mosquito net... and found myself face-to-face with a jaguar.*'

Four travellers meet in Bolivia and set off into the Amazon rainforest on an expedition to find a hidden tribe and explore places tourists only dream of seeing. But what begins as the adventure of a lifetime quickly becomes a struggle for survival when they get lost in the wilds of the jungle.

The group splits up after disagreements, and Yossi and his friend try to find their own way back without a guide. But when a terrible rafting accident separates them, Yossi is forced to survive for weeks alone in one of the most unpredictable environments on the planet. Stranded without a knife, map or survival training, he must improvise shelter and forage for wild fruit to survive. As his skin begins to rot from his feet during raging storms and he loses all sense of direction, he wonders if he will make it back alive.

It's a story of friendship and of the teachings of the forest, and a terrifying true account that you won't be able to put down.

'*an unnerving memoir of an adventure in Bolivia that quickly turned into a tragic struggle for survival*'   ABTA magazine

'*Every so often an inspirational tale pops up that is simply better or more frightening than anything Hollywood can create. Lost in the Jungle...is one of those*'   SUNDAY EXPRESS magazine

Featured on BBC Radio 4's 'Excess Baggage'

Have you enjoyed this book? If so, why not write a review on your favourite website?

Thanks very much for buying this Summersdale book.

www.summersdale.com